The Grounding of Positive Philosophy

SUNY series in
Contemporary Continental Philosophy
Dennis J. Schmidt, editor

SUNY series Hegelian Studies
William Desmond, editor

The Grounding of Positive Philosophy

The Berlin Lectures

by

F. W. J. Schelling

Translated and with an Introduction and Notes by
BRUCE MATTHEWS

STATE UNIVERSITY OF NEW YORK PRESS

Published by
State University of New York Press, Albany

© 2007 State University of New York

All rights reserved

No part of this book may be used or reproduced in any manner whatsoever without written permission. No part of this book may be stored in a retrieval system or transmitted in any form or by any means including electronic, electrostatic, magnetic tape, mechanical, photocopying, recording, or otherwise without the prior permission in writing of the publisher.

For information, address State University of New York Press,
194 Washington Avenue, Suite 305, Albany, NY 12210-2384

Production by Ryan Morris
Marketing by Michael Campochiaro

Library of Congress Cataloging-in-Publication Data

Schelling, Friedrich Wilhelm Joseph von, 1775–1854.
  [Lectures. English. Selections]
  The grounding of positive philosophy : the Berlin lectures / F.W.J. Schelling; translated and with an introduction and notes by Bruce Matthews.
     p. cm.—(SUNY series in contemporary Continental philosophy) (SUNY series in Hegelian studies)
  Includes bibliographical references and index.
  ISBN-13: 978-0-7914-7129-6 (hardcover : alk. paper)
  ISBN-13: 978-0-7914-7130-2 (pbk. : alk. paper) 1. Philosophy, Modern-History. 2. Positivism. I. Matthews, Bruce, 1962– II. Title.

B2858.M38 2007
193–dc22   2006024607

10 9 8 7 6 5 4 3 2 1

FOR ADELINA MINOR

Contents

Acknowledgments	ix
Editorial Apparatus and Standard Abbreviations	xi
Translator's Introduction	1
The Singularity of F. W. J. Schelling	1
Expectations in Berlin	6
An Existential System of Philosophy	15
The Grounding of Positive Philosophy	24
Schelling's Negative Philosophy	33
Existence as the Inverted Idea	37
Hegel Critiqued	54
Abduction as the Method of Positive Philosophy	68
Towards a Philosophical Religion	81
Translator's Note	85

The Grounding of Positive Philosophy: The Berlin Lectures

On Philosophy	91
On the Academic Study of Philosophy	101
Metaphysics before Kant	113
Kant, Fichte, and a Science of Reason	127
The Difference between Negative and Positive Philosophy	141
History of Negative and Positive Philosophy	155
Metaphysical Empiricism	171
The Grounding of Positive Philosophy	193
Notes	213
Index	227

Acknowledgments

Numerous people have been essential in helping see this project through to its completion. The initial support and encouragement of Louis Dupré, as well as the continuing guidance and inspiration provided by Manfred Frank, have been invaluable. Quite early on, Andrew Bowie graciously offered much needed advice and criticism regarding the translation, while William Desmond saw enough value in the project to lend his considerable support. Others who helped at various stages include Edward Beach, Agnes Heller, Johannes Fritsche, Reiner Schurman, Peter Heath, Michael Vater, Robert Brown, and of course Joseph Lawrence. David Clarke's mastery of Latin proved invaluable, as well as Jean Matthews's prowess as an editor. Heidi White and Edward Rackley were always there in times of need. Adelina Minor provided more assistance than she could ever have imagined. Finally, gratitude and thanks to Robin Osler for bringing grace and beauty into life, and for putting up with my extended absences.

Editorial Apparatus and Standard Abbreviations

[ ]	Insertion by the translator.
[57]	Pagination referring to the German text of *The Grounding of Positive Philosophy*, in the second division, third volume (II/3), of the *Sämmtliche Werke*, ed. K. F. A. Schelling (1856–61). References to *Schelling's Werke* in the 'Translator's Introduction' specify respective part and volume.
i., ii., iii.,	Footnotes by Schelling. Footnotes inserted by Schelling's son, K. F. A. Schelling, editor of his father's collected works, are indicated by '-ED.'
1, 2, 3,	Notes by translator.
GPP	F.W.J. Schelling, *Grundlegung der Positiven Philosophie: Münchener Vorlesung WS 1832/33 und SS 1833*, ed. Horst Fuhrmans (Turin: Bottega D'Erasmo, 1972).
PO	F. W. J. Schelling, *Philosophie der Offenbarung 1841/42*, ed. Manfred Frank (Frankfurt am Main: Suhrkamp, 1977).
WMV	F. W. J. Schelling, *System der Welalter: Münchener Vorlesung 1827/28 in einer Nachschrift von Ernst von Lasaulux*, ed. Siegbert Peetz (Frankfurt am Main: Vittorio Klostermann, 1990).
A 800/B 828	Immanuel Kant, *Critique of Pure Reason*, trans. N. K. Smith (London: Macmillan and Co., 1964).

Translator's Introduction

I do not at all expect to be judged according to prejudices and provisional remarks alone. Whoever seeks to listen to me, listens to the end. It could very well be that in this case he would find something completely different from what, commensurate with his existing and somewhat narrow opinions, he expected to find.

(II/3, 143)

THE SINGULARITY OF F. W. J. SCHELLING

We would all do well to heed the words of advice Schelling offers his Berlin audience in 1842. As anyone who has ever wrestled with his works can attest, doing justice to the philosophical complexity of this original thinker is a huge challenge. The first and most obvious hurdle in conveying his philosophical views is simply Schelling himself: a child prodigy whose scholarly career spanned more than sixty years, he was at the center of, and yet outlived, both Romanticism and German Idealism. Over these many decades, the prodigious scope of his writings covered a wide spectrum of interests that reached from the natural sciences of physics and chemistry, biology and medicine, to philological work on myth and the history of religions; from aesthetic theory and criticism, to the work for which he is best known—philosophy and theology. In each of these fields, his works sparked intense interest and even sharper debate and controversy. By the time he arrived in Berlin, in the very twilight of his career, all these works lay behind him. In addition, over the few decades preceding his belated yet triumphant assumption of Hegel's old position, Schelling had hardly published anything that would shed light on the ongoing development of his philosophical system. Yet, through at times almost stenographic notes of his lectures, various accounts of his new positive philosophy had made their way into the public arena, thereby providing material upon which all interested parties could base their opinions, be they accurate or, as Schelling terms it, "somewhat narrow" (II/3, 143).

As Schelling makes clear in the words cited above, expectation plays a crucial role in the shaping of such opinions. Supported by the *Vorverständnis* of our unavoidable prejudice, the very act of expectation itself assumes its object to be predictable in that our anticipation seems, as if by habit, to aim at forming an interpretation that will confirm and conform to past experience. In this way, the schema of continuity and its benefit of predictability absolve us from having to risk encountering what is unexpected and new. As he made clear very early in his career, Schelling finds such a monochromatic view of life, in which one longs for a predictable and risk-free world, unattractive on several levels, for not only does such a philosophy make "history a mere illusion," but it condemns all of us to a life under the "law [of]…iron necessity," an existence whose ultimate outcome, according to Schelling, can only be a life of complete and utter "boredom" (I/1, 472). This antipathy toward boredom expresses one of the defining characteristics of Schelling's philosophical work, namely his contention that reason is incapable of exhaustively parsing the exuberant dynamic of existence. The "first impression [that this]…so highly contingent thing we call the world [makes on us]…can in no way be an impression of something that has emerged through the *necessity of reason*."[1] That there is a world at all, and that this world has precisely this vibrant explosion of life in all of its ongoing differentiation, communicates to Schelling a truth of existence that precedes the application of reason's web of order and necessity. "*In every respect*" he writes, "*the world looks much less than a product of pure reason. It contains such a preponderant mass of that which is not reason*, that one could almost say that what is rational is what is *accidental*."[2] What is not accidental, what appears to Schelling as much more essential to life than reason and thinking, is desire and action. In the Berlin lectures, he repeatedly stresses this obvious yet all too frequently overlooked fact that since thinking is not action, logic cannot be the author of history. Rather, only those beings free to act enjoy a history; a fact demonstrated by "the acts and deeds of exceptional individuals," which, for Schelling, are "something that cannot be comprehended through reason alone" (II/3, 143). Necessary but not sufficient, reason loses its power to explain when confronted with the freedom of existence that is revealed in the deeds of real individuals. Returning to the hermeneutical task at hand, taken on his own terms as a free and arguably exceptional individual, we cannot comprehend Schelling's deeds, thoughts, and philosophy through reason alone. Something more is required, and a good starting place would be to call into question some preconceived notions about who Schelling was and what his philosophy means.

In the standard reading of nineteenth-century German philosophy, Schelling is associated with German Idealism, a school of thought that grew out of Kant's work and sought to perfect the latter's 'critical idealism' into an 'absolute idealism' capable of unifying all fields of knowing within one self-enclosed system of philosophy. As a stepping-stone from Fichte's 'subjective idealism' to Hegel's 'objective idealism,' in this reading the young Schelling serves as an essential moment in the movement's efforts to create a complete science of reason whose final form would be as universally valid as its method would be necessary. As the story goes, it was only later, after Hegel had demonstrated the brutal elegance of such an absolute idealism, that Schelling broke with this school of thought and turned his efforts to unsuccessfully critiquing and repudiating the tenets of this former colleague. While this reading of Schelling lends itself to the quick dismissal his complex thoughts have traditionally enjoyed, it is just too simple an account to be true.

To begin with, far from ever having been an evangelist of an absolute philosophy and necessary method, Schelling had always insisted upon the irreducible plurality and open-ended nature of doing philosophy. For example, consider what he wrote in 1795, some forty-five years before his Berlin lectures, on the proper relation of a philosopher to his vocation:

> Nothing upsets the philosophical mind more than when he hears that from now on all philosophy is supposed to lie caught in the shackles of one system. Never has he felt greater than when he sees before him the infinitude of knowledge. The entire dignity of his science consists in the fact that it will never be completed. In that moment in which he would believe to have completed his system, he would become unbearable to himself. He would, in that moment, cease to be a *creator*, and would instead descend to being an instrument of his creation. (I/1, 306)

The young Schelling provides us here with a succinct articulation of one of his most cherished core convictions, which remains constant throughout his career, an ethical conviction vis-à-vis the *dignity* of philosophy, which in defending its inexhaustible meaning is diametrically opposed to the dream of finality and completeness found in a Hegel or Kant (as, for example, when the latter writes of attaining with his critical idealism the same degree of certainty and unchanging completeness of Aristotle's logic and Newton's mechanics). Kant locates the dignity of philosophy in its power to transcend the unique contingencies of existence, which for Schelling constitute the very nature of both our existence as free individuals and the unlimited richness of knowledge. Dignity for Schelling derives in part from the manner and integrity with which we tackle this fact of our human existence. Since freedom is the alpha and omega of all philosophy for Schelling, the process of engaging in the creative enterprise of philosophy must be as unending and vigorous as life itself. Dignity demands we refuse the temptation to surrender our role as creator for the less risky role of imitator, dependent as it is on a doctrine or method of our own, or worse, of someone else's making. This demands we refuse the self-gratifying conceit of a settled knowledge, and instead respect the magnitude by which existence exceeds our capacity for comprehension. Contrary to what many would have us think of Schelling and his role in the development of absolute idealism, he rejects all claims to a universally valid and perfected system of philosophy as nothing other than a product of vain delusions of grandeur:

> What philosophy is as such cannot be answered immediately. If it were so easy to agree about a definite concept of philosophy, one would only need to analyze this concept to see oneself at once in possession of a philosophy of universal validity. The point is this: philosophy is not something with which our mind, without its own agency, is originally and by nature imbued. It is throughout a work of freedom. It is for each only what he has himself made it; and therefore the idea of a philosophy [is] only the result of philosophy itself; a universally valid philosophy, however, [is] a vainglorious figment of the imagination [*ein Hirngespinst*]. (I/2 9)

The delusive claim to a universally valid philosophy is for Schelling the result of a particular type of *Geisteskrankheit* that compels a philosopher to find more reality in the reflected world of abstraction than in that of lived experience. A symptom of this particular type of intellectual disease manifests itself in the inhibited and restrictive mentality characteristic of the mythic consciousness, in which the creations of our mind are accorded a reality independent of our own. Once this projection becomes accepted as fact, one forgets that one's system is just that, namely one's *own* unique creation. Schelling speaks to this mythic pathology in his *Stuttgart Lectures* of 1810, when he notes that claiming one's own creation as universally valid is "most illiberal," if not downright "scholastic [*Schulsystem*]" (I/7, 421). Since philosophy is always a creative work of freedom, Schelling argues that "philosophical systems are simply the works of their creators," which, in an important sense, are really only comparable to "historical novels (for example, Leibniz's system)" (I/7, 421). Problems arise, of course, when the authors of such systems forget their own freedom as creators and mistake their creative narratives for works of nonfiction. And it is in this sense that, beginning in 1827, Schelling took to calling Hegel's system a fiction because the latter believed he had completed a system whose method and truth were universally valid by themselves.[3] The inhibiting and restrictive effects this system imposes on thinking parallels the effect *myth* has on consciousness in that both rob consciousness of its freedom for self-determination (II/2, 123, n. 1). Hegel achieves this effect through a *logical animism* that conflates the animate with the inanimate, whereby the human agency of a "living, real subject" is projected onto the "necessary self-movement…of the logical concept" (I/10, 212). The resulting mythic thought is typified by what Lévi-Strauss calls "anonymous thinking"—thinking that is no longer animated by the conscious decisions of an individual but rather by an impersonal and transcendent force. In Schelling's critique of Hegel's fiction, anonymous thinking is driven by the self-movement of the logical concept via its autonomous negation, which "operates in men's minds without their being aware of the fact."[4] The outcome is that, as Schelling points out, the creator of such a fiction or myth "descends to being an instrument of his creation."

Schelling refused to sink to such a level, choosing instead to accept philosophy as an infinitely creative task whose dignity and worth are demonstrated through its capacity for further development and differentiation. This point returns us to Schelling's words of advice to his audience in Berlin in 1842: "[w]hoever seeks to listen to me, listens to the end" (II/3, 143). Schelling's demand to be heard "to the end" follows from his understanding of the organic nature of his philosophy, shaped as it is by the organic nature of existence. Ontologically, he conceives of 'being' as an ongoing process of creative development, which, as a continuous creation, entails the continued emergence of *new* forms of being. Incessantly freeing itself from its momentary limits, existence is sustained and driven onward by what Schelling calls the "exuberance of being." *Existêmi* (existence), understood etymologically as an *arising* or *standing out of*, is in this sense ecstatic in that it continuously stands out beyond any momentary equilibrium. In this process, the ontogeny of being survives only if it continuously engenders new growth in a process of becoming, whose stasis would mean its cessation, and therewith its death. This same organic dynamic informs Schelling's idea of human nature: our existence as individuals is a continuous process of self-differentiation, wherein the possibilities of the future project out of the static reality of the past and present (hope). As Schelling repeatedly emphasized, the "task" of life, education, and culture is "to free oneself from oneself."[5] We exist as individuals only when we overcome ourselves, when our actions transcend past habits and thereby generate a richer and more differentiated self.

Applied to the task at hand, Schelling's philosophy in general, and these lectures in particular, must be approached as the record of a relentlessly original individual whose long life was dedicated to the continuous development of his philosophy. As fruitful as this positive suggestion for reading Schelling might be, it nonetheless sets for us a daunting challenge. As he told his students in Berlin, "the content of these lectures is just not suited to the format of a typical textbook: it does not consist of a series of finished propositions that can be put forth individually. Rather its results are generated in a continuous but thoroughly free and animated progression and movement" (II/3, 20). His lectures represent a progression and movement of thought which, in 1842 Berlin, only *began* with the introductory lectures translated here, and then continued for the next *year and a half* through the course of *three* consecutive semesters. Again, accepting his own terms, I am tempted to suggest that Schelling's work is just not suited to a standard academic treatment because these lectures do not constitute a discrete text designed to stand on its own.[6] The problem is even more acute given the attenuated scope of a translator's introduction that limits any attempt to do justice to the full complexity of his philosophy. While acknowledging these limitations, I nonetheless want to offer a few historical sketches and interpretive suggestions, which I hope will offer a productive opening for reading and appreciating Schelling's Berlin lectures on *The Grounding of Positive Philosophy*.

EXPECTATIONS IN BERLIN

Hegel's brilliance dazzled Berlin, and like a supernova his death in 1831 left behind a black hole in the intellectual and cultural life of Prussia's capital. Immediate attempts to find a suitable replacement for his chair were doomed to failure. The only professors foolish enough to take on the challenge were orthodox Hegelians with a penchant more for confessing allegiance to their master's teachings than advancing any original philosophy of their own. Failing to find a suitable replacement among the followers of Hegel, all eyes turned towards Munich, where Schelling, Hegel's one-time friend and supporter, was busy upsetting the Bavarian ecclesial authorities with his unorthodox brand of philosophy. A contemporary wrote not long after Hegel's death, "[a]fter the choice for the new professor of Hegel's chair completely failed, all the world turned with fiery eyes toward the universally longed for Schelling."[7] This universal longing for Schelling extended to the highest reaches of German society. As early as 1833 the philosophically inclined crown prince Friedrich Wilhelm IV wrote of calling Schelling, whom he considered the "*geistreichesten* man of the German fatherland," to Berlin to take over Prussia's most prominent position in philosophy.[8] So when in 1841 death once again made Fichte's former chair vacant, the now King Wilhelm IV brought the reluctant Schelling to Berlin with an offer he could not refuse: guaranteed freedom from the royal censors, plus the highest salary ever offered to a university professor at that time.[9] The sixty-five-year-old Schelling negotiated these terms directly with the king's ambassador to Munich, C. J. Bunsen, whose enthusiasm for Schelling almost drips off the words he used in his appointment letter, where he proclaims, for example, that Schelling "should not come as a common professor, but as the philosopher chosen by God and called to be the teacher of this age."[10] These great expectations were shared by the King himself, who hoped that Schelling's philosophy would put an end to the "dragonseed of Hegelian Pantheism," and its "facile omniscience."[11]

This brief account of the constellation of forces that brought Schelling to Berlin in 1841 raises several important issues. There is an obvious question that refuses to be ignored: given Schelling's ripe age of sixty-five, and the very important fact that he had not published a significant work of philosophy in over thirty years, why would so many expect so much from a thinker who, on the face of it, appeared to offer so little? If one accepts the credibility of this question, one may well conclude that Schelling's appointment was the last gasp of conservative traditionalists fighting to turn back the clock to a time when philosophy believed more than it doubted. Kant's successful inversion of the balance of power between belief and reason had unleashed an unstoppable quest for knowledge that culminated in Hegel's reduction of faith to logic. Ever since Jacobi first introduced the specter of "nihilism" in 1790 to describe the debilitating results of converting philosophy's wisdom into epistemology's knowledge, the more traditional elements of German culture had fought to maintain the integrity of the religious beliefs that held their culture together.[12] The unresolved tensions that animated the battle between the "rationalists" and the "Pietists"—tensions that the then twenty-year-old Schelling himself had surveyed in his earlier *Letters on Dogmatism and Criticism*—were still at work forty-five years later and had, in fact, grown in their intensity. In this reading, the appointment of the aging Schelling was seen by the rationalists as an almost poignant act of desperation on the part of the old guard to fend off the inevitable dawning of a new age of reason. Once again, just as in the 1790s, it appeared as if there were only two possible choices: revolution or a reactionary conservatism. Although this reading jibes well with the most recent accounts of Schelling's appointment in Berlin, it fails to do justice to both the complexity of his actual position and the historical context surrounding what Karl Jaspers has described as the last great event of the German university, that actually engaged the interest of the educated public.[13]

Indeed, a closer examination of the historical record leads to a different question: if Schelling was so philosophically over the hill, why did so many care so much about his return to the center stage of philosophy? Could it be that there was good reason to expect that Schelling would finally correct the excesses of idealism as manifested in the Hegelians' panlogism, and therewith restore a sense of balance and purpose to philosophy's role within society?

After King Ludwig of Bavaria invited him to teach in Munich in 1826, Schelling began a new cycle of productivity equal in intensity to that of his youth. In these years, he feverishly sought to articulate and develop a more comprehensive philosophy that would address the demands of his day by drawing on the truths he found in his study of the world's mythic, religious, and philosophical traditions. The spirit of modern philosophy clearly tended toward formal, critical, and thus *negative* results, and it was precisely the force and vitality of the *positive* that Schelling believed had been sacrificed by his erstwhile collaborators Fichte and Hegel. Modernity's demand for quantifiable forms of knowledge called for the divorce of sensuous intuition from its reflective articulation in the universal concepts of the natural sciences; a divorce that abandoned the needs of the human spirit for an integrative meaning and purpose of existence. In Munich Schelling began to critique this negative tendency, arguing that philosophy devoid of anything positive can only be thetic, that is, a formal system of definitions.[14] As an a priori science, it follows that such a system ultimately proves to be one extensively developed petitio principii, since as a purely immanent science it can begin and end only with itself. Following from its definition as logic, such a science cannot begin with actual existence but must rather "withdraw into itself so as to presuppose nothing" (*WMV*, 80).

Word of the general contours of Schelling's new work spread quickly after his inaugural lecture in Munich during the winter semester of 1827–28. With Schelling's 1834 publication of a brief introduction to a work by Victor Cousin, in which he set forth his first public critique of Hegel, the stage had been set for the inevitable clash of Hegel's defenders and Schelling's supporters. The German literati, who were repulsed by the anemic abstractions of Hegel's system and fed up with the "facile omniscience" of his disciples, had found their champion in Schelling, whom they now hoped would provide them with a real future for philosophy. As Karl Rosenkranz acknowledges in his *Letter to Pierre Leroux*, "the news that Schelling was coming to Berlin" had "delighted" him:

> I looked forward to the fight that this occasion must cause. I rejoiced in quiet over what by all appearances would be the toughest test of the Hegelian system and its adherents. I reveled in the feeling of progress, which for philosophy must spring from this. I greeted this challenge as a phenomenon never before encountered in philosophy, where a philosopher should have the power to step beyond the circle of his creation and to grasp its consequences, which in the history of philosophy until now is without precedent.[15]

A report of Schelling's appointment in a Parisian journal in 1841 informs us that "[t]he most famous German philosopher, and without a doubt the greatest living thinker, Schelling, has been called by the King of Prussia" to be professor at the University of Berlin. After detailing the difficulties Schelling was leaving behind in Munich, where his critiques of Catholic dogma had almost lead the Bavarian King to ban him from lecturing, the article continues with the following analysis of the obstacles he would encounter in his new northern home:

> Schelling's arrival in Berlin will expose him to other conflicts and, as one even now can predict, of a no less sensational type. Those who have spent but a little time with philosophy know how bad these days the relations are between Schelling and the Hegelian school. For one thing, in a small publication of 1834, Schelling spoke quite contemptuously about the person and fundamental thoughts of his great rival, and quite sharply about the hordes of his followers, which he dared to describe as feeble minded.

On the other hand, in Germany there is a new school of philosophers who support Schelling's new system, and claim that it surpasses Hegel. Now this is a matter that the Hegelians, of the *genus irritable*, can in no way deal with. Not only do they not think of confessing themselves to be feeble minded, they rather contend that with Hegel philosophy is complete, since the formula which explains all things has been discovered, and one must now simply apply it. And if there are still feeble minds in the world, then they are those who have not yet grasped this, and deceive themselves about being able to surpass Hegel.[16]

This report's predications proved to be dead on target. Schelling's brief introduction to Cousin's work had taken direct aim at Hegel's system, and in so doing had shown the direction in which his philosophy had been evolving during his years of silence. After defending his claim to having introduced the groundbreaking idea of a dynamic historical process in his *Philosophy of Nature* (1799) and his *System of Transcendental Idealism* (1800), Schelling proceeded in his Cousin introduction to criticize Hegel for having completely drained this dynamic process of its living, empirical reality. He writes of "[a] later arrival, who by nature seemed to be predestined to create a new Wolfian system for our age, who by instinct, as it were, swept away that which was empirical…[and]…in place of what was living and real…posited its opposite, the logical concept, to which through a strange fiction or hypostatization, he ascribed a similar sort of necessary self-movement" (I/10, 212).

Schelling makes clear that this "feeble minded" transcription of the natural self-movement of the living human subject to a subject construed as a logical concept was Hegel's own "astonishing invention" (I/10, 212). Like watching a runner attempting to sprint on ice, Schelling saw Hegel's efforts to derive nature as the result of a logical process to be almost comical, if it were not for the destructive consequences that followed from this "strangest fiction" (I/10, 212). As if compounding Hegel's obsession with order and method, his followers now demonstrated an almost fanatical zeal in their efforts to, in the words of Engels, "protect the grave of the great master from insult."[17] Thus did the avowed critics of religion's dogmas prepare to attack Schelling with nothing other than a religious zeal, devoid of any awareness that the ferocity of their assaults was almost as effective as any government censor in quelling dissent from their party line. And the attack from the Young Hegelians was fierce, employing the rhetoric of brute force, as when an anonymous author claimed that Schelling "was beaten into the grave" by Hegel in 1807.[18] In a strange twist of irony, their agenda was being advanced not by an appeal to reason, but through the use of the dogmatic rhetoric of ecclesial authority and the appeal to the immature ego's need to belong to a group. In the rather shrill words of Engels:

Our concern will be to pursue the course of his thoughts and to protect the grave of the great master from insult. We do not shy away from the fight. Nothing more desirable could happen to us than for a while to be the *ecclesia pressa*. Here the temperaments part ways. What is true remains preserved in the fire, what is untrue we gladly miss amongst our ranks. Our opponents must concede that never have so many youths thronged to our colors, and never has the thought that governs us been on our side so much as it is now. Thus do we wish to stand with confidence against our new enemy.[19]

Disregarding the more ideological dimensions of this philosophical "fight," the Young Hegelians had serious reasons to suspect that Schelling's appointment signaled the beginning of a conservative backlash, spearheaded by the king and the religious authorities, against their critique of religion which, for Marx at least, was the "presupposition of all critique."[20] Just judging the book by its cover, the full title of Schelling's lectures speaks of a *philosophy of revelation*, which strongly suggests some sort of philosophical return to a Christian orthodoxy, a suggestion reinforced by the resounding chorus of support for Schelling's arrival in Berlin from theologians, who had recently come to feel like an endangered species in the face of Hegel's deadly logical formulas. The party line from this camp saw Schelling's positive philosophy as "the necessary corrective for the recent discovery of criticism, before which no book of the new testament is safe"; a criticism which they held to be responsible "for the barrenness" of their "entire theological science."[21] As hard as it may be for us to grasp now, when Marx and others spoke of critique, they were not talking about a mere academic matter of no concern to general society. On the contrary, in the then nonsecular Prussian state, the possibility of critiquing religion also meant the possibility of critiquing the very center of ideological power that held the state together. This is why the state had censors, and why Schelling insisted that he have unconditional freedom from such censors while lecturing and working in Berlin.

Schelling's entire position vis-à-vis the government's suppression of freedom of inquiry demonstrates how this thinker refused to be neatly subsumed under this or that category, be it political, theological, or philosophical. The Hegelians' fears that Schelling's arrival announced a clampdown on intellectual and political freedoms proved baseless; on the contrary, he actually helped convince the government to lift censorship of the main journal of the Young Hegelians, the *Halleschen Jahrbücher*—an action that complements Ruge's conclusion, based on personal conversations with Schelling, that Schelling was "completely liberal" when it came to religion and politics. Moreover, this conclusion would have come as no surprise to Bavaria's governing powers in Munich, whom Schelling openly defied in 1838 through his refusal to follow their ban against philosophy professors lecturing on theological issues.[22]

Indeed, if Schelling was a vehicle for reactionary conservatives, why were his lectures such a problem for the conservative government in Munich? Could it be that he too was engaged in a critique that, in good Socratic fashion, called into question too many religious conventions, thereby upsetting the government's ministers in Munich? If we answer this question in the affirmative, we must then ask why theologians in Berlin were looking for help in combating criticism from a philosopher whose freedom of teaching had been threatened due to the government in Munich giving into Catholic protests who were against his philosophy of revelation. Even taking into consideration the very real differences between Catholic Bavaria and Protestant Prussia, a philosophy of revelation that cannot be taught in a university would not appear to be a philosophy that a conservative theologian would look to for help in combating secular critiques of religion.

This constellation of opposing factions looking to the same thinker with very different expectations speaks to the importance of Schelling's lectures in 1841 Berlin. The hopes placed on Schelling's shoulders were immense because they were animated and driven by spiritual crises partially unleashed by Hegel's conceptual dismemberment of the cultural enterprise that had previously sought to unite and integrate the opposing claims of philosophy and religion. Consider Hegel's most popular work, *The Phenomenology of Spirit*. The prevailing understanding of this work at this time was that it was a description of a victorious process, in which the rational concept achieves total control over every domain of human experience through its knowing subsumption of every possible predicate under its ever-expanding sphere of determination. Yet this victory of rational knowing over ignorance appeared to many to have been purchased at the price of the reality and essential importance of spiritual, of *geistige* experience.[23] The numinous power of the *mysterium tremendum*—the sensuous experience of the sacred that animates the soul of every spiritual person—plays no role in Hegel's logic. Indeed, it is not allowed to play a role because as the prototypical 'other' of conceptually mediated experience, the numinous is by definition not qualified to participate in the dialectical development of the absolute. In his lectures on the *Philosophy of Religion*, Hegel is quite clear about the asymmetrical relation between logic and faith: "One must know only what the essential category of thought is here. Faith is also knowledge, but an immediate knowledge. Thus the antithesis reduces to the abstract determinations of immediacy and mediation, which we have to refer to only in the logic where the categories of thought are considered according to their truth."[24] In Hegel's logic, a "truth" must always be mediated; that is, it must be a reflexive moment immanent to the self-explication of the concept.[25] There are simply no other possibilities for truth, epistemological or otherwise; the existentially very real alienation of faith and reason experienced by the "ordinary abstract understanding…vanishes in the speculative notion" of Hegel's logic.[26] Thus is the reality of the numinous castrated and folded into the necessary progression of Hegel's method. As even the first pupils at his gymnasium would have known, for Hegel "[t]here can be but *one method* in all science, in all knowledge. Method is just the self-explicating concept—nothing else—and the concept is one only."[27]

The hubris of this position led many to draw damning comparisons between Hegel and Goethe's *Faust*, pointing out how Hegel's philosophy culminated in the very state of omniscience that Goethe decried. "It really appears to be the case," Leroux wrote, that Hegel "presents himself as Faust,…the philosopher who in vain searches for wisdom," yet is "capable of transforming himself into Mephistopheles,…so that after the completion of this strange operation he can say: see here, Faust has finally reached the solution to his problem."[28] And although Goethe never commented directly on such a family resemblance between Hegel and the characters of his *Faust*, he did express his thoughts about Hegel's reduction of *Naturphilosophie* to his *Logic*, finding it impossible "to say anything more monstrous" than Hegel's "annihilation [of] the eternal reality of nature by means of a miserable sophistical joke."[29]

Yet what for Goethe was a monstrosity was for Hegel's followers anything but a sophistical joke. On the contrary, deriving certainty from the strict application of their teacher's method, they too arrived at the summit of perfected knowing, an Archimedean position from which they claimed to be able to see clearly the underdeveloped nature of the unenlightened regions of human existence that stretched out below them; an absolute standpoint from which the Young Hegelian believed he could critique every and all other human activities, particularly religion. Implicit in Marx's contention, for example, that the critique of religion is the precondition of all criticism, lies his acknowledgment of the central role this practice plays in the life of humanity—a role which Marx fought furiously to destroy, and which others struggled just as hard to sustain.

Leroux perhaps spoke best for those who demanded more from philosophy than just destructive critiques when he wrote that "the dangers that now threaten philosophy" come not "from the direction of her natural enemies, the adherents to all the idolatries of the past, but from the direction of those who pose as philosophers, and who now unfortunately believe that philosophy has its goal in calling everything into doubt, and in not believing in anything."[30] The unrealized vision of German Idealism's quest for a unified and integrated philosophy capable of harmonizing the oppositional claims of reason and intellect, faith and the will, and of coordinating the prismatic claims made by these very different powers of our humanity, appeared threatened by Hegel's monotone method of "grey upon grey," wherein, with the triumph of epistemology over wisdom, of knowledge over faith, there was nothing more left to believe in.[31]

It was this nihilistic milieu that fed what Rausch called the "widespread longing for Schelling." For many he was a giant of the golden age of German Hellenism, whose genius and wisdom gave them hope that perhaps he would be the philosopher who would reunite and resuscitate what Hegel had so effectively separated and drained of life. The future force behind modern anarchism, the Russian philosopher Michail Bakunin, gives voice to such feelings when he writes to his family in the summer of 1841: "You cannot imagine with what impatience I have been waiting for Schelling's lectures. In the course of the summer I have read much of his works and found therein such an immeasurable profundity of life and creative thinking that I am convinced he will now reveal to us a treasure of meaning."32 Sören Kierkegaard was also among the ranks of those who saw in Schelling a sort of savior figure who would rescue their age from meaninglessness. He writes of the desire for a connection of philosophy with the real world, with the reality of our lived human experience; a connection he cannot find in a universal logic. There is a "sighing"—the metaphor of longing once again—a deep need and desire to have something real, not just an idea. And again, there is the extraordinary expectation projected onto the old Schelling:

> I am so thrilled to have heard Schelling's second lecture—indescribable. Long enough have I sighed and the thoughts within me sighed; and then as he spoke the word "reality," and of the relationship of philosophy to reality, the fruit of those thoughts within me jumped for joy as if they were of Elizabeth. I remember almost every word he said from that moment onward. Maybe here clarity can occur.... I have now placed all my hope in Schelling.33

What unites Bakunin and Kierkegaard is the longing for a philosophy that would once again offer the hope of a meaningful connection to reality and a creative future. Clearly, the intensity of these longings and hopes exceeds the anemic limits of pure reason, spilling over into the realm of existence and, most importantly, the sphere of the religious. Whereas Hegel and his school had consigned the religious *Vorstellung* (*representation*) to the hinterland of underdeveloped ideas, it was clear from its very title that Schelling's positive philosophy, with its subsidiary philosophies of mythology and revelation, incorporated into its field of investigation the entirety of all religions. Schelling's stated goal was to philosophically explicate the phenomena of religion without, however, castrating their numinous power. This reconciliation would then usher in a new era of productive peace between the perennially antagonistic camps of philosophy and theology. Finally, from the many written accounts of Schelling's Munich lectures, most of his audience in Berlin was aware that his positive philosophy culminated in the challenge of creating a new way of doing philosophy, which would lead to what he called a *philosophical religion*.

This challenge of moving beyond the past and into a new and different future appealed to a wide spectrum of the educated classes not only in Germany, but throughout Europe as well. In a review of Schelling's Berlin lectures in a French journal, Leroux emphasizes that Schelling's task is "above all to solve the problems which move the human spirit today."[34] Problems of the human spirit that Leroux believed could only be addressed if philosophy reinvigorates itself by integrating the creative power of the sacred:

> [O]ne should realize that Schelling is not facing backwards. He has assembled himself in the phalanx of those great spirits who all with different formulations announce a *new religion*. I repeat: there will come a time in which there will not be one or more German or French philosophies, but rather there will be but one philosophy, that is at the same time a religion.[35]

What was hoped for was the declaration of a new interpretive framework that, unlike Hegel's system, would not repress humanity's desire for meaning that transcends the present. Such a framework would offer the hope of a new and transformed future, while integrating this longing into a meaningful unity that encompasses all the varied dimensions of human existence. The intensity of the desire for some way of making meaning in a world rendered meaningless by reason's excesses speaks to the crises of the human spirit that Leroux and others clearly experienced, both personally and culturally. A crisis that Schelling himself acutely sensed. As he wrote in 1834, "German philosophy is still in the grips of a process" whose "explanatory crisis still lies ahead of it" (I/10, 223). The crises that he foresaw would occur only if philosophy proved itself incapable of countering the growing force of cultural nihilism; a possible future that could only be avoided if philosophy could somehow offer a viable system that promised a new redemptive paradigm.

To do this philosophy was going to have to offer up something more than a formal science of concepts, animated only by the sheer force of logical negation, and thus devoid of any positive meaning for humanity's existence. While a necessary element of any complete philosophical system, a formal system of concepts controlled by the necessary dictates of logic alone was incapable of doing justice to the contingencies and complexities of human experience. The Kantian ideal of completeness had to be redefined so that it would no longer refer to an idealized state of static immutability, devoid of all development. Completeness needed to be conceptualized as dynamic and processional, referring to a perfect state of ongoing and never ending development whose results would be as unpredictable as they were creative. Such a redefined conception of completeness was to be found in the system principle of freedom which animates all of Schelling's thinking. The challenge was to account systematically for the reality of this freedom, particularly as it manifests itself in the generation of the new, whether this is in terms of the first creation from the past, the creation of the present, or of creations yet to be realized. If experience refuses to be reduced to the elegant necessities of mathematical expression; if the boredom of a perfected nature and final answers is not the ultimate goal of philosophizing; and if we are not to be forever doomed to advance while looking backward to the past, then it is imperative that philosophy develop new ways of articulating a more complex understanding of our reality. It is precisely this challenge that Leroux and others hoped Schelling would prove capable of meeting in his "existential system" (*PO*, 125).

AN EXISTENTIAL SYSTEM OF PHILOSOPHY

In the Berlin lectures on *The Grounding of Positive Philosophy*, Schelling claims that he has always worked within a system whose goal of completeness demands an ongoing struggle between two complementary methods, namely the negative or critical and the positive or dogmatic. "Convinced of this" he writes, "I maintained already in 1795, in the *Philosophical Letters on Dogmatism and Criticism*, that…in opposition to this criticism (and thus was the critical philosophy labeled as a system) there will someday appear an entirely different, far more adroit dogmatism than that of the mistaken and half-hearted former metaphysics" (II/3, 84).[36] Jacobi introduced this opposition in a debate about the scope and power of reason, which he cast in the form of a simplistic dilemma, wherein one is forced to choose between a "rational nihilism or irrational fideism."[37] Schelling argued against such a divisive approach in his *Philosophical Letters*, advocating the replacement of Jacobi's binary "either-or" with a complementary and more encompassing "both-and": philosophy can do justice to the dignity and richness of human existence only when it can integrate these opposing frameworks into one system. Although the negative enterprise of critique is needed to maintain philosophy's allegiance to truth, it often devolves into meaningless skepticism if it is incapable of dealing with existence and the world of human action in which our very freedom testifies to the contingent status of meaning in our lives—a contingent status that in turn requires some form of dogmatic belief system through which we can integrate the chaotic and fragmented regions of our existence into a meaningful whole. We can submit our individual judgment to the necessary dictates of logic in the sphere of abstract thinking and theory, but "the extralogical nature of existence rebels so decisively against this," that the attempt to "explain the world and…[our]…own existence as the mere logical consequence of some kind of original necessity" renders impossible any coherent account of the freedom through which we determine *for ourselves* what we are to believe in (II/3, 95).

Freedom, as always, is the driving force behind Schelling's positive philosophy. Reinterpreting Kant's division of philosophy into its theoretical and practical employment, Schelling's understanding of positive philosophy flows seamlessly from Kant's own demarcation of the sphere of practical philosophy made in the first *Critique*: "[b]y 'the practical' I mean everything that is possible through freedom."[38] Positive philosophy addresses the rebellious "extralogical nature of existence" that refuses to conform completely to the order of necessity. At the same time, however, through his negative philosophy Schelling is also dedicated to mapping out the logical nature of existence that constitutes the legitimate sphere of necessity's influence and control. If philosophy is to remain a vital and relevant power both in the lives of individuals and society, it must be capable of accounting for how both of these forces work together. Due to our instinctual drive to create meaning, both the negative and positive philosophies are inescapable because they are required to create the oppositional tension that drives the continuous development of philosophy. Indeed, it was the skeptical insight of criticism itself that enabled Schelling to see "why these two systems must necessarily arise beside each other" (I/1 306). This necessity yields the possibility of a comprehensive philosophy that would not only account for the philosophizing subject's abstract thoughts and representations but would also address and integrate the positive reality of existence that supports and transcends the *cogito's* reflections.

The essential role that the actuality of existence [*Wirklichkeit*] plays within Schelling's work is one of the most important yet difficult aspects to grasp. Unfortunately, the complexity of Schelling's understanding of existence, caused in large part by his originality as a thinker, has led many to just ignore this fundamental dimension of his work and simply file his philosophy away under the catchall category of German Idealism. Although this is certainly an expedient strategy, it ignores the richness of his contributions and the rebellious role he played in this decisive chapter of philosophy's history. Given our current task, a brief look at some of these earlier ideas will help us to better appreciate the continuity of the arguments he advances in Berlin against the absolute idealism of Hegel's negative philosophy.

As discussed earlier, Schelling's opposition of criticism and dogmatism expresses a frustration with the limits placed on philosophy by Kant's transcendental doctrine of method, which, according to his "disciplined reason," is allowed to work only in the abstract world of the 'concept': "[p]hilosophical knowledge is rational knowledge from concepts" (A 713/B 742). Only the concept can satisfy Kant's demands for a philosophical knowledge that must be universal, necessary, and certain. Intuition, be it sensual or intellectual, is therefore an unacceptable source of philosophical knowledge, since according to Kant, intuition concerns itself with what is particular and contingent.

This expulsion of intuition unmoors philosophy from its roots in existence and nature, releasing it, as it were, to ascend into the intoxicating air of universality, from whose dizzying altitude the reality of the individual, and the chaotic power of freedom and creativity, vanish. Filtering out such contingent impurities enables Kant's transcendental idealism to function like a sort of conceptual knowledge-machine, which, as the third *Critique* would have it, effectively demotes the sublime yet nonlinear order of our organic existence to the second-class status of the mere sensuous world. This world then, agreeing with traditional dual-plane constructs of a Plato or Augustine, is valued as less real than the conceptual cathedral of pure reason. Since Kant's epistemology is incapable of processing that which is simultaneously the cause and effect of itself, he accords the purpose-driven actions of organic life—and therewith freedom itself—a merely regulative status, to be dealt with only as if they were forces constitutive of our world. By dividing our world into the noumenal and phenomenal, Kant set us on a course that, due to its repression of the organic, guaranteed "the negative and the positive in philosophy had to separate," with the former laying claim to dominance over the latter (II/3, 75).

In this reading, Kant's Copernican Revolution initiated the final chapter in modernity's disastrous efforts to elevate the order of the subject over the order of nature—a chapter that Schelling helped to compose in its early stages, leaving it to Hegel to complete. As he confesses in Berlin, "[i]n truth, I had attempted in this philosophy nothing other than the next possible thing after Kant, and was inwardly quite removed from accepting it—no one will be able to cite an assertion contrary to this—as the *whole* of philosophy in the sense in which this later occurred" in Hegel (II/3, 86). His remove from the inverted world of idealism is plain to all familiar with his *Naturphilosophie*—the unique philosophy that was the focal point of his first three books and to which he devoted much more time and energy than he spent on his short essays on transcendental idealism.[39]

Of particular relevance is the vehement protest he voices in the *Naturphilosophie* against philosophers for whom the only reality is the reflected, and thus *inverted*, world of the concept. Writing in 1797 he puts the matter as follows: "[h]e who feels and knows nothing real within and beyond him, who in general only lives from concepts and plays with concepts, for whom his own existence itself is nothing other than a matter of thinking—how can such a person speak about reality (like the blind about colors)? (I/2, 215).[40] The grey upon grey monotone concepts are but schematic outlines of the world, lifeless and anonymous representations stripped of all vitality and color due to reflection's removal of intuition from the realm of philosophical knowledge. Echoing Hamann, Schelling sees in Kant's removal of intuition the emergence of a conceptual philosophy that makes reflection an end in itself rather than a means to an end (I/2, 14). As he argued in his *Magister*, reflection is a "necessary evil" of thinking itself that emerges in the genesis of knowledge and freedom.[41] We become aware of this power of reflection in the moment of "alienation" [*Entzweiung*] in which we find ourselves in "contradiction with the world" (I/2, 13, 14). This split, this separation of self from world, denotes both "the beginning of reflection" and "the first step to philosophy," since without this alienation and separation "we would have no need to do philosophy" in the first place (I/2, 13, 14). But once engaged in reflection, the philosopher "separates what nature had always kept unified, separating object from intuition, concept from image," and finally "himself from himself" (I/2, 13). In making "himself into an object," however, "the *whole* person no longer acts," because he has elevated one part of his being "in order to reflect on the others" (I/2, 13). Now an end in itself, this enthronement of reflection to a "position of control over the entire human" inevitably leads, on the psychological level, to the "intellectual sickness" of inaction due to overanalysis (I/2, 14). On the epistemological level, the exclusive reliance on reflection is a "divisive business," which "makes permanent the separation between humanity and the world, in that it considers the world as a thing in itself, which neither intuition or imagination, nor understanding or reason, is capable of reaching (I/2, 14).

As an alternative to such a simplistic and anemic concept of philosophy, Schelling accepts reflection as a "necessary evil" that a "true philosophy" will always consider a "mere means" to an end. Therefore, reflection is nothing other than its "own destruction" via the overcoming of the very disjunct at the root of our separation and subsequent alienation" (I/2, 14). To accept reflection as such he must construct a genetic epistemology that will integrate sensual and intellectual intuition into Kant's conceptual architectonic. What must be accounted for is the movement of the self from its original condition of wholeness to its more differentiated state of reflective activity. Schelling undertakes this challenge in the developmental history of self-consciousness advanced in his *Transcendental System of Idealism* (1800), wherein reflection arises in the self only after the more primary stage of "productive intuition":

> Since our whole philosophy proceeds from the standpoint of intuition, not that of reflection, occupied, for instance, by Kant and his philosophy, we shall also derive the now incipient series of acts [*Handlungen*] of the intelligence *as* acts, and not, say, as concepts of acts, or as categories. For how these acts attain reflection is the problem for a later epoch of self-consciousness. (I/3, 456)[42]

In the second "epoch" of productive intuition, the self engages in the "unconscious act of producing" the "primary representations" of the object world of existence (ibid.). Roughly equivalent to Aristotle's account in the *De Anima* of "the perception of proper objects" (428b21), Schelling here seeks to account for the self's unerring apprehension of objects before the reflective assignment of concept *qua* predicate. It is this preconscious activity, operating at the limbic level of involuntary action, that forces us to perceive and represent the external world. The force of necessity that generates this conviction of an external object world is not only much stronger than thought, but it also serves as the paradigm for the force of necessity itself, which accompanies the more tenuous connections of our logical judgments. This inversion of modernity's ordering of certainty places existence before representations, noting the undeniable fact that "we are just as insuperably and unshakably firm in our conviction of an existence beyond us—although this is communicated to us only through our representations—as we are of our own existence" (I/2 216). What makes our conviction so unshakable is that the sensuous intuition of the object world forms the very basis for the subsequent production of our concepts of these objects. Consequently, in Schelling's developmental epistemology, there is no dualistic gap that would require a correspondence theory of truth to bridge such a separation.

At this involuntary level of awareness, the unity of intuition and object is such that the act of intuiting and "the object are originally one" (I/3, 506). It is only in the next epoch of reflection that the result of this productive act—the concept—is differentiated from the generative act itself. This is an act of separation that Schelling considered the most elementary of judgments, and which is "designated very expressively through the word *Urtheil* [judgment], in that through this act what has thus far been inseparably united is now separated into concept and intuition" (I/3, 507).[43] Concepts arise for us in the separation of the act of producing from what is produced, "when we separate the acting as such from the outcome," which we then call "the concept" (I/3, 506).

Schelling provides us here with the process whereby the unconscious act of productive intuition serves as the generative ground of the resulting concept. The ordering of this developmental progression stands in stark contrast to what is seen from the standpoint of reflection, which, beginning with the divide between concept and intuition, must then account for how the two correspond to each other. A philosophy such as Kant's begins and works within the already formed world of the reflexive self. But this analytic starting point enters into the process too late, missing the beginning, the self coming to know itself. This fact undermines his account of how these transcendental concepts conform to the actual object world of existence. "A philosophy which starts from consciousness," Schelling writes, "will never be able to explain this conformity, nor is it explicable at all without an original identity" of the object and the concept, "whose principle necessarily lies beyond consciousness" (I/3, 506). Within Schelling's developmental monism this question does not even arise, "inasmuch as this question presupposes an original difference between the two" (I/3 506). Indeed, from this standpoint, the very fact that correspondence can occur on the abstract level of reflection indicates that concept and object must share the same structural identity on a more fundamental level. The horizontal picture of correspondence is just too static and one-dimensional to generate anything more than a circular argument of how the two relate. To provide a criterion whereby concept and intuition can be judged to agree or disagree we need a prior field of unity that transcends this duality. We need a vertical dimension, a genetic process of knowing, whose starting point will provide us with the basis for explaining the necessity with which our concepts involuntarily match up with our intuitions of the external world. Schelling achieves this by his principal of the "original identity" of object and concept, which, because it is prior to the act of judgment, supplies the basis for adjudicating correspondence and agreement between different things. As he makes clear, this principle of the original identity "necessarily lies beyond consciousness." This last point is critical. Under threat of circularity, the ground of consciousness cannot itself be consciousness, just as the ground of reason cannot itself be located within reason, and the ground of reflexivity cannot itself be accounted for in reflexive terms. The attempt of such an immanent grounding, as we will see, always proves circular and thus futile.[44]

Schelling's strategy of providing a transcendent grounding of thought in the unconscious limits of existence testifies to his conviction that philosophy must primarily deal with the actual world of human experience, a conviction which again sharply contrasts with the modality of possibility which determines Kant's transcendental world of the "I think" (nowhere in the latter's table of categories does actuality [*Wirklichkeit*] appear). For this to happen, Kant would have to begin his construction on a foundation beyond thinking, in that which is other than thinking, in that which in Schelling's words is "immediately given" through the very thing Kant forbids philosophical knowledge, namely intuition. Following Fichte, Schelling's paradigm of the "absolute certainty whereby all other certainty is mediated" is the proposition "I am" (I/3, 347, 343). Turning the Cartesian epistemology on its head, Schelling begins in the facts of existence and action, not of reflection and speculation. In this position the highest element in our knowing must be intuition, since only intuition provides us with unmediated certainty of the given actuality of our existence: "Nothing is for us actual, other than what, devoid of all mediation through concepts, devoid of all consciousness of freedom, is immediately given. But nothing gets to us immediately other than through intuition, and therefore intuition is the highest element in our knowledge" (I/2, 216). Radically empirical, the necessary force of certainty that delimits all philosophical activity ultimately derives from experience, namely, our actual existence. The undeniable constraints and limits which define our existence thus serve as the experiential paradigm for the necessity of a priori concepts, which, after the fact of experience, we then create through a process of abstraction (of separation in the sense of *Urtheil*) as we reflect backward upon what has already been.

Using the explanatory concept of the unconscious, Schelling expands the field of the empirical to cover both those experiences that we take notice of, as well as those that fall below the liminal level of conscious awareness. Seen from this standpoint, the apparent opposition between a priori and a posteriori knowledge disappears:

In that we displace [*versetzen*] the origin of the so-called a priori concepts beyond consciousness, where we also locate the origin of the objective world, we maintain upon the same evidence, and with equal right, that our knowledge is originally empirical through and through, and also through and through a priori. (I/3, 527)

Just as experience occurs on the two interdependent levels of conscious and unconscious knowledge, in terms of its origin, is as thoroughly a priori as it is a posteriori. Schelling continues: "To become aware of our knowledge as a priori in character, we have to become aware of the act of producing as such, in abstraction from the product. But in the course of this very operation, we lose from the concept, in the manner deduced above, everything material (all intuition), and nothing save the purely formal can remain" (I/3, 527). We do have formal concepts, which we can call a priori concepts, but these concepts do not exist prior to experience. They originate in experience and reach their seemingly ironclad certainty only after the fact, after they have been refined and distilled as it were, into formal concepts through the process of abstraction. In this process the raw material of intuition, the actuality of experience, is removed, thereby excluding the actual being of experience from the reflexive operations of the thinking subject. Thus from the standpoint of the thinking subject reflecting upon actual experience, the process of knowing, of applying predicates to things, appears to have begun here in reflection, and to have been initiated by the thinking subject. It is precisely in this moment, when the thinking subject begins to operate in the inverted world of reflection, that it naïvely assumes that the beginning of this reflected world is in fact the beginning of the actual world. The *cogito*'s "I think" thus becomes the confession of allegiance to the naïve belief that this thinking is the initiator, the prime mover as it were, of this subject's world. The task of a "true philosophy," however, is to expose this illusion created by reflection, thereby dethroning reflection as an end itself so it can be put back into its proper role as the necessary means to the end of its own overcoming. According to Schelling, the very word itself signals this inversion: just as left is right in a mirror image, in reflection what appears as cause to the thinking subject is actually effect.

Schelling's developmental history of the self coming to consciousness seeks to get beyond this inverted world of reflexivity so that philosophy can return to its primary task of providing a comprehensive and integrated understanding of existence. In doing this, the beginning is crucial: initial conditions determine the subsequent development of the entire system. According to Schelling, the fact of existence must somehow determine these initial conditions. Consequently, he insists that existence precedes reflection in the same way that the immanence of intuition precedes the concept. Concepts arise through the act of separating the result of intuition from its productive activity, a process in which intuition provides the positive undifferentiated material that the separated concept then reflexively determines and limits. For Schelling, the positive undifferentiated material of our knowledge is the unbounded and thus absolute fact of existence, "that something *is*" (I/2, 216). This simple yet sublime fact of the world's existence—that we can even know this fact—is not the result of the subject's magical epistemological efforts, but is due rather to the nature of the existing world to which we belong and from which we have evolved. That we can determine and thereby limit this positive fact of existence is the result of the common ground we share with our world, a shared identity that is always the basis for the judgment of difference that emerges through the reflective inversion of abstraction: to recognize myself in a mirror I must already have an awareness of myself that precedes the inverted reflection before me. The apparent dualism between intuition and concept, which defines the standpoint of reflection, disappears from the genetic position of production in which the formal concept emerges out of the material of intuition.

Schelling claims that it is this common ground that, in uniting humanity with the world, provides us with the epistemological basis of our knowing. We are a part of the larger organization of nature in which we participate, a fact on whose account our knowledge of the world is, in this fundamental sense, what Schelling calls a "knowing with" [*Mitwissenschaft*] or "*conscientia*" (I/9, 221). The common ground that unifies us with the world, this identity, locates the starting point of all thinking and deliberation in that which is the condition of reflexive thinking, namely, the intuitive realm of unmediated certainty. This realm is an epistemological ground zero to which Schelling cites Aristotle's "fitting words" that "the starting point of thinking is not thinking, but something stronger than thinking" (I/2, 217).[45] What is stronger than the possibility of the thinking subject's reflections is the fact of existence, whose chaotic reality is the ground of the *cogito*'s reflexive determinations.[46]

It is from the standpoint of this natural ordering of existence before the *cogito*'s reflection that we can understand Schelling's use of the terms "positive" and "negative" in his *Naturphilosophie*. In his *Weltseele* of 1798 he writes that "our philosophy cannot proceed from the mechanistic (what is negative), but rather must start with the organic (what is positive)" (I/2, 349). Positive here refers to nature's self-organizing systems of creation as opposed to the stable results of such generative systems. Inspired as he was in these early years by Spinoza, we should understand this contrast of the positive and negative through Spinoza's opposition of a progressive *natura naturans* to a regressive *natura naturata*. Like the difference between a movie and a snapshot, the positive of *natura naturans* is nature as a whole in its productive activity, whereas *natura naturata* is the result of this producing reflexively determined in its static forms. In the same way as the static concept relates to productive intuition, the unbounded productive activity of *natura naturans* is the positive yet undetermined ground of the resulting product, whose articulation as *natura naturata* occurs through a limiting and thus negative force.

Refusing to accept Kant's bifurcation of our world into that of a phenomenal nature and an otherworldly noumenal freedom, Schelling considers the creative power of organic life itself to be "the schema of freedom" (I/1, 249). This integration of Kant's dual-plane cosmology into one actual world sets off a whole series of chain reactions within Schelling's system. As life is the schema of freedom, and freedom the beginning of all philosophy, life itself and its teleology of purpose becomes constitutive of existence; a position that informs Schelling's commitment to his *Naturphilosophie* and its attempt to plant his philosophy firmly in the actual world of organic life. From this position Schelling always sought to make clear his "distance" from the subjective idealism of Fichte, as when he equates "the positive" with "life" and "experience" (I/7, 32), or when he simply states that "the philosophy of nature presents what is positive immediately in nature" (I/7, 6). As he insists in 1802, there "are not two worlds, but rather only one true world that is not external or above the phenomenal world, but is itself within it" (I/7, 274). It is impossible for the subjective thinker who doubts the existence of other minds and the external world to realize that the kingdom of reason is itself rooted within the embodied world of sensuous nature, since "[h]ow such knowledge is possible cannot be realized as long as all knowledge is viewed as subjective, as if it too didn't belong to the world" (I/7, 144). This last phrase captures perfectly Schelling's critique of those philosophers who, in good Gnostic fashion, assume from the outset that their thought is not a natural product of this world in which we live. This otherworldly alienation from the lived world of existence, which since Descartes has characterized the ethos of modern philosophy, *inverts* the relation between thinking and being, making the later dependent on the former with the result that the positive world of existence becomes as inscrutable as the object of the transcendental ideal. In the 1820s, Schelling again takes aim at how this alienation manifested itself in that school of thought from which, as we saw above, Schelling claims to have always been far removed. He writes of how:

> German Idealism carried this thought out to its most absurd conclusions, thereby denying the agreement between philosophy and the philosophy of nature that namely philosophy should account for the world. However, in doing this idealism deals with the world of lived experience just as a surgeon who promises to cure your ailing leg by amputating it. If philosophy refuses to amputate existence, then it must begin by ascribing being to those elements of nature that are not known. (*WMV*, 94)

This is the challenge Schelling refuses to ignore: how to coherently speak about "those elements of nature" that we are incapable of knowing according to the propositional structure of discursive thought. If, as Aristotle argued, the "starting point of reason is not reason, but something stronger than reason"; if, as Schelling maintained, the starting point of consciousness is not consciousness, but something stronger; and if the beginning of thinking is not yet thinking, but actually something stronger—if this correction of the inverted reflection of the thinking subject's relation to the world of existence is accepted, then philosophy must admit that it is incapable of reflexively integrating the fact of existence into a purely conceptual structure.

Admitting this impotency of reason is not, however, a satisfactory resting place for philosophy. Rather, a way must be found to face the difficult epistemological challenge of integrating "those elements of nature that are not" capable of being reflexively "known" due to their positive nature, a challenge which, if it is to be successfully met, cannot be dealt with through an appeal to some immediate access to being that absolves Schelling from the difficult task of justifying his position. The challenge Schelling has before him is to provide a positive account of why the condition of all knowing cannot itself be known. It is this challenge that Schelling claims to meet in his Berlin lectures on *The Grounding of Positive Philosophy*.

THE GROUNDING OF POSITIVE PHILOSOPHY

What Schelling means by a positive, free science of thinking, is perhaps best seen in his use of Kant's antinomy of pure reason, which illustrates the unavoidable presence of both the negative and positive philosophies. What for Kant were simply the "self-contradictions that reason allegedly falls into regarding the cosmological ideas," are for Schelling further evidence of the many ways in which "the opposition of the negative and the positive philosophies" manifests itself (II/3, 145). Following Spinoza's axiom according to which *omnis determinatio est negation* (all determination is negation), Schelling holds that a science of reason can only determine objects through negation, a position we might now elaborate by pointing to Saussure's concept of language as a diacritical system of signs. These signs can only articulate relations of difference, devoid of positive meaning, in which each word is defined negatively as its reflexive other. In contrast to such a mechanistic and (like Spinoza's philosophy) completely deterministic system, Schelling's positive philosophy is animated by a freedom of thinking that, with a more comprehensive scope than that of reason's reflexive mechanism, is (like Saussure's speaking subject) capable of making positive determinations of meaning through its power to make assertions [*Behauptungen*].[47] Schelling writes:

The thesis of the Kantian antinomies positions itself consistently on the positive side, the antithesis on the negative side. Nothing is required to allow the world to continue into infinitude or indeterminacy—for in doing this strictly speaking nothing is posited, since to posit the absence of all limits [*Grenze*] basically means not to posit something, and thus properly speaking, to posit nothing. In contrast, to posit a limit is to do something; it is an assertion [*Behauptung*]. Yet the antinomy as contradiction arises only through the fact that what is really not an assertion (the antithesis) is put forth as an assertion, whereas the other one, which is actually an assertion (the thesis), is put forth as an assertion of reason. Reason, which according to its nature cannot assert, can also not posit a limit, and conversely the philosophy that asserts a limit must proceed beyond reason and know more than what by virtue of reason alone is *to be known*. (II/3, 145–46)

Kant's account of the "collision of reason with itself" (II/3, 146) is for Schelling proof that the master from Königsberg employed a parochial and too limited view of the scope and nature of philosophy. As a critical endeavor, Kant locked philosophy within the limits of reason's determinative power of negation. This limitation demonstrates for Schelling the truncated and thus anemic nature of Kant's architectonic, insofar as a pure structure of negations hopelessly begs the question: *what is being negated?* As Kant himself points out in his attempt to render the transcendental ideal coherent, "no one can think a negation determinately, save by basing it upon the opposed affirmation" (A 575/B 603). As parasite to host body, determinate negation requires the real and actual opposition of a positive object; an opposition which requires affirmation not merely as its initial condition, but also as the irreducible other of negation. This other provides the disjunctive friction that sustains the never-ending process of predication. However, according to Kant, reason, and thus philosophy, is incapable of providing what he himself acknowledges is the very condition of all predication, namely, the positive object of such predication. According to Kant, the antinomies' affirmative theses are illusions, and thus cannot supply the very "opposed affirmation" Kant himself here insists upon. Consequently, just as Aristotle accused the Eleatians of circular reasoning in their attempt to explain logic by means of logic, Schelling here charges Kant with the similar fallacy of attempting to account for the "opposed affirmation" of reason's negations through a purely negative science.

Schelling claims that the only consistent way out of this *Teufelskreis* (vicious circle) is for philosophy to integrate and make use of "that which is more than reason" through a new, truly "positive science" (II/3, 146). According to Schelling, Kant's antinomies simply articulate the opposition between reason and what is more than reason, namely, existence. However, a comprehensive philosophy must integrate both realms of thinking and existence in their proper order and arrangement. Schelling uses Kant's resolution of the third antinomy of freedom as his model for completing the difficult task of integration. In this resolution Kant argues, through the use of the disjunctive form of reasoning, that both the thesis and the antithesis are to be held as true.

Kant never succeeded in truly integrating the positive force of freedom into his theoretical architectonic, opting instead to relegate its articulation to his practical philosophy. According to Schelling, Kant's conviction that his propaedeutic science "starts out purely from itself," as a "pure science of reason," prevented him from seeing that theoretical philosophy itself must be capable of integrating the demands of a positive philosophy, so that it could provide "a significance for action [*die Praxis*]," and thus deliver the conditions "for the ethical life" (II/3, 146). Schelling knew there must be a way of bringing Kant's practical concerns, most importantly freedom, into the systematic constructs of his theoretical philosophy, and it was the overcoming of Kant's bifurcated architectonic that Schelling understood as the goal of his life's work. The account Schelling provides of the history of post-Kantian philosophy is illustrative of this.

What Kant bequeathed to his successors was far from a formal science of reason due to its lack of a clear principle that would unite his three a priori sources of knowledge, namely, sensible intuition, the concepts of the understanding, and the ideas of reason. Fichte demanded an absolute *prius* (*origin*) for these three faculties, and located it in the 'I' of human consciousness; a standpoint from which he then attempted to provide "a common derivation of all a priori knowledge from one principle" (II/3, 56). It was then an obvious and necessary step for Schelling to sublate this "limited form according to which the I was but the I of human consciousness," in order "to arrive at the true *universal prius*," the Absolute I (II/3, 55). This idea of an absolute reason, "in which no longer the *philosopher*, but rather reason itself knows reason," liberated Kant's *Critique* from its dependence on "what was simply given," thereby elevating it to the "wholly independent and autonomous science" that Kant had aspired to, that of "an unconditioned science of reason" (II/3, 57). Yet Schelling designates this pivotal point in the development of German Idealism as the beginning of its gradual decline into a dogmatic metaphysics of the kind that Kant's *Critique* had hoped to have forever discredited. Schelling lays the blame for this squarely on Kant, insofar as he "extended what he had proved only of *reason* to *philosophy*" as a whole, and thereby "tacitly assumed that there is no other philosophy than pure rational philosophy" (II/3, 83).

In doing this, Kant put philosophy in an impossible situation since, according to Schelling, it is impossible that the human spirit could ever satisfy itself with a purely critical and thus negative response to the most profound questions of human existence. Refusing to reduce philosophy to logic, Schelling argued that the "propensity to understand, so deeply embedded and insurmountable in humanity," inevitably drives us to seek out a positive response to the riddles of human existence (II/3, 75). "Even Kant himself," he tells us, "after he had completely eliminated the positive from the theoretical philosophy, introduced it again through the back door of the practical" (II/3, 84).

From the historical distance of some forty years, Schelling claims, as we saw above, that he was never completely convinced of the worth and value of an absolute negative science of reason, even at the height of his own efforts to construct one. Making a veiled reference to his fragmentary work on such a science, which in 1801 he called a *System of Identity*, he unequivocally states that he never accepted negative science "as the *whole* of philosophy in the sense in which this later occurred" in Hegel (II/3, 86). Calling to mind his *Naturphilosophie* and the extensive attempts he made therewith to do justice to the positive facticity of our natural world, Schelling claims that the error in this earlier work "was not to have placed what is positive *outside*" a negative system (II/3, 89). Citing such frustrations with the limits of his earlier work, he claims he "abandoned" his own system and "left [it] for the time being to those who stood ready to appropriate it" (II/3, 86). This is of course a reference to his then friend and colleague Hegel, who since 1800 had been living and working with him in Jena. In Berlin almost forty years later, Schelling now claims that if his mistake then had been to leave the positive within the confines of his absolute system, "so this was surpassed by the ensuing (Hegelian) presentation, but only through the perfection of that error" (II/3, 89). And it is in this sense that he presents Hegel's system as the most fully developed articulation of a fundamental orientation that has always been present within philosophy itself.

Schelling argues that the difference between a philosophy "that grasps the essences of things" and one "that explains the actual existence of things" has been present within the history of philosophy "since time immemorial" (II/3, 95). For example, from the negative standpoint of a science of essences, Heraclitus "sought to explain everything…through reason," whereby he argued "that nothing ever endures, but rather…everything only flows or moves like a river, τὰ ὄντα ἰέναι τε χαὶ μένειν οὐδέν" (II/3, 96).[48] Such a strategy reflects the essentially mobile nature of the theoretical employment of pure reason, insofar as it only supports "a science that…abides at nothing" (ibid.), and thus finds itself always caught up in the never ending movement of discursive thought.[49] Together with the Eleatians, such "rational philosophers" find themselves trapped within a "circular movement," whereby they fall subject to Aristotle's criticism "that although their science is only logic, they nevertheless sought with it to *explain* logic itself" (ibid.).[50]

Schelling introduces Plato's work as representative of philosophizing that goes beyond the merely logical to deal with what is positive. By this he means a philosophy that is "empirical in the widest sense of the word, in which the *thatness*" of existence "is first, and the *whatness*" of its essence "becomes second and thus secondary" (II/3, 100). It is in reference to this secondary knowledge of the essence of things that Socrates claims his 'unknowing': while "others boasted" of such knowledge, with "which they believed really to know,"

Socrates merely added that "he is aware that this knowledge [of the essences] is no real knowledge" (II/3, 98). This claim of unknowing thus only refers to a "science that occurs solely in thought," such as "geometry, which no doubt for this reason Plato, in the famous genealogy of the sciences (*Republ.VI*), counts not as an ἐπιστήμη, but only as a διάνοια" (II/3, 99).[51] But in advancing this conception of an "ignorant science," Socrates "thereby posits external to this…a positive science," capable of a positive knowing (II/3, 102).

The object of this positive science is the "exuberant nature" of existence; a force which serves as the attractive power that draws thought "outside itself," thereby liberating thought "from its necessary movement" in the a priori sciences, so that it might begin a new "science of free thinking" (II/3, 102). And it is only this philosophy of "free thinking" that is creative and powerful enough to meet the challenge of actually making meaning within our individual lives. While the evolution of negative philosophy is indeed required for philosophy's continued development and relevancy, it alone is incapable of achieving this outcome. While negative philosophy can provide the necessary discipline for academic exercises of logical thinking, it proves insufficient when applied to the realm of existence.[52] The clear delineation of where each philosophy has jurisdiction is thus essential to the success of Schelling's project.

Schelling praises Kant for having established the limits of what a pure science of reason [*Vernunftswissenschaft*] is capable of achieving. Such a science has as its object reason itself, and not experience. Turning in upon itself, reason discovers what Schelling calls "the infinite potency of cognition," which, as the *prius* of all thought, contains within it the principle "of an a priori knowledge of everything which is [*alles Seyenden*]" (II/3, 57). What reason knows a priori, however, is only the essence [*Wesen*] of what is; a knowledge and an essence whose natural environment Kant perfectly captured in his virtual world of possible experience. Possible experience, however, is not real experience, and while reason proves quite successful in differentiating itself within its own sphere of thinking, it is incapable of grounding that sphere, and worse, it is rendered catatonic when faced with articulating the dynamic facticity of real existence.

Kant himself had argued in the first *Critique* that only a precritical or "dogmatic procedure of pure reason" can presume "to make progress with pure knowledge, according to principles, from concepts alone."[53] Drawing a distinction between knowing and thinking, we can say that reason is never capable of knowing that what it thinks actually exists. For this it must have recourse to what is beyond the domain of the a priori, namely actual experience. Thus in everything which is real there are always two decisively different aspects to be distinguished: "what a being is, *quid sit*, and that it is, *quod sit*. The former—the answer to the question *what* it is—accords me insight into the *essence* of the thing," whereby I gain "an understanding or a concept of it." The "other insight however, *that* it is, does not accord me just the concept, but rather something that goes beyond just the concept, which is existence [*Existenz*]" (II/3, 58).

This later insight into the *quod sit* is what Schelling considers to be a true cognition, in which there is positive knowledge of what is transcendent to, and thus more than, the concept, namely existence. The former insight into the *quid sit* generates only a "thought," which while "still by no means knowledge" in the positive sense, is nonetheless "a thinking knowledge" used in "a mere science of thought" such as geometry (II/3, 99). This *Denkwissenschaft* is, as Kant put it in his *Logic*, a form of science in which we "know only the cognitions but not the things presented by them," thereby generating the idea of "a science of that whereof our cognition is not knowledge."[54] This is exactly the form of science which negative philosophy assumes is thought a priori, in that it is a science of the essence of things a priori from the standpoint of pure reason. Such a science of reason is negative since it only operates in the a priori realm of possibility, being fully incapable of realizing or proving "any *present* existence, e.g., the existence of *this* plant or this stone" (II/3, 171). As Kant was at pains to demonstrate in his first *Critique*, Anselm fails to rebut the fool, essence does not include the predicate of existence, and the concept of one hundred Thalers, unfortunately, does not *tout suit* generate one hundred fungible Thalers. In stark contrast to the old metaphysic's dogmatic use of reason, Kant's use of pure reason employs an exclusively conceptual architectonic that restrains reason's desire to expand its domain into the realm of existence. In a point that is decisive for our treatment of the Berlin lectures, Kant insists that his *Critique* "is indeed *negative*," in that it restricts the *cogito's* seemingly instinctual drive "to progress" into the positive world of experience (an instinctual need whose paradigm expression is dogmatic reason's attempt to derive existence from essence in the ontological argument for the existence of God).[55]

Schelling lauds Kant for performing an invaluable service for philosophy when he demonstrated that reason can only ever attain to the concept of reality, whether it be of the world, the soul, or God. "Kant showed in general how futile it is for reason to attempt through inferences to reach beyond itself to existence." Schelling calls this illegitimate expansion of reason beyond its rightful borders dogmatizing (II/3, 83). And it is the failure of philosophy to recognize and check the excesses of such a dogmatizing logical strategy that has lead to what Schelling considers the "final crisis" of German Idealism (II/3, 32). As a central player in the history of this movement, he is quite clear about his desire to help move philosophy beyond this crisis. The essential first step in this process is to recognize the proper limits of the negative philosophy vis-à-vis the positive philosophy. In doing this, however, Schelling not only seeks to develop and advance a new positive philosophy of existence, but he also wants to overcome the shortcomings of previous sciences of reason through an improved and more robust negative philosophy. This is of course connected with his understanding of how philosophy had to further develop: the way out of philosophy's crisis demanded that these two different powers of philosophical inquiry come together in a unified system capable of sustaining their continual productive interaction; a system in which the opposing acts of negation and affirmation are integrated without ever suppressing each other's essential role in engendering philosophy's future growth. This demand, in keeping with his earliest attempts at creating a unified philosophy of nature and spirit, calls for the construction of a unified system capable not only of integrating difference, but of sustaining and encouraging its further development.

The way in which Schelling goes about the further development of his system is both predictably complex and true to the "dignity of his science," which, as he claimed in his youth, "consists in the fact that it will never be completed" (I/1 306). Consequently, only the impending end of his life could put an end to his incessant attempts to further refine and better articulate his system. Given the number of different iterations that emerged from this ongoing activity, the best way to approach Schelling's later work is to examine the development of his positive philosophy as demonstrated in his writings and lectures from 1810 onward.

This date designates the start of Schelling's struggle to put down in writing the very beginning of all that is positive, namely the process of creation whereby God and world come into being. Expanding his 1808 analysis of human freedom to encompass all creation, his goal in 1810 is as simple as it is problematic: conceptualize a historical philosophy that, while freely initiated, also integrates the orders of necessity that structure our existence. Under the working title of *The Ages of the World*, he constructs a three phased cycle of creation through which three ages, first god, then world, and finally humanity, come to be. Each of these three ages emerges out of the same dynamic of desires for wholeness, differentiated unity, and completeness. These desires draw each successive phase out beyond itself in the ecstatic emergence of the next, more complete stage of development. In this triadic movement the third and final phase of an age thus becomes the jumping off point for the beginning of the next, more fully developed age. When considered individually, each of these three triadic cycles can be seen temporally as past, present, and future, or ethically as what could possibly be, what must be, and what should be.

Thus, the first age of God creating his own positive being moves simultaneously through three phases: the pronominal being of God's initial capacity to be comes to know itself in the second moment of reflexive predication, which itself is made possible by the third phase of copulative or transitive unity of subject and predicate. The resulting unity of possibilities emerges in the 'inverted triad' of the three creative potencies that generate the positive and actual world of nature and humanity.

The ensuing age is that of the mythic process—the world—in which the three inverted potencies of nature's creative force engender a fragmented human consciousness that is dominated by the real unconscious power of nature. In this inverted consciousness, humanity is carried along by a mythic form of thinking that appears to consciousness as objective. While this process plays itself out within consciousness, consciousness itself, since it does not understand this process, sees it as an objective power of necessity over which it has no control and thus no freedom.

This age of the world transcends itself when God reveals the possibility of free action. Overcoming the earlier inversion of the creative potencies, God and humanity transition to the third and final age of freedom, in which human consciousness becomes capable of liberating itself from its being, and thus capable of freely deciding to bring back into harmony the positive potencies of creation. This harmony, if ever achieved, would yield the most completely creative environment for world, god and humanity (if not achieved, it will lead to what Schelling early on called "the annihilation of nature," and therewith, of course, ourselves [I/5, 273]).

Although Schelling never published *The Ages of the World* during his lifetime, he did offer lectures bearing the same title and similar content in Munich during the winter semester of 1827–28. By 1833, however, he had dropped the title *The Ages of the World* in favor of *The Philosophy of Mythology and Revelation*. And the three series of lectures he offered under this title betrayed the three phases of *The Ages of the World*: the first was the introduction to the entire cycle, *The Grounding of Positive Philosophy*; the second was treated in his lectures on *The Philosophy of Mythology*; while the third and final phase was detailed in *The Philosophy of Revelation*. As the full title of the Berlin lectures translated here indicates, *The Grounding of Positive Philosophy* presents us with the final version of the first phase of his lecture series, in which Schelling seeks to provide us with the foundation [*Begründung*] for positive philosophy. Whereas the philosophy of mythology and revelation remained essentially the same over the last decades of Schelling's life, the introduction to the entire cycle underwent significant changes, the cause of which brings us back to Schelling's attempt to rehabilitate negative philosophy.

Horst Fuhrmans provides us with the earliest version of Schelling's introduction in the form of a student's almost stenographic account of his Munich lectures of 1832 and 1833.[56] In light of its breadth, scope, and sheer volume, Fuhrmans calls this version the "large introduction." Here Schelling begins his presentation of positive philosophy with a critique of the negative systems that have dominated European philosophy since Descartes. In this larger version of the introduction, Schelling critiques those modern systems which, in inverting the *cogito*'s relation to being, reduce positive being to the negative activity of the thinking subject.

But as much as Schelling believed his critique of negative philosophy to be valuable, he was still acutely aware of the fact that he had yet to resolve the problem of how the negative and the positive philosophies relate to each other as an integrated whole. If he was to maintain the integral ordering of the philosophy of mythology and revelation—an ordering that presupposes the necessity, worth, and value of myth—then it follows that as the philosophical analogue of myth, negative philosophy itself must also have a meaningful role to play within his system. In the larger introduction, however, Schelling had only provided a critique of negative philosophy: having exhaustively detailed its shortcomings, he had failed to advance an account of its necessity and positive function.

This unresolved tension became more acute with the sudden death of Hegel in 1834; an event which indicated to Schelling that the post-Kantian movement of German Idealism had finally reached its end. The reality that he was the only surviving member of this generation of thinkers only reinforced his conviction that German Idealism was in the death throes of its "final crisis," precipitated in large part by its dogmatic belief that philosophy is ultimately nothing other than a science of knowing. Schelling locates the source of this mistaken position in a misinterpretation of Kant's critical program vis-à-vis the ontological argument; specifically in Hegel's attempt to ground his absolute idealism in a power of thinking whose efficacy Kant had repudiated: whereas Kant denied thought's ability to derive existence from its own immanent activity, the entire superstructure of Hegel's absolute idealism depends on it.

Kant's Copernican Revolution demonstrated a possible process through which our conceptual network, guided by the a priori categories of our understanding, reflexively shapes how things appear to us. The fact that there is nothing to be known that is not caught within our conceptual network suggested to Hegel that ultimately being itself is reflexively knowable. If such a position were to be embraced, a philosopher would then have the possibility of fully articulating the entire spectrum of our reality in a self-enclosed and immanent system of conceptual thought; a majestic conceptual construction whose completed unity would ultimately be demonstrated by the perfection of a final idea that emerges as the result of this reflexive process of determination.

Of course Hegel could pursue such a methodology only by dismissing Kant's *Critique* and its denial of thought's ability to magically generate actual existence. It was this failure to heed the conclusions of Kant's *Critique* that led Schelling to move the starting point of his introduction to positive philosophy from Descartes and modern philosophy, to Kant and German Idealism. For while Schelling was critical of Kant on many points, he considered his own life's work as an attempt to more fully develop the central insights of Kant's critical program. As we will see below, he compared the development of Kantian philosophy to the construction of a medieval cathedral: although it takes more than one generation to complete such a monumental project, each successive generation is guided in their work by the organizing principles set down by the original architect. Kant's critical program was a propaedeutic, setting negative boundaries for where philosophy could not go. What remained to be completed by ensuing generations were positive determinations of where philosophy can and should go. To do this Schelling required not only a positive philosophy, but he also needed to rehabilitate negative philosophy in order to show how it too was an essential and necessary component of a more developed and comprehensive philosophy. Only in this way could Schelling provide a way out of the crisis philosophy found itself in, an escape, as it were, out of the completed order of Hegel's logic. This liberation would once again release philosophy's subversive power to imagine alternative futures capable of freeing us from the restraining limits of the past and present.

SCHELLING'S NEGATIVE PHILOSOPHY

Standing on their own, neither the positive nor the negative philosophy can claim sovereignty over the entire domain of philosophy. They must somehow relate, yet in a way that will not merely repeat Kant's error of elevating one over the other (the theoretical over the practical), nor fail to provide an account of how the two work together. They must enjoy shared structures and dynamics that will justify their inclusion into a unified, systematic account of philosophy. The point of connection between the two, as it has always been for Schelling, is the assumed isomorphic structure—the identity—between thinking and being. This structured identity not only enables a new account of the negative science itself, but also allows for a transition to positive philosophy. It is here, in the reconfiguration of this identity of negative thinking and positive being, that Schelling introduces one of his most radical ideas, whose trajectory once again runs directly counter to the prevailing tendency of modern philosophers to limit their systems to the disciplines of logic and epistemology.

To guarantee systematic coherence between these two seemingly opposed regions of necessary thinking and free existence, Schelling proposes as axiomatic the proposition that "the highest speculative concepts" must always be "simultaneously the most profound ethical concepts" (II/3, 67). In returning ethics to its foundational role in philosophy, Schelling makes the point that logic alone is insufficient to account for the isomorphic identity of thinking and being. Rather, the structure of this identity must be somehow essentially ethical, a quality that must therefore be shared by both modes of negative and positive philosophy.

True to his established practice, this attempt at reconfiguration leads Schelling back to the beginning of his philosophy, since the conditions inherent in the beginning of any developmental system establish the parameters for its further evolution. Following the contours of his earliest system, Schelling does not turn to a negative force for his beginning impetus, but rather to the affirming positive force manifest in the will's *desire*. In contrast to Hegel's attempt at a *creation ex nihilo*, beginning as it does with the negation of a negation, Schelling's negative philosophy begins with the affirmation of a negation, or better, the affirmation of a *void*. The starting point of his negative science is a wanting [*ein Wollen*], since according to Schelling only the dynamic of desire and wanting can account for the initial conditions of a real beginning. As he much more eloquently phrases the matter, "all beginning lies in an absence, [and] the deepest potency, which holds fast to everything, is nonbeing [*das Nichtseyende*] and its hunger for being" (II/1, 294). In the wanting of desire, Schelling discovers a way of conceptualizing a beginning that is robust enough to encompass the presence and absence of being and nonbeing as one. And as the hunger of desire, this beginning satisfies his requirement that the highest speculative concepts also be ethical, for if freedom is going to be the determining principle of his entire architectonic, then even the necessary science of reason itself must be initiated in a free act of desire.

Logical operations of a double negation are indeed capable of engendering a positive in the monochromatic world of abstract possibility. But in the unruly hues of embodied existence it is not logic, but rather "[w]anting itself" that is the "purest example" of "the transition *a potentia ad actum*." This example captures the living dynamic of a beginning that does justice to our actual experience of being "capable of freely deciding" to become "originator[s] of a course of action" (II/3, 68). Such decisions are motivated by a wanting for something that leads us out beyond ourselves, thereby expanding our sphere of experience and knowledge. Reason follows this desire in wanting to move beyond its initial and immediate content of an inchoate intermingling of being and nonbeing. Reason does so, however, only as a desiring will, that, due to its ambiguous content, does not know precisely what it wants. Schelling presents this volatile initial mixture of being and nonbeing as the "amphibole" of reason's "infinite capacity to be" [*unendliche Seynkönnen*]. In this *prius*, in this potency, we encounter his attempt to articulate the inherently ambiguous dynamic of reason's immediate content that drives the disorderly beginning of thought's movement. What we encounter here is Schelling's alternative to Descartes' *cogito*, in which there are no bedrock propositions demonstrating clear and self-evident ideas. We begin neither in the ready-made world of pristine reason nor the vacuous desert of pure nothingness. Rather, we begin in an indeterminate but potent origin whose disordered ambiguity is much more commensurate to the reality of our experience. This immediate content of reason, this infinite capacity to be, is for Schelling the embryonic seed of all being. In this first moment it shows us a reason that, since it is "open toward everything" and thus "excludes nothing," is "free towards all that is" (II/3, 75). In excluding nothing, the immediate content of reason betrays its roots in an environment that is *other than* reason itself. Far from being the science that presupposes nothing, for Schelling, "philosophy is the science that must presuppose everything."[57]

Due to the inherent ambiguity of the immediate content of reason, the first task of Schelling's negative philosophy is to establish how this content itself can belong to being. Thus the first movement in this science is to make the transition from this unmediated state of possibility to an actual determinate concept of the being of this potency; an emergence of determinateness that occurs only when we make it happen, in that "the concept of being must" first "be produced"

(II/3, 77).[58] Schelling pulls this off by constructing an initial movement in which thought's potency "steps out of its capacity [*Können*]" and "into the sphere of becoming" (II/3, 69). Apropos the desirous nature of Schelling's reason, he employs Kant's logic of organism to generate this concept, wherein the whole of this idea of being must be presupposed in order to enable reflexive understanding to articulate, after the fact, the constituent members of being. Thus "in order to arrive in our thought at being itself" we must dissect its "original unity," thereby allowing the constitutive moments of being's emergence to become distinct in "their own right" (II/3, 78). Schelling's strategy of dissection follows the three-step analysis he perfected during his years of work on the *Weltalter*, in that here too he lays out, in a timeless succession, the emergence of: 1) the subject of being, 2) its object, and 3) their coupling "as one inseparable subject=object" (II/3, 77). The progression of this emergence is thus heuristic: since only all three make up the original unity, Schelling's sequential account of their emergence must be understood as the only order in which the clarity of reflective thought can present their simultaneous emergence.

He begins with the first moment in which "[i]mmediately, i.e., presupposing nothing, nothing other than the subject can be thought" (II/3, 78). This follows of itself since a subject is indeed the only idea that "presupposes *itself*. i.e., allows nothing to presuppose it" (II/3, 78). Consequently, this subject of being, in the "pregnant sense" of the "cause of all being," is "the potency of that which it already *Is*...immediately and without transition" (II/3, 77). But here, in the singular moment of thinking the subject, before the structure of predication, there is no movement, since in this first moment there is not yet a second element toward which thought can transition. In this limited sense the subject here is "provisionally being," thereby providing Schelling with the presence of "what *Is*, the ὄντως ˮΟν, as the Greeks very significantly named it" (II/3, 70). In thinking this singular subject, however, as what *Is*, we allow it "to be a potency *for itself*, i.e., to be the potency of its *own* being" (II/3, 79). In thinking it *for itself*, as what *Is*, we immediately propel it out beyond its pure potency, and "think of it as passing over into being" (II/3, 79). With this, the movement of thought really begins, since with this transition a 'void' is exposed within this subject: in thinking it for itself [*für sich*], thought makes its first distinction, and thereby creates a lack or absence of that which is not the subject. This absence, in turn, can only be filled by the second determination of that which is not a subject, namely, an object whose relation to the subject can only be articulated through the third and final determination of a transitive copula, which unites both elements "as one inseparable subject=object" (II/3, 77).

The successive determination of these last two elements demonstrates the dynamic nature of reason's movement once it steps out of its immediate state of potency and into the sphere of becoming. For with the emergence of the object and the transitive bond of the copula, reason is now faced with "this otherness [that] is not to be separated from that which is being itself: the former is unavoidably assimilated simultaneously *with* the later in the first thought" (II/3, 70). With this, being takes on as its ever-present companion what is *not* in being, and thus always has "the capacity not to be" (II/3, 79). The ineluctable otherness of this contingent and thus relative nonbeing is inescapable since it is that which reason never posits, "but is rather only what is not not to be posited" (II/3, 70). This capacity not to be provides the dissonance of appearance and reality, of *Seyn und Schein*: in its discursive movement thought has "only the appearance of being, for it presents itself as that which is not, as soon as it becomes something different" (II/3, 69). It is the variance between that which is being, actual, and thus unchanging, and this otherness of appearance, possibility, and contingency that now propels thought in its discursive movement, throwing our thinking into Heraclitus's rushing stream of thoughts. But as the current of every river flows towards a destination, this torrent of thought also has a telos.

Its goal is that which truly is, "being itself in its purity, being exalted beyond all doubt" (II/3, 79). And the only way that reason can arrive at this pure being is by "allowing" this otherness "to emerge and really pass over into its alterity, in order to liberate in this manner [the] true being…[of] the ὄντως Ὄν" (II/3, 70). In this way, this science aims at the "elimination of what is contingent" in order to free being itself from the virtual world of possibility (II/3, 79). The process of elimination is thus critical, and therewith negative: it advances by removing contingent being and all "that lies implicit or *potentia* in the general and indeterminate concept of being" (II/3, 70). Ultimately, this negative philosophy results in the concept of being itself [*das Seyende Selbst*], but due to its negative nature it can generate nothing "other than a *negative* concept of that which being itself is" (II/3, 70). Because of its thoroughly critical nature, negative philosophy has no other concept for being itself "than that of what is not nonbeing" (II/3, 70). The result of this science of reason is a concept of being itself, which it can only define negatively in terms of the apparent being that it has now successfully eliminated; a point which Schelling uses to show how actual being itself remains "outside" the movement of reason, making itself known to reason only at the "end" of this process, "as the result of this elimination" (II/3, 71). From this standpoint, it is of no concern to Schelling whether this concept is "something real," since "from the height which I look out at it a priori, it is merely what is possible" (II/3, 71).

The concept Schelling has as the *result* of his negative philosophy is of course the same concept Kant generated within his negative science of reason, namely, the concept of a necessary being, a necessary idea of reason that, as Kant demonstrated, reason will always find "not as its contingent, but rather as its *necessary* terminus" (II/3, 62). This necessary terminus of reason, however, has no more special claim on existence than any other concept. Negative philosophy can only ever generate a "logically mediated concept—in thought" of this necessary being and is thus incapable of demonstrating the existence of its highest idea (II/3, 79). To know that "this being itself *exists above*" the merely logically mediated concept "can no longer be the task of the negative science, but of a different one, that in contrast to the latter is to be called a positive science" (II/3, 80). And it is to this positive philosophy that we now turn.

EXISTENCE AS THE INVERTED IDEA

Kant characterized his critical philosophy as a "quite special, though purely negative science," whose purpose was "to remove an obstacle which stands in the way of the employment of practical reason."[59] Schelling understood this purpose as limiting the static necessities of reason to their proper sphere of conceptual thought in order to create an opening within philosophy, wherein the positive reality of our free existence could further develop. In Schelling's reading, Kant's work was a negative propaedeutic designed to clear the way for a reinvigorated and thus positive philosophy, which would deal with the actual world of existence. The key word here is *actual*, for it is only if philosophy can make the transition from the negative sphere of the possible to the actual world of existence that its constructions will evolve from an aggregate collection of conceptual elements into a true system. In the Berlin lectures, Schelling claims that it is this task to which he has devoted his life and to which these lectures are devoted: the presentation of his final attempt at developing a comprehensive system of philosophy that will integrate the seemingly opposing worlds of essence and existence, thereby providing Kant's negative philosophy with its proper foundation. Comparing Kant's architectonic to that of a gothic cathedral, Schelling makes clear both his allegiance to the principle of its design and his appreciation of the seemingly unending task of successfully completing it:

> I know that this architectonic, in its *perfect* execution, particularly in the countless details of which it is capable and indeed even demands, all of this is only comparable to the works of the old German architecture, which cannot be the work of one person, of one individual, and for that matter, not even of one epoch. Yet even the Gothic cathedrals left uncompleted in an earlier age were taken up again by a later progeny and constructed according to their principle. Although aware of this, I nonetheless hope not to withdraw from this world without having also consolidated the system of the negative philosophy in its true foundation, and as far as it is now possible for me, to have further developed it. (II/3, 90)

Schelling seeks to consolidate Kant's critical philosophy within its true foundation, which he believes can only be supplied by a positive philosophy. To perfectly realize this architectonic and supply it with its proper foundation demands that its detailed infrastructure be constructed systematically; Schelling felt Kant had failed to meet this internal consistency satisfactorily because he himself did not always construct his system according to the principle of his architectonic. The principle to which Schelling refers is of course the transcendental ideal, which, appropriately, he cites as the "genetic connection" of his work to that of the old master, claiming that the "point in the structure of the Kantian Criticism" that serves as this "genetic connection ... lies in Kant's doctrine of the ideal of Reason" (II/I, 283, n.1).

This ideal of reason, the transcendental ideal, supplies Kant with the conceptual power to systematically unite "all order in the world as if it had originated in the purpose of a...supreme intelligence" (A 686/B715). By infusing "all order in the world" with the unifying intent and purpose of one "author," the transcendental ideal should serve as the foundation of Kant's critical edifice, providing the unconditioned totality required to support and sustain reason's negative science in its ongoing effort to completely determine our knowledge of the world. As a modern reinterpretation of traditional metaphysics' *form of all forms*, this necessary idea of reason must be unconditioned since it serves as the transcendental substrate, which, as the common ground between the noumenal and the phenomenal, should unite and integrate Kant's theoretical and practical efforts into one coherent system. Decisive for Schelling's positive philosophy is Kant's requirement that this ideal of reason serve as the transcendental prototype of all being, in that as the "idea of the primordial being" (A 579/B 607) it is the positive subject, the *"ens realissimum"* (A 578/B 606), that serves as the host body for reason's parasitic negations *qua* determinations. As Kant himself made clear, his critique of reason is dependent on what he calls transcendental theology's "concept of God" (A 632/B660), which, as merely a regulative ideal, functions as the ground and basis "for the complete...[and]...unconditioned...determination of things" required by reason (A 580/ B 608).[60]

But how is it possible for a regulative ideal to execute such a foundational role? This question becomes even more acute when Kant demands that this unconditioned totality support and determine all the things of the world "as their ground, not as their sum [*Inbegriff*]" (B 607).[61] It is hard to overestimate the extent to which this distinction shapes Schelling's thinking. For in distinguishing between the necessary ground and the *Inbegriff* of all things "that follow from it" (A 579/B 607), Kant makes clear the difference between an original unconditioned necessity and a derivative yet still unconditioned "sum-total of all possible predicates" (A573/B 601). But in demanding an original status for this necessary being, Kant sets for himself a goal that appears impossible to achieve from within his negative science. For an original ground cannot be reconciled with the regulative function of an ideal, which, as an ideal, is much more suited to delivering the sum-total of all possible predicates as the result of an ongoing process of determination. Moreover, it would appear that an unconditioned ground must be more than merely possible, that it must be actual, that is positive, if it is to serve as the ground and basis for the determination of all things by reason. This absence or lack of an actual positive basis to support and receive all possible predicates is what Schelling calls "a hole in Kant's critique," which he believes his positive philosophy can fill, and indeed, with system resources Kant himself provides, yet fails to employ consistently (II/3, 168).

Accepting Kant's claim that only an unconditioned ground can supply reason with a systematic "unity of the grounds of explanation" (A 612/B 641), it follows that this idea itself cannot be the result of an additive process, since such a process would be never-ending, generating instead only what Kant calls a potentially unconditioned ground. An actually unconditioned ground, in contrast, provides an absolute measure, which Kant calls a "*Grundmaß*."[62] Such an absolute measure is categorically different from the members of the series it initiates and supports, insofar as it is the starting point of a process "to which other members" of that series "are subordinated" (A 417/B 445). As Kant makes clear in the *Critique of Aesthetic Judgment*, an Absolute of this kind lies *jenseits* (beyond) any external reflective measure that depends on relative comparisons. As unconditioned, this *Grundmaß* is a measure "that is only equal to itself."[63] Kant describes how this works in his account of how the sublime generates a fundamental measure whose scope and force exceeds our powers of conceptualization. Calling this unlimited force "exuberance" [*das Überschwengliche*], Kant states that it is, "as it were, an abyss" for our conceptual powers, insofar as they "fear to lose themselves therein."[64] While what Kant here describes is the encounter of our reflexive faculties with the sublime, the functional purpose of this *Grundmaß* in the third *Critique* parallels that of the unconditioned ground of the transcendental ideal in the first: both supply a ground that is *jenseits* the series they ground, and which serves as the unifying and thus absolutely positive starting point of the reflective process of negation *qua* determination. Applying the very same terms in Berlin, Schelling goes a step further and maintains that the ground of explanation, and thus of reason, cannot itself be immanent to reason's operations. It must instead be *jenseits* of the series it grounds, so that this ground can be neither reflexively appropriated or conceptually articulated, since *per definitum* it must precede our discursive analysis of it. Such a reading of the transcendental ideal dovetails with Kant's own demand that this *ens realissimum* must serve reason as its *ground* and not as its *sum*.

This last point has immense ramifications for Schelling's understanding of the relation between being, as the condition of the possibility of signification and the positive carrier of predicates, and the negative determinations of predication. Following Kant's account of the progressive synthesis of an actual unconditioned, in which this real unconditioned is transcendent to the series it grounds, Schelling reaches the conclusion that this unconditioned being stands in an *asymmetrical* relationship to the relative negations of predication.

In the regressive synthesis, wherein the potential unconditioned emerges at the end of the synthesis as its immanent result, the being of that unconditioned is of the same status as the negations that constitute the series: all are merely *possible*. Because of this, in such a series the being of this unconditioned enjoys a symmetrical relation to its negations: its being can be translated and reduced to the sum of all its constituent moments of negation qua predication. But the *actual* unconditioned of the dynamic progressive synthesis, as the ground of this series, is incapable of being reduced to such a negative status. This point will prove decisive in Schelling's critique of Hegel's system.

Due to the limitations of Kant's critical method and its programmatic reliance on a regressive method of synthesizing the unconditioned, his "purely negative science" only generated a negative account of this absolute, which, as a potentially unconditioned, can only be conceived as the *result* of a reflexive process. This is an internal inconsistency that Schelling had already noted while still a student in Tübingen, when he wrote to Hegel that "[p]hilosophy is not yet at its end. Kant has provided the results: the premises are still lacking."[65] The defect in reasoning that Schelling points to here is, as we will see, virtually the same formal flaw in reasoning that he finds in Hegel's account of a reflexive process of determination resulting in the immanent generation of the Absolute. Schelling finds the remedy to this defect in reasoning in a nexus of Kantian concepts and methodologies, which, ironically, were deemed by Kant as inappropriate for use within his own negative philosophy.

True to his claim to be following the principle of Kant's architectonic, Schelling employs these discarded concepts and methodologies in order to provide a positive account of synthesizing an unconditional ground. In order to supply philosophy with the "premise" he quite early on claimed was lacking, he employs Kant's *progressive method* of synthesis to account for an unconditioned ground that is actual, as opposed to being a mere possibility of thought. For whereas negative philosophy is solely concerned with articulating "what is capable of being comprehended *a priori*," positive philosophy "deals with what is not capable of being comprehended *a priori*,...transforming precisely that which is incomprehensible *a priori* into what is *a posteriori* comprehensible" (II/3, 165). Thus the key to understanding the different methodologies of negative and positive philosophy is to be found in the two different ways Kant offers to synthesize the unconditioned, namely the regressive and the progressive (A 411/B 438).

While Kant found the a posteriori application of the progressive method gratuitous, since this method begins with the inexponible concept of the unconditioned, Schelling saw in this method the only way of accounting for the absolute alterity of the positive foundation of philosophy. Coupled thereafter with the regressive method of Kant's preferred analysis, Schelling believed he would finally be capable of satisfying the demand he set for himself years earlier in his *Letters on Dogmatism and Criticism*. By incorporating both of these complementary methods, one regressive and negative, the other progressive and positive, he seeks to integrate the negative demand of reason for the reflexive articulation of a necessary being, with the positive demand for the *emphatic knowledge* of that being's actual existence. Whereas the a priori method of negative philosophy employs an immanent thinking that never goes beyond itself, the a posteriori method of the positive uses a transcendent thinking whose ecstatic pull draws thought outside itself into the arena of freedom and existence. As Schelling explains in the Berlin lectures:

> Negative philosophy is only a *philosophia ascendens* (ascending from below), from which one immediately realizes that it can only have a logical significance, [whereas] positive philosophy is a *philosophia descendens* (descending from above). Both *together* first complete the entire sphere of philosophy, as one could, if you still required further explanation or elucidation, easily trace this duality back to the customary division in the schools of theoretical philosophy into logic and metaphysics, in that the first is fundamentally only logic (logic of becoming), while everything truly metaphysical fell entirely into the other division (of the positive philosophy). (II/3, 151)

The distinction between a *philosophia ascendens* and *descendens* correlates seamlessly with the methodologies of each philosophy. The regressive method of the negative is an immanent ascension of reflective thought to the idea of that which exists in a necessary manner, while the progressive method of the positive begins with what necessarily exists, what is transcendent to thought, and then embarks on the never-ending demonstration of the nature and meaning of this existence. Once again, informed by his understanding of the connection between freedom and metaphysics, the ethical interest emerges as the center of gravity of Schelling's construction. What is predictable, what transpires necessarily according to a calculus, can be adduced a priori and thus determined in a closed and immanent movement of thought. In the realm of freedom and history, however, the matter is decisively different in that thought here is transcendent to the actual present and is thus truly metaphysical. Schelling elaborates on this central distinction in his earlier lectures on the grounding of positive philosophy in Munich:

> This is most easily seen when we consider that the primary object here is of existence, of free decision and deed: all decision and action is grounded in an inner experience that always includes a thinking that goes beyond the scope of the present reality, that is, it aims at a future configuration of events and is thus metaphysical. It is a thinking that goes beyond itself into decision and action, and is thus a transcendent thinking. In contrast, the *a priori* operations of negative philosophy occur in an unchanging

network of pure thought, and thus do not "happen." As static and unchanging, this thinking does not go beyond itself, instead remaining an immanent thinking with itself as its own object. (*GPP*, 101)

This immanent thinking, concerned only with itself, is dictated by the necessities of its method, with the result that self-reflexive thought is incapable of developing anything *new* and is thus locked out of the dynamic realm of existence and historical development. Reason here spins in its reflexive web a possible world in which, however, "there is no time-sequence,…no *before* and *after*" (A 553/B 581). To this degree, Schelling associates the thinking of negative philosophy with the necessary and restrictive logic of *myth*, in which consciousness lives in the cyclic time of "a continuous eternal happening" (I/10, 160). In contrast, the creative thought of his positive philosophy supplies the means to account for the unpredictable freedom of *decision*, which is *revealed* or made manifest only in action and deed. This freedom is not the "negative" freedom of mere "independence of empirical conditions," but is rather the "positive…power of originating a series of events" (A 553/B 581). It is a power of thinking to be able to transcend itself and break out of the static limits of immanent reflection. Only when both types of thinking, immanent and transcendent, are integrated into one coherent system will a philosophy emerge that is robust enough not only to deal with the vicissitudes of existence, but also to generate the creative power required to realize what is truly metaphysical within a world that supports such change and development.

How this is possible, and how Schelling executes these methods in his negative and positive philosophy, is best understood if we once again return to the details of Kant's architectonic and examine his account of how each method synthesizes the unconditional. This occurs in the first section of *The Antinomy of Pure Reason*, the *System of the Cosmological Ideas*, where Kant integrates these methods into his architectonic by associating each with categories of the understanding. The regressive method employs the mathematical categories of quantity and quality to synthesize a homogeneous unconditioned which emerges as the immanent *sum-total* of a series, whereas the dynamic categories of relation and modality are used by the progressive method to conceptualize a heterogeneous unconditioned that, as such, is the transcendent *ground* of its series. The first method of synthesis begins with the conditioned and then, turning backward, ascends to "the totality of the regressive synthesis *in antecedentia*," to finally arrive at the absolute unconditioned as the mathematical *sum-total* of that series (A 409/B 436; A 411/B 438). Conversely, the progressive method of synthesis proceeds *in consequentia*, beginning with the unconditional unity of the "dynamical whole" of nature and then proceeding forward, advancing into the future, moving "from the first consequence to the more distant" (A 411/B 438). Whereas the regressive method only finds the unconditioned at its terminus as *a result* of its method, the progressive method begins with the unconditioned as its *ground*. Presupposing the timeless and linear continuity of a mathematical reality, the regressive synthesis begins with extensive magnitudes in which "the representation of the parts makes possible, and therefore necessarily precedes, the representation of the whole" (B 203/A 163). The progressive series, in contrast, begins with the *inexponible* concept of the dynamic self-organization of nature and then proceeds to the progressive synthesis of its continuously evolving parts.

Reconfiguring Schelling's spatial metaphors, it is clear that the *philosophia ascendens* of negative philosophy employs the regressive method to chase after the chain of conditions in *antecedentia* until it *results* in a potential unconditioned. The *philosophia descendens* of positive philosophy, on the other hand, makes use of the progressive method, which begins with the actually unconditioned of existence as the *ground* of its process and then *in consequentia* abductively argues for the emergence of a meaningful narrative, whose ultimate worth can only be demonstrated in reference to the future.[66] The immanent absolute synthesized by the regressive method is an *aggregated totality*, equal to the sum of its parts, as it consists of a "series in which all the members without exception are conditioned and only the totality of them is absolutely unconditioned" (A 417/B 445). Yet because this is only a *comparative series*, it has no real "limits or beginning," and thus falls into an "infinite regress"(A 418/B 445). Lacking the oppositional alterity of a heterogeneous and thus transcendent ground to its synthesis, the regressive method proves incapable of generating more than the mere thought of an absolute. An absolute which, by definition, must always remain potential, trapped in its own infinite regress toward an existence necessitated by its concept but to which it cannot ever attain. Alternatively, as Schelling phrased the matter in 1833, "on this regressive path I come only to a relative, not to an absolute prius" (*GPP*, 433). And this is precisely the problematic shortcoming Schelling associates with Kant's negative concept of the most supreme being as *Inbegriff*, or sum-total of all possible predicates. It begs the question: is the existence of a positive subject required to support the infinite number of predicates demanded by his transcendental ideal?

The situation is quite different with the *absolute measure* [*Grundmaß*] synthesized by the dynamic categories of the progressive method. According to Kant, the dynamic categories begin with an "absolutely unconditioned" whole that is transcendent to the sum of its parts; a fact that allows us to conceptualize a discontinuous relation between heterogeneous elements, namely, the reflexive parts and the absolute unity. Schelling reads Kant here as suggesting that these categories of experience could be used to integrate the actual alterity of an inexponible and thus nonconceptual content that is supplied by "the dynamically unconditioned" (A 420/B 448). A positive philosophy that employed this progressive method would then, at least methodologically, be capable of supplying an unconditioned ground, located in that which necessarily exists, which would be transcendent to its conditioned consequences. As

Schelling makes clear in 1833, "I can prove that being which Is indeed only a posteriori, but again *only in a progressive* sense, i.e., *per posteriorem*, only through its *consequences*,— and because it is what can only be known through its consequences, it cannot be known *before* its consequences...*a priori*" (*GPP*, 433).

For Kant, however, this is not an option. This "self-subsisting whole" synthesized by the progressive method is *inexponible*, which means that it cannot be reflexively analyzed. The simultaneity of the reciprocal interaction among a self-subsisting whole's constituent members cannot be parsed by the sequential reflections required by Kant's model of subsumptive knowledge (A 419/B 446, n. b). Kant's ideal form of scientific knowledge is determined by the mathematical categories' categorical form of judgment, whose power to generate certain conclusions stands in stark contrast to the dynamic categories' disjunctive form of judgment. This latter form of judgment is only capable of generating *problematic* conclusions and informs the abductive inferences of the progressive method.[67] This would be no problem for Kant if, as he does in the first section of the *Antinomies*, he were to reject this form of problematic judgment and never employ its logic of *disjunction* elsewhere in his conceptual architectonic. But this is impossible due to Kant's demand for "systematically complete unity," which he can only account for if he uses the disjunctive logic of an organic whole (A 677/B 705).[68] Thus, later in this very section, Kant will employ this problematic form of reasoning to explain perhaps the two most important elements of his architectonic, namely, the antinomy of freedom and—the lynchpin of his entire structure—the transcendental ideal.

First, consider how Kant treats real existence through the relational form of the dynamic categories of reciprocity and community, both of which are informed by the logic of disjunction. Second, it is the disjunctive form of reciprocity that Kant uses to resolve the antinomy of freedom, whereby the necessity of the phenomenal and the freedom of the noumenal are both granted sovereignty in their respective domains. Third, Kant employs the disjunctive forms of reciprocity and community to account for the simultaneous reciprocity of the parts that make up the whole of a living organism. And finally, consider how Kant uses this form of judgment to explain how the transcendental ideal unites the disparate forms of knowledge into one systematic whole. All these operations, while essential to Kant's program, are determined by a logical form whose conclusions he himself concedes are of *a problematic status*. That is, the conclusions of such judgments do not generate a consciousness of necessity, but rather, as Kant puts it in his *Logic*, they only produce a "consciousness of the mere possibility" of necessity.[69] Yet Kant uses this problematic form to explain how the ideal of pure reason unites his entire system of apodeictic truths, writing that "reason, in employing the transcendental ideal as that by reference to which it determines all possible things, is proceeding in a manner analogous with its procedure in disjunctive syllogisms" (A 577/B 605).[70] Indeed, this must be the case, since the reciprocal interaction of distinct parts can only be comprehended if they are simultaneously thought of as belonging within the same whole, that is, the ideal of reason. But it is the very *simultaneity* of the coordinated interaction that, because it refuses to submit to the sequential analysis of the regressive method, forces Kant to label this form of thinking problematic. And this, once again, follows from his epistemological framework: Kant's blanket exclusion of inexponible concepts derives from his prohibition against any nonconceptual, that is, *intuitive*, content being admitted into his reflexive superstructure of concepts. Even the universal a priori axioms of mathematics are demoted to the status of inexponible concepts within Kant's epistemological hierarchy, since their "knowledge content" can be apprehended "only in pure intuition" (A 300/B 357). Consequently, they are derivative of Kant's synthetic a priori principles of reason, from which, as pure discursive concepts, we can "apprehend the particular in the universal through concepts" devoid of all intuition (A 300/B 357).

In limiting philosophy to the immanent use of exponible concepts, Kant removes the possibility of thought ever transcending the infinite regress inherent in the regressive method. This becomes painfully obvious in his treatment of the three ideas of reason, namely, world, self and God. As we have seen above, within the limits of the regressive method each of these ideas can only synthesize the infinite regress of a potential absolute. The result of this infinite process is thus a problematic idea, whose proof moves in circular fashion since it must use as the ground of its demonstration the very idea it seeks to prove. Having recourse only to a potential absolute, Kant himself acknowledges that all of these three ideas of reason are "problematic" (A 417/B 445 n. a). The cosmological idea of the world, *Weltbegriff*, rests on the law of causality. Because this world is a cosmos capable of being synthesized by mathematical categories, this idea only generates a potential absolute. This limitation forces Kant to admit that his proof of this law is *circular*, insofar as "it has the peculiar character that it makes possible the very experience which is its own ground of proof, and that in this experience it must always itself be presupposed" (A 737/B 765). In similar fashion, since Kant must posit a self that is only potentially absolute in its unity of consciousness, he is again forced to employ the conclusion of the proof of that unity, "which is what was to be explained," but which again "must itself be presupposed" as the ground of its own proof (B 422).[71] Finally, as we saw above, this point becomes particularly problematic for Kant when he moves to account for the unity of his concept of God, namely, the transcendental ideal. Because Kant's methodology can only synthesize this idea as the result of a process of complete determination *qua* negation, he is forced to presuppose this idea as the *positive ground* of his entire critical edifice (not to mention all predication, and therewith, language itself).

Here we arrive at what Schelling considered to be the most serious problem in Kant's conception of the transcendental ideal, namely, Kant's failure to explain how the idea of God could be *both* ground and sum of his system. The root of this problem lies in Kant's failure to distinguish between that which necessarily exists (ground) and the most supreme being (sum *qua*

Inbegriff]. It is precisely in the clarification of this distinction that Schelling claims his positive and negative philosophies offer up their greatest contribution to the Kantian structure, in that they offer a more coherent account of how the idea of the transcendental ideal, God, is to be understood.

Just as the old metaphysics before him, Kant requires the concept of a necessary being, and not only because it "is based on a natural, [and] not on a merely arbitrary idea" (A 581/B 609). Like all consequent thinkers, Kant requires this idea to account for the very *stuff* that his system will work with. And like most traditional metaphysicians, Kant is not content to just accept the simple concept of that which necessarily exists. He has to infuse the transcendental ideal with a more robust nature if it is to fully account for how his system provides the possibility of the entirety of all knowledge. As it "includes in itself all reality," it must also provide the ideal's positive object: the "transcendental substrate" of the "unlimited" that is the *positive content* to be negated by the determinations of all possible predicates (A 578/B 606; A 575/B 603). Only if we have this positive concept of an *unlimited substrate* can we think the possibility of conditioned things, for we can think these things only through determining them, which, *per* Spinoza, we can only do through negation. And since "no one can think a negation determinately, save by basing it upon the opposed affirmation," this concept of positive being, of the "*ens realissimum*," is for Kant the condition of the possibility of all thinking; a fact that in turn demands that this *ens realissimum* be regarded as "original":

> "For all negations (which are the only predicates through which anything can be distinguished from the *ens realissimum*) are merely limitations of a greater, and ultimately of the highest, reality; and they therefore presuppose this reality, and are, as regards their content, derived from it. All manifoldness of things is only a correspondingly varied mode of limiting the concept of the highest reality which forms their common substratum, just as all figures are only possible as so many different modes of limiting infinite space. The object of the ideal of reason, an object which is present to us only in and through reason, is therefore entitled the primordial being (*ens originarium*). (A 578/B 606)

As original, as the unconditioned ground of all determination, the object of this necessary ideal of reason must be *inexponible* in order to meet Kant's demand that it determine all things "as their ground, not as their sum" (A 579/B 607). And indeed, Kant seems to suggest that this object of the transcendental ideal is opaque to the discursive analysis of the regressive method when he notes that the "transcendental object…is and remains for us inscrutable" (A 614/B 642). Yet if it is inexponible, and in this sense inscrutable, it would follow that in a very important sense it cannot be present "in and through reason." Due to its "inscrutable" nature, it would seem problematic to speak of correctly applying predicates to it, since we have no clear criteria to determine the truth of our judgments about it. Moreover, as we have seen, reason in its regressive employment is incapable of generating an *actual* unconditioned ground, and instead generates only a *possibly* unconditioned, which of course emerges only as the *sum* and *result* of a regressive synthesis. It seems that Kant's own logic demands what it also forbids: it demands an *actual* unconditioned, and thus necessary being, but is incapable of synthesizing one. Yet the very demand to seek the condition of all things leads Kant's regressive analysis inexorably back through the chain of conditions to this inscrutable unconditioned being. Schelling notes that even Kant himself is forced to acknowledge this point, and in terms that suggest to Schelling how he can proceed beyond Kant. Citing the first *Critique*, Schelling writes:

> Kant calls the unconditional necessity which, as he says, we so indispensably require as the *supporter of all things*,…which precedes all thought, the true abyss for human reason. "Eternity itself," he continues, "in all its terrible sublimity, as depicted by Haller,[72] is far from making the same overwhelming impression on the mind; for it only *measures* the duration of things, it does not *support* them. We cannot put aside, and yet also cannot endure the thought, that a being, which we represent to ourselves as supreme amongst all possible beings, should, as it were, say to itself: 'I am from eternity to eternity, and outside me there is nothing *save* what is through my will, *but whence then am I?*' All support here fails us." (II/3, 163, citing A 613/B 641)

Here Schelling provides us with Kant's own account of the groundlessness of this necessary idea of reason. The unconditioned necessity of the *ens originarium*, like eternity, throws us into an intellectual vertigo that both Kant and Schelling find *sublime*. Schelling's choice of words is as strategic as it is significant, as he himself points out, "I quote these words because they express Kant's profound feeling for the sublime nature of the being that precedes all thought" (II/3, 163). This unconditioned necessity, according to Schelling, is thus transcendent to thought since it is that "which precedes all thought." More importantly, he uses Kant's term of the sublime, since only this term can adequately express the fact that both ideas are an absolute *Grundmaß*, which, as Kant wrote in the third *Critique*, exceeds our capacity of reasoning, creating, 'as it were, an abyss' for our conceptual powers insofar as they 'fear to lose themselves therein.' When faced with the overpowering magnitude of an actual unconditioned, reason rightly fears it will lose its capacity to properly function, since by definition reason cannot reflexively synthesize such an inexponible concept; as a measure "that is only equal to itself," a *Grundmaß* cannot be reduced to any other magnitude.[73] And this is *precisely why* positive philosophy must begin with this actual unconditioned, which, as that which precedes all thought, cannot be the *result* of a logical process, but must instead be the *ground*, the condition, and thus the beginning of all such processes, a beginning which Schelling calls the *fact of existence*, namely, the unthinkable condition of all thought.

As such, this unconditioned being is the positive ground of its concept, not a reflective consequence of thought. As the absolute condition, the absolute subject of all predication, this unconditioned being itself cannot be predicated. Yet while we are incapable of saying *what* it is, we can, however, say *that* it exists. As that which necessarily exists, this being qua Absolute Subject must be free of reason's restrictive necessity: reason, as negation, must itself be supported, and thus *limited*, by the unlimited, positive freedom of this *ens realissimum*. It is reason's demand for a positive existing being of unconditioned necessity that ultimately forces reason to acknowledge its inability to ground itself from within its own sphere of reflexive thought, a failure of self-grounding which occurs when reason's compulsive movement comes face to face with the necessary concept of that which groundlessly exists, and before which nothing can be thought. This is what Kant calls the abyss of human reason, and what Schelling terms *das Unvordenkliche*: "that which just exists is precisely that which crushes everything that may derive from thought, before which thought becomes silent, and before which reason itself bows down" (II/3, 161). It is perhaps here that we can see most clearly Schelling's *inversion* of the modern ordering of the *cogito* to being; a position that he presents us with in the following excerpt from the Berlin lectures:

> We can produce everything that occurs in our experience, a priori, in mere thought, but as such it exists of course, *only* in thought. If we wanted to transform this into an objective proposition—say, that everything in itself likewise exists only in thought—then we would have to return to the standpoint of a Fichtean idealism. If we want anything that exists outside of thought, then we *must* proceed from a being that is absolutely independent of all thought, which precedes all thought. Of this being, the Hegelian philosophy knows nothing, it has no place for this concept. Kant has in mind that which necessarily exists, to the extent that it is at the same time *God*. At the beginning of the positive philosophy we must still disregard this, and seizing it as that which just exists, we discard the concept of *God* precisely because it is a contradiction to posit on the one hand that which just exists, and yet also to posit it as *something* with a *concept*. For either the concept must come first, and being must be the result of the concept, so that it would then no longer be the unconditional being, or the concept is the result of being and we must then start from

being, devoid of the concept, and precisely this is what we want to do in the positive philosophy. But in God it is precisely *that*, by virtue of which he is what groundlessly exists, that Kant calls the abyss of human reason—and what is this other than that before which reason stands motionless, by which reason is devoured, in the face of which it is momentarily nothing and capable of nothing? (II/3, 164)

That which simply exists, that which just is [*das bloß Seyende*], is that which overthrows the *cogito's* claim to founding being. There is an identity between thinking and being, but this identity includes within itself difference, which in this context is the precedence of being over thinking. That which simply exists is that positive being that exists before all thought and the actual reality upon which all thought feeds. Or, as Schelling reminds us, "it is not because there is thinking that there is being, but rather because there is being that there is thinking" (II/3, 161).

Anticipating the obvious objection that this concept, whose essence is to have no concept, cannot itself be thought, Schelling responds that "[o]ne can concede this in a certain sense and say that for precisely this reason it is the *beginning* of all real thought—for the *beginning* of thought is not yet thought itself" (II/3, 162). We have seen Schelling state this position before, as when over forty years earlier, in 1798, he cited Aristotle's "fitting words" that "the starting point of thinking is not thinking, but something stronger than thinking."[74] Thought, reason, logic, and the concept: none are independent in the sense of being self-grounding. Rather, each operates in a context dependent on what is *irreducibly different*: thought occurs only in an embodied intuitive awareness, reason only emerges out of ambivalence, the same is true for logic vis-à-vis the fundamentally alogical character of existence, and the concept "exists" only in the individual personalities of human beings. These existential factors are opaque, unique, and thus transcendent to the universal and transparent realm of pure reason.

What is transcendent to the negative reflections of reason is the positive historical world of existence. As the supporter and bearer of thought, the being of this existence always exceeds reason's attempts at circumscribing its borders. Thinking is movement, but it is not self-propelled; rather, thought is carried along incessantly from predicate to predicate by the power of what Schelling calls the infinite potency of cognition. Like Kant's unconditioned absolute, the *actus* of this potency is transcendent to the series of its members, but transcendent only in the sense that it is absolutely other than thought: as the pure actuality of reality [*Wirklichkeit*], that which simply exists excludes potency, and thus the *possibility* indicative of thought. This is why the groundlessness of this actual existence is the abyss of human reason. Like the sublime, this absolute measure, this "exuberant being," forces reason's discursive movement to cease in the face of the total absence of all possibility in its object, since this object is the thought of that which cannot *not* be thought.[75] That which groundlessly exists is thus an idea that can only be called "the inverted Idea" [*Umgekehrte Idee*], since with this idea "reason is set outside itself" (II/3, 162). It is an inverted idea because instead of leading thought onward through its own possible self-reflexive determination, it *halts* that movement by confronting reason with a reality beyond itself. Confronted with this alterity, reason is drawn out of its self-involved reflexivity to become, as Schelling says, "free of itself," since in this instant it is "no longer its own object" (II/3,165). Upon encountering the other of actual existence, set free from the narcissistic mirror play of self-reflection, reason breaks out of its rotary motion to become "absolutely ecstatic" (II/3, 163):

> That which just exists is in its way also that which exists of itself, αὐτὸ τὸ ὄν, that is if we accept this Greek ὄν in its verbal sense. To this extent one cannot attach being to it as an *attribute*; what is *elsewhere* the predicate is here the subject: it is itself in the position of the subject. Existence, which appears as accidental in everything else, is here the essence. The *quod* is here in the position of the *quid*. It is thus a pure idea, and nonetheless it is not an idea in the sense that this word enjoys in the negative philosophy. That which just is [*das bloß Seyende*] is being [*das Seyn*] from which, properly speaking, every idea, that is, every potency, is excluded. We will thus only be able to call it the inverted idea [*Umgekehrte Idee*], the idea in which reason is set *outside* itself. Reason can posit being in which there is still nothing of a concept, of a whatness, only as something that is absolutely *outside itself* (of course only in order to acquire it thereafter, *a posteriori*, as its content, and in this way at the same time to return to itself). In this positing reason is therefore set outside itself, absolutely ecstatic. And who has not, for example, experienced the ecstatic dimension of Spinoza's philosophy, and of all of the other teachings proceeding from that which necessarily exists! (II/3, 162–3)[76]

Faced with the absolute measure of that which groundlessly exists, thought is forced outside of its immanent movement in an experience that Schelling fittingly describes as ecstatic, as an exuberant breaking out of the static orbit of reflexivity into the discontinuous domain of actual existence. That which *just is*, the pure subject, the Greek's αὐτὸ τὸ ὄν, is the inverted idea because it reverses thought's artificial inversion of cause and effect, of essence and existence, so that "existence" again becomes "the essence," and is realized as the actual source and foundation of reason's activities. The dynamic at work parallels how Kant, in the third *Critique*, uses the clash between the absolute measure of the sublime and reason's relative determinations to turn the latter's static self-reflexivity *inside out*, thereby creating an integrative form of judgment that aims at systematic unity.[77] The absolute and thus unconditioned measure of the sublime lays bare the actuality of existence that, compared with the mere possibility of thought, can only be described as "exuberant," as in Kant's "*das überschwengliche*," and Schelling's "*überschwengliche*" existence (II/3, 126). Finally, just as Kant describes the encounter with the sublime as an overpowering shock [*Erschütterung*], Schelling connects this ecstatic moment of reason becoming free of itself with Plato's account of the transformative experience of awe and wonder [*thaumazein*] (I/9, 229).

The inverted idea gestures, as it were, at the outermost boundary of predication, at an experience that is its real ground, and is not just a thought, since, under penalty of circularity, the impetus to thought cannot itself be a thought. This is a critical point that bears repeating: the unity or identity of thought and existence can only be accounted for if we begin before reflexivity divides and conquers our awareness of this unity of experience. As we have seen, if we abstract from this unity of experience, and attempt to account for the identity between thought and existence from within this reflexive relationship, we are faced with the impossible task of demonstrating their correspondence. The only other possible way of accounting for the correspondence between idea and world is to locate the ground of this identity in an experience prior to thought's reflexive negations. And while emphatically distancing himself from the mystical standpoints of Böhme and Jacobi, Schelling nonetheless grounds positive philosophy in an experience that is not mediated by thought. In part his reasons for doing this are, as we have seen, due to theoretical considerations, yet the most significant factor in Schelling's argument is ethical. In accordance with Schelling's position that every principle of philosophy must be as ethical as it is metaphysical, the proof of this inverted idea of the Absolute Subject must have an *ethical dimension*.

Accepting this inverted idea as the condition of all predication, we have seen why a reflexive proof of its status as such is impossible due to its inevitable circularity. Like Kant's proof of causality, "it has the peculiar character that it makes possible the very experience which is its own ground of proof, and that in this experience it must always itself be presupposed" (A 737/B 765). Since 1794, the very circularity of this type of proof has always demonstrated for Schelling its ethical dimension, in that reason's incapacity to break out of such circles indicates that the objects of such proofs are actually objects "of free action" [*Handelns*], whose reality is not demonstrated through a deductive proof, but is rather *realized* through "the moral activity of people" (I/1, 243).[78] The simple being of the inverted idea, in its pure simplicity as Absolute Subject, is thus the condition of all free action, since, as we have seen, this Absolute Subject is essentially forever free of being exhaustively predicated.

In saying this, however, we obviously predicate this simple being, but we do so with a predicate of freedom that, as such, does not limit the Absolute

Subject, since as free it can always be other than it is. In this way, the inverted idea provides the grounding for both the negative philosophy's reflexive operations, as well as the positive philosophy's free interpretation of the meaning of existence. The freedom manifest in this simple being serves as the common "band" which unites thought and being (II/1, 355).[79] For it is this freedom which animates the ecstatic, never-ending process of being overcoming itself, the process of being freeing itself from itself. It is in the encounter with this simple being that the reason of negative philosophy experiences this: when faced with its other, it is liberated from its own self-reflexive indulgence, and set free to deal with objects other than itself. The same occurs within the field of the historical experience of positive philosophy, in every individual, through the very process of education and culture: "Even man must tear himself away from his being in order to begin a free being.... To free oneself from oneself is the task of all education [*Bildung*]" (*PO*, 170).

With this, it should be clear why the truth of this inverted idea cannot be demonstratively proved: as freedom is the condition of all ethical action, the simple being of the inverted idea can only be approached and experienced freely. This is why Schelling insists that "positive philosophy is the truly free philosophy" that can only be proposed "to everyone freely," with the consequence that "whoever does not want it, should just as well leave it alone" (II/3, 132). If the inverted idea of simple being reveals to reason the positive field of free creation, then the reality of the freedom which animates this field of experience cannot be dependent upon anything, much less the necessary conclusions of a valid deductive proof. Free action is an experience that cannot be compelled by logical necessity anymore than political freedom can be imposed on a country through military force.

For both theoretical and ethical reasons the truth of the inverted idea cannot be dealt with as one would deal with a 'normal idea.' Consequently, "[t]hat there can be no supposition before the pure subject is not to be proved, [rather] one must experience it" (II/1, 326). According to Schelling, the experience of the groundlessness of being must give rise to an ecstatic feeling of awe and wonder, a point which makes clear the extent to which Schelling hasn't forgotten his Pietistic roots, and the degree to which his conception of philosophy differs so decisively from that of the rationalist genre typical of modernity. In its most comprehensive scope, philosophy is not a deductive science that generates demonstrative proofs of its truths that could then be used to compel others to accept such truths, as one does, for example, in geometry. Just as much an ethical enterprise as a theoretical one, the most important truths of positive philosophy must be freely accepted, commensurate with one's experience. Refusing clear and certain ideas as both a beginning and an end of philosophy, Schelling constructs his philosophy around the central role of the ecstatic experience of wonder. He does this not only because he believes wonder *attracts* and nourishes the human spirit, but also because only wonder can "lead thinking out beyond itself" (*GPP*, 82). Turning once again to his old ally Plato, he writes:

> 'The pathos of philosophy is wonder.' The need for wonder is universal to all humans, [and] for this reason they esteem the artist, the poet. A consequence, a merely logical necessity, truly produces a disposition opposed to such an affect. *Only that which comes from the deed of an incomprehensible will generates wonder.* (*GPP*, 82)

The only arena in which we encounter such a will is the historical arena of human existence, and, more specifically, in the actions of humans, from which we can infer, a posteriori, the previous decision of a free will. As a result of a freely made decision, it is the unexpected deed that generates the amazement that momentarily suspends reason's compulsive movement, and therewith creates the possibility of reason's further development:

> In these words of Socrates speaks the need of a great soul that puts an end to all talk and thought; and this of course cannot be something that is self-explanatory. The wish of rationalism is precisely the opposite. What is self-explanatory is what cannot be other than it is. But that which can never be other than it is, is incapable of producing wonder or amazement (*GPP*, 255).

This realization of the brute facticity of existence is for Schelling an actual experience of transcendence that draws us out beyond the immanent and habitual orbit of thought and experience. With this realization of its *other*, whose reality Schelling attempts to grasp in his notion of the *inverted idea*, the self-reflexive mirror play of reason is stopped, and reason is drawn out of itself, becoming "free of itself" since it is "no longer its own object" (II/3, 165). Turning away from itself, reason creates the possibility of encountering what is other than itself, namely, the unpredictable field of free action.

Through this encounter with the transcendent actuality of existence, Schelling makes the transition from the rational mechanism of negative philosophy to the existential arena of the positive, wherein the free actions of historically embedded people move to center stage. Escaping from the mirror hall of self-reflexivity, reason now enters the field of choice and risk, on which it now faces the difficult task of differentiation, of engaging in real change and development of the type that typifies historical individuals.

The wish of rationalism for a perfectly complete und unchanging system of thought promises for Schelling nothing less than the nightmare of absolute boredom. What is stronger than thinking? Wonder, amazement, ecstasy: all are volatile and ambiguous catalysts capable of breaking through the mediation of reflective thought, and thereby actually tying directly into our existence. Herein lies the connection between ecstasy and alterity: reason's encounter with both entails the *risk* that accompanies all real freedom, a risk that in turn is the necessary condition for a philosophy that is not mythic, that like its political counterpart, ideology, silences present and future debate by locating certainty and closure in the nonhistorical and thus static now of eternity.

With this inverted idea, some forty-six years after his letter to Hegel, Schelling provides us with his final draft of the premise missing from Kant's critical edifice, a premise of brute *existence*, whose alterity to thought provides Schelling with the actual conflict and opposition necessary to drive a real dialectical process. This process's trajectory of development betrays the unpredictable markings of living freedom. And it is precisely from the perspective of this chaotic field of the reciprocal interaction of thinking and being that Schelling aims his critique of Hegel's mythic animation of the logical concept.

HEGEL CRITIQUED

Toward the end of the first *Critique* Kant distinguishes between the dogmatic and polemical uses of reason. He is at pains to make this distinction due to his rather sober conviction that reason "itself is incapable of conclusively" proving its claims "κατ ἀλήθειαν," as truth (A 739/B 767). Having decided that the mathematician's method of constructing concepts and proofs is inapplicable to philosophical knowledge, Kant offers up as proof of his claims a type of deduction that is modeled on the juridical practice of his time used to establish deeds and titles to property. As he here somewhat covertly acknowledges, nowhere in the speculative employment of reason is there "to be found a single synthetic judgment" or principle "directly derived from concepts," that is a priori and apodeictically certain (A 736/B 764). Contrary to claims made in the beginning of the first *Critique* to be supplying us with the supreme "example" of "all apodeictic (philosophical) certainty" (A, xv), Kant, at the end of this work, lets on that his exemplary synthetic judgments and principles emerge only when possible experience is *presupposed*. This circular shortcoming of his a priori principles leads Kant to give them their rather surprising title of "dogmas." Thus, in its "dogmatic (nonmathematical) employment," the best a philosopher can do is to offer up a persuasive case that will win a "verdict," reached through "the agreement of free citizens" living within reason's jurisdiction (A 739/B 767). Kant further specifies the polemical use of philosophy's dogmas. The occasion for such polemical use of reason arises when a philosopher has to deal "with the claim of a fellow-citizen" (A 739/B

767), which for Kant was his case against Hume. In such a situation, the best that can be hoped for is to justify a claim "κατ ἄνθρωπον" (as concensus), whereby "the contention is not that...assertions may not, perhaps, be false, but only that no one can assert the opposite with apodeictic certainty or even, indeed, with a greater degree of likelihood" (A 739/B 767). In the dogmatic use of reason engaged in polemic, the best outcome we can hope for is a verdict based on probability. There are no clear and conclusive proofs as found in mathematics and logic, but rather only verdicts whose probable certainty always leaves them open to future appeals and possible overturning.

I would like to suggest that it is in this Kantian spirit of polemics that Schelling makes his case against Hegel. The specific charge of Schelling's suit accuses Hegel of having usurped the freedom of reason—upon which, according to Kant, reason "depends for its very existence"—and set in its place the "dictatorial authority" of a fictitious, even *mythic*, system of logic (A 739/B 767). And just as it was for Kant and Hume, there will be no clear and undeniable proof with force enough to demonstrate, "with apodeictic certainty," a clear and conclusive victor. The deed and title in dispute concern the very nature of what it means to do philosophy, and as such, the starting points of each side might appear so far apart as to render virtually impossible any attempt at finding a common argumentative ground upon which to determine a victor.

Such difficulties noted, the crux of the disagreement has to do with the identity of thinking and being, and the type of unity *qua* truth that philosophy has to offer us based on this identity. Hegel maintains that this identity reveals reason's capacity to ground itself in a reflexive system of thought that not only demonstrates the truth of being's dependence on thinking, but that, in demonstrating this, successfully brings philosophy to its final completion. To do this, Hegel's transcendental ontology must demonstrate the identity of identity and difference through the reflexive structure of judgment *qua* predication. Pushing Spinoza and Kant's treatment of predication as negation to its logical extreme, Hegel maintains that every finite thing can only be defined negatively as the other of itself. For example, the object world demonstrates its finitude through the self-negation of its apparent positive character. If we grant this, then the identity of identity and difference follows: difference is the other of itself, that is, identity. Likewise for thinking and being: thinking is the reflection of what it is not, namely, being. In this process, thought reveals its power to reflect what it is not as, in truth, itself (even though at first it does not appear to be being). If being and thinking conform to such a reflexive structure, Hegel can then proceed to integrate the infinite and the finite, thereby avoiding the awkward hiatus between the two, since in his system the other of the finite world of relative objects is the infinitude of thought. The identity of thought and being, of the infinite and the finite, is thus exhaustively accounted for within this one philosophical system. In the act of absolute knowing that crowns this necessary progression, the Absolute Idea appears in which reason realizes its absolute other as, in truth, *itself*. This truth that is beyond all negation and determination, is the truth of the positive immediacy of reason's other, namely, simple being. And with this, the Absolute Idea releases itself into nature, which is the other of the *Idea*.

Schelling has no qualms with the general contours of Hegel's logic since he recognizes in much of this process his own earlier work that Hegel studied in Jena. To this extent Schelling agrees with Hegel, but only as long as the discussion is about what a science of reason can do and prove within the possible experience of *thought*. Where Schelling most obviously disagrees with Hegel is in the latter's attempts to derive the actual world of existence from the virtual world of the logical concept. As we have seen, identity for Schelling is always construed as the condition of God's revelation through creation. Identity must therefore always be understood as supporting both the beginning *and* the ongoing process of creation. This is something that Schelling can only conceptualize through the slight asymmetrical identity of being and thinking in which the expansive force of the ideal always has a slight edge over the contractive force of being. Only in this way is there a real and irreducible difference, a real opposition between the two, which, as a form of ontological discontinuity, is the condition of creation and its ongoing differentiation. If this were not so, if there were no real difference and opposition between being and thinking, then creation as we know it would immediately cease to be.

What sets this process of creation in motion is not, for Schelling, a logical operation, but is instead a *wanting*, whose erotic dynamic thrives in the tensive interplay of opposing forces and contradictory predicates. In agreement with Diotima's account of *eros*, this desire can live nowhere else but in this tensive field that arises out of the interplay of having and wanting.[80] With this in mind, what Schelling finds so fantastic in Hegel's position is his claim of its absolute status. Of course while Schelling always argues that his constructions are true, like a good art critic he never makes the claim that this truth is somehow universally or necessarily true. And here the words Schelling put to paper while still in Tübingen, some forty-seven years before the Berlin lectures, bear repeating:

> Nothing upsets the philosophical mind more than when he hears that from now on all philosophy is supposed to lie caught in the shackles of one system. Never has he felt greater than when he sees before him the infinitude of knowledge. The entire dignity of his science consists in the fact that it will never be completed. In that moment in which he would believe to have completed his system, he would become unbearable to himself. He would, in that moment, cease to be a *creator*, and would instead descend to being an instrument of his creation. (I/1, 306)

Note that Schelling's center of focus is not his creative ability, but rather the infinitude of knowledge and the dignity of a science that remains true to the unlimited source of its further development. What "upsets the philosophical mind" is when one claims that this infinitude of knowledge actually lies in the "shackles of one [limited] system." Proving quite consistent with this earlier position, Schelling's initial critique of Hegel's *Phenomenology of Spirit* raises several of these same concerns, but articulated now in the aesthetic terms of creation and literary fiction:

> Most philosophical systems are merely the creations of their authors—more or less well thought out—comparable to our historical novels (e.g., Leibnizianism). To proclaim such a system as the only possible system is to be extremely restrictive, [and results in] a dogmatic system. I assure you that I do not intend to contribute to such [thinking]. (I/7, 421)

In making this point Schelling is once again repeating his conviction that all philosophy begins in a free act of the individual, and that, as such, any resulting system that emerges can make no claim to being "the only possible system." His goal in this is consistent, namely, "to liberate philosophy from that stagnation into which it unavoidably" lapses, "owing to ill-fated inquiries into a *first principle of philosophy*.... [For] true philosophy can start only from free actions, and abstract principles, as the mainstay of this science, can only lead to the death of all philosophy" (I/1, 242). Schelling's position follows from his understanding of what it means to be human, in "that man was born to act, not to speculate, and that therefore his first step into philosophy must manifest the arrival of a free human being" (ibid.). A philosophy that touts its unflinching adherence to a necessary method as the most powerful proof of its truth can, for Schelling, "only lead to the death of all philosophy." The bottom line is pragmatic, in the sense that, ultimately, Schelling is concerned with the possibility of moral action, which is rendered meaningless if philosophy removes from its heart the freedom and uniqueness of the individual. And this is precisely what follows if one advances "a universally valid philosophy" that, in its execution, effectively subsumes the rich and yet unstable course of history under only one narrative of a necessary method (I/1, 243).

Given these two very different positions vis-à-vis the nature and task of philosophy, it is to be expected that Schelling responded so strongly against Hegel's system, modeled as it is on the formal methodologies of a deductive science. Such an understanding of what philosophy should be emerges clearly in the following correspondence, written at the beginning of Hegel's career, while he was still headmaster of a Gymnasium in Nuremberg: "I am a schoolmaster who has to teach philosophy—who, possibly for that reason, believes that philosophy like geometry is teachable, and must no less than geometry have a regular structure."[81] Whereas Schelling looked to the free domain of ethics and art for guidance, Hegel took as his exemplar the "regular structure" of geometry. And while Hegel believed the world to be essentially rational, necessarily emerging in a logical emanation from the Absolute Idea, Schelling contended that far from "*a product of pure reason,*" the world appears to "contain such a *preponderant* mass of that which is *not reason*, that one could almost say that what is rational is what is accidental" (*GPP*, 99). Thus for Schelling, to pursue a philosophy conceived as a product of pure reason, that manifests itself in a complete and self-enclosed system of speculative thought, is tantamount to losing oneself in the construction of an "accidental" appendage to our existence (as in a historical novel, or other genres of fiction). The proper task of philosophy as Schelling sees it is to integrate precisely that which stands opposed to reason and the concept, namely, the contingent historical facts of the world:

> Nothing is more comprehensible than the concept, and whoever takes this as the object of their development has chosen the most malleable material. The real concept is only an *actus* of thinking. What is incomprehensible only begins with that which is *opposed* to the concept.... Consequently, right from the start, philosophy needs a *real* opposition.... The world does not consist merely of categories or pure concepts, it does not consist of concrete concepts, but rather of concrete and contingent things, and what is at stake is what is not logical, what is other, which is *not* the concept, but rather its opposite, which the concept as it were, only unwillingly accepts—this is what is at stake. Here philosophy must pass its test. *Hic Rhodus, hic salta.* (*GPP*, 225)

Clearly Hegel and Schelling, onetime friends and colleagues, enjoy different orientations toward existence and reality, which, in turn, reflect strikingly different conceptions of what philosophy should be. Schelling speaks to this when he pulls into play Hegel's temperament in a suitably polemical critique of the latter's philosophy published in 1834. After providing an account of his own philosophy's "living interpretation of reality," which, through the use of the Absolute Subject, sought to provide a natural "means of progress," and an "empirical definition" to his system, Schelling remarks that:

> A later arrival, who nature appeared to have predestined to [create] a new Wolffianism for our time, had as it were instinctually removed this empirical factor so that, in place of what was living and actual, which had been the characteristic indicative of the earlier philosophy, he instead posited its opposite (the object), the logical concept, which goes out and beyond itself in order to then return to itself, and to which through a

strangest fiction or hypostatization he ascribed a similar necessary self-movement. (I/10, 212)

Cutting through the more obviously polemical elements, the charge Schelling levels against Hegel is that he strips philosophy of everything living and real in order to arrive at the "regular structure" of the development of a logical concept. This move robs Hegel's system of the resources needed to account for how it begins and develops, and forces him to engage in the "fiction" of an animated logical concept, whereby his system somehow lies in its conceptual nature, bouncing back and forth between two strictly opposed extremes. This first act of creative invention, however, is compounded by what Schelling calls Hegel's second fiction, which is Hegel's account of why and how the completed logical concept makes the transition into the empirical world of nature. Continuing in the same polemical vein, Schelling writes:

> The self-movement of the concept...held out as long as the system advanced through logical space; but as soon as it had to make the difficult step into reality the path of the dialectical movement broke off totally. A second hypothesis becomes necessary, namely, that the idea—one knows not why, unless to interrupt the boredom of its merely logical existence—allows its moments to fall apart, so that through them nature could arise. The first presupposition of the philosophy that allegedly presupposes nothing was thus that the pure logical concept has the property or nature, *of itself* (since the subjectivity of the philosopher should be totally excluded), to change into its opposite (to, so to speak, overthrow itself), in order to again change back into itself; a deed that one can think of a real, living being, but of a mere concept one can neither think nor imagine, but can really only *assert*. The breaking off of the Idea, that is, of the perfected concept, from itself, was the second fiction, since this transition (into nature) is no longer a dialectical transition, but of a different sort for which it would be difficult to find a name, for which in a purely rational system there is no such category, and for which even the creator himself in his system has no category. This attempt to go back to the standpoint of the scholastics...and to begin metaphysics with a *pure* rational concept that excludes everything empirical, and then [later] to introduce the previously rejected empirical nature through the backdoor of the Idea becoming different or untrue to itself: this episode in the history of modern philosophy, even if it didn't serve to further develop philosophy, has at least served to demonstrate anew that it is impossible to get at reality [*Wirklichkeit*] through a *pure* philosophy of reason. (I/10, 212–13)

Engaging in a bit of demythologizing, Schelling seeks to expose Hegel's animistic *Begriff* for what it is: a fiction playing the leading role in the revival of the old scholastic maneuver known as the 'ontological argument.' Siding with Kant's charge that this old rationalist workhorse is incapable of demonstrating that existence follows essence, Schelling accuses Hegel of having based his entire system on a misinterpretation of this argument. Hegel's philosophy does not, as it claims, enjoy a presuppositionless beginning, since his system is itself presupposed as the latent content of the concept. Hegel's first fiction occurs through an inversion of the order of nature with that of the subject, whereby the extralogical reality of being is reduced to and conflated with the subject's reflexive concept of being. In doing this, Hegel does not demonstrate the identity of the concept with being, but rather only the identity of the concept of being with the same concept in the possibility of the idea (the starting point, it should be noted, of Schelling's negative philosophy). Since Hegel's concept of being excludes everything, his philosophy can only relate to being as a limiting negation of that being. Consequently, Hegel must presuppose being as the latent implication of the concept's reflection, thereby beginning his construction with a being that is itself already presupposed as the undeveloped result of his reflexive method. And this is where the *ordo inversus* takes over: that which presents itself as the first and immediate content of reflection is, from the standpoint of nature, a second order creation dependent on a being prior to and different from the concept. Following Schelling's line of argumentation, Hegel's philosophy would be true only if reality itself were stood on its head.

The need for this inversion leads to Hegel's second fiction, which, for Schelling, is perhaps the greatest defect of Hegel's system, namely, his awkward attempt to conceive nature as the externalization of an abstract idea. Writing in the Berlin lectures, Schelling draws attention to Hegel's "astounding category of the release [*Entlassens*]. Yet is this release not a figurative expression? What this release itself is about is not explained" (II/3, 122). Schelling charges that the only way one can conceptualize this transition from logic to nature is to engage in a circular argument in which both fictions, that of the presuppositionless yet self-moving concept, and its ultimate generation of an extralogical existence, are at their core animated by a similar *petitio principii*.[82] A *petitio principii* which, as we have seen, in its essence demonstrates the inability of the reflexive model of thought to ground itself.

The first circle of reasoning emerges out of Hegel's attempt to articulate a logical *creatio ex nihilo* through the use of a negation that should then drive the dialectic of his system's development. Before initiating this process of negation, however, Hegel must prepare the field of being for its becoming. To do this, he posits the simple immediacy of being as nothingness, implying that it is not conditioned by any determination and, as such, is unconditioned. For if this were not the case, then being and nothingness would not have a symmetrical relationship, since any determination (negation) of being would emerge as a positive within the reflected nothingness, thereby destroying the simple purity of the beginning. Faced with the challenge of grasping this simple and thus unconditioned being, Schelling charges Hegel with grounding the first moment of his *Logic* in an act of intuition, noting that "with the first step of his *Logic*" Hegel "already presupposed intuition" (I/10, 138). For how else does one comprehend simple, unmediated being, devoid of all predication, save through intuition? Hegel, however, insists that this simple immediacy is actually an expression of its other, namely, "of reflection," which "relates to the difference" in this immediacy as the determinacy of what is being mediated.[83] This is not, Hegel claims, due to this category of being suffering the reflexive determination as the other of itself, thought (as is the case with every other predicate). Rather the inverse is true: immediacy comes to be as the result of reflection's negation of its own self-relation. In order for Hegel's system to remain devoid of presuppositions, the order of reality must be inverted so that immediacy is derivative of reflection, and thus is the result of the mediation of reflection. It is important to note that Hegel can only conceive of this reflection as the self-relation of negation.[84]

With this we enter into the first circle of Hegel's reasoning, which arises through what Dieter Henrich calls "autonomous negation."[85] As advanced in his *Greater Logic*, Hegel's program is to derive identity and difference from one conceptual structure. The key player in this derivation is the category of reference: the Universal (unity) refers only to itself, while the particular (difference) refers to something other than itself. What refers only to itself has an immediate reference, whereas that which establishes a relation with something other than itself has a mediate reference. Since both references, however, must be derived from the unity of one thought, Hegel must somehow show that the reference to something other than itself is actually an instance of *self-reference*.

The single-phase relation of immediacy must therefore be exposed as identical to the two-phase reference of the differential relation, thereby proving the unity of immediacy and mediation. Henrich calls the operation employed to achieve this transition from the immediacy of the negative to that "which it is not," the operation of "autonomous negation."[86] Henrich's characterization of this operation of negation as *autonomous* follows from Hegel's insistence that his philosophy begins from a self-sufficient principle that presupposes nothing. The possibility for such an autonomous negation derives from negation's alleged capacity for self-reference, which, according to Hegel, circumvents the need for an independent Other that would be the *positive* object of negation. Whereas in classical logic a double negation requires an initial position to negate— and then only yields an affirmative result that is the *same* as the initial position—Hegel claims that in his logic *double* negation is autonomous since it produces a result that is *different* from the nothingness of the initial condition. According to Hegel, it is the *variance* of difference generated by negation's self-relating which drives the immanent logical movement that animates the unfolding of his entire *Logic*. At its end, in its terminus, the fully mediated and determined idea reveals itself to be the essence of the immediate being that negated itself in the first moment of the system. As Hegel writes, the absolute concept is "essentially a result" that "only at the end" is "what it is in truth."[87] And herein lies the circle in its largest circumference: where is the criterion that would allow us to make the judgment that the essence, so articulated, corresponds with the original unmediated being, if this original unmediated being is completely indeterminate?

The condition of the possibility of knowledge is reflexive division: a judgment that joins what is separated into a unity is true. As we have seen, the correctness of this bringing together must occur according to some criterion, namely, a common basis or identity. According to Schelling's epistemology, the truth of correspondence between subject and object cannot emerge as the result of reflection but must instead, like Kant's transcendental ideal, be the ground that is always presupposed by it. Obviously, as the science that presupposes nothing, Hegel's philosophy wants to offer us an alternative way of generating such a standard for truth. At this level of his system, the truth of being is essence: essence is the criterion that allows us to judge and know being. But for Hegel, being is also the ground of essence and, as Schelling points out, that which is the ground of something must be *different* from that which it grounds: "[g]round is in comparison to that of which it is the ground, nonexistent" [*Grund ist gegen das, dem es Grund ist, nicht seyend*] (*GPP*, 440). Given Schelling's point, how can this difference concerning the ground be overcome by an essence that must also articulate itself as the original immediacy of being? If one obeys the logic of negation, the complete presentation of unmediated experience can only demonstrate its truth by negating itself in its return to unmediated experience. Its truth can only be demonstrated by the negation of that demonstration, but from this it would follow that its truth can only be articulated by the silencing of that articulation, a structural limitation that follows from Hegel's exclusively reflective method. This primary and most fundamental demonstration generates no criterion to establish the identity of itself and its content, that is, of essence and being, a fundamental shortcoming, as we have seen, of the reflexive model of reasoning.

Examined from a less abstract level, given negation's original void, it is as impossible to prove mediation to be the truth of immediacy as it is to prove that my mirrored reflection is my reflection if, like Hegel's negation, I am devoid of any previous positive self-awareness. A "correct" judgment is impossible in such an instance since there is no criterion to adjudicate the correct correspondence of subject and predicate. Hegel has supplied an account of a separation through negation—of *teilen*—but without accounting for the original unity [*Ur*] that suffers that separation and that, most importantly, supplies the *ground* for judgment. As we saw above in Kant's analysis of the *ens realissimum*, all negations presuppose a positive reality from which they derive their content (A 578/B 606). The transcendental ideal must therefore be the ground of all possible predicates. Predication *qua* separation alone is incapable of generating a criterion whereby disparate predicates could be said to enjoy a true relationship to each other: with no common ground transcendent to their difference there remains no criterion upon which to judge their agreement (as well as no way even to judge their *difference*). As such, reflexive negation is incapable of generating a subject that these predicates could signify. Hegel's science of thinking is, in this sense, nothing more than a "category, that is, a predicate theory," in which one begins with the category "poorest in content" and ends with the "highest, richest category," that still, however, contains "nothing other than predicates, without something about which they can be asserted, a subject" (II/1, 335).

The second *petitio principii* occurs when Hegel attempts to explain how reflexive negation generates the actual world of existence. According to his logic, negated being becomes but the *relata* of the essence's relation and therefore an immanent object of reason: in the essence's relation, negated being is shown to be reflexive in that it dissociates into two reflexes. Each of these *relata*, however, is in itself nothing, instead deriving its status only in its relation to its correlate. In a critique of Fichte's use of a similar logic of negation made in 1802, Schelling argues that the proposition that each of these correlates enjoys its being not in itself but only in its correlate robs them of their being, and perpetuates the "circle...within which a nonbeing receives reality through a relation to another nonbeing" (I/4, 358). Such a relation—one that bestows being only through the self-engagement of relative nonbeing—is of course a tautology. Negation alone is incapable of the immanent generation of self-reflexive truth since it requires a ground transcendent to its own operations to protect itself from its complete perfection, that is, its complete destruction as each correlate cancels its reflective other, and thus itself, resulting in the *absolute* nothingness of Plato's οὐκ ὄν. In agreement with Kant's analysis of the transcendental ideal as the ground of all negative predications, the only self-relation negation can suffer is that of a *relative* nothingness—Plato's μὴ ὄν—whereby negation is able to base its resulting truth on a positive ground that, as such, transcends and thus supports the defining limits of negative determination.[88] In the name of self-preservation, negation must presuppose being with the result that it can only ever enjoy relative nonbeing (μὴ εἶναι). As stated above, being and nothingness are not symmetrical. Hegel's circular reasoning thus reads: the self-sublation of negation determines being, but only if being already exists in the positive sense as its ground before negation occurs. And Schelling accuses Hegel of using this same reflexive method of negation to produce not only consciousness, but also the actually existent world of nature and the Absolute *qua* God.

Although Kant had already determined God as the final necessary concept of reason, he had done so with too much reliance on tradition, and not in a scientifically methodical manner. Schelling applauds Hegel for having successfully generated this highest concept "by virtue of an objective method" that, unfortunately, lent this concept "the semblance" of an actual cognition of a reality and not just the thought of yet another concept (II/3, 173). The methodical nature of Hegel's logic proved strong enough to justify almost every step of this process, but only as a merely conceptual endeavor: "It was from beginning to end an *immanent* philosophy, that is, it progressed in mere thought and was by no means a *transcendent* philosophy" (II/3, 73). Thus, when Hegel successfully confirmed Kant's position that God is a necessary idea of reason, all this achieved, according to Schelling, was "to rob God of all transcendence and draw him into this logical thinking, into a merely logical concept, into an *idea itself*" (II/3, 73). As a logic, Hegel's method was incapable of doing anything other than generating an idea of God. Although this final idea was determined as "something *transcendent*, since it stood out beyond this science," it nonetheless remained locked within the immanent categories of that logic (II/3, 73). Schelling continues:

> Yet precisely this advance from relative nonbeing to being, to that which according to its nature or *concept* is being, was viewed as a successive realization of the concept of being, as the successive self-actualization of the idea, whereas in fact it was merely a successive elevation or intensification of the concept, which in its highest potency remained just a concept, without there ever being provided a transition to *real* being [*wirklichen Daseyn*], to existence. (II/3, 72–3)

As an idea, this concept of God as a necessary being enjoys no real being or existence, since ultimately it contains within it nothing other than the possibility of such a necessary being. As the result and sum of a method of self-negation, this idea of God can only be, at best, the idea of that which cannot *not* be.

Hegel claimed more than this however, namely, that he had demonstrated that, in its self-relating, negation returns to itself, and in doing this grounds and shows the truth of the actual being of its immediacy. Schelling counters that the determination of the Absolute as "the essence that is" must be completely devoid of any positive content if the being of this idea arises only through the self-negation of the essence. Thus Schelling agrees with Hegel to the extent that this idea of God—understood as self-negation—does indeed constitute the necessary concept of that which cannot *not* be. Where he disagrees, however, becomes clear in his charge that as the result of an immanent method, the idea that begins in thought can only ever remain an idea in thought: "What has once begun in thought can only continue in thought, and can never advance any further than to the *idea*" (II/3, 162). And even in this advance, Schelling claims that Hegel's method is incapable of grounding its truth with its own principle. Schelling makes this point particularly clear when he turns to Hegel's attempt to build into his system a transition from his completed logic to the actual world of nature.

As we have seen, beginning in the void of self-negation, Hegel's process does not begin with truth, but instead with that which only at its *terminus* is true. Thus the truth of every moment of its movement is, until its end, a relative truth. Each successive development is, in good Aristotelian fashion, pulled ahead by the emergence of the relative final cause that is a result of that phase. Following the inverted logic of reflection and this inverted sequence of final causes, Schelling makes the obvious but embarrassing point that, given this inverted sequence of relative final causes, "then inorganic nature is the cause of matter, the organic is the final cause of the inorganic, the animal world is cause of the plant world, and humanity [is the cause] of the animal world" (*PO*, 133). This is of course the sequence of *final* causes in Hegel's logic. However, once it reaches its climax in the Absolute Idea, it must then correct its inversion and allegedly become the *efficient* cause of the actual world of nature, whereby, remaining consistent, "thus would man appear as the efficient cause of the animal kingdom, etc." (*PO*, 133). At the end of this process, Hegel's Absolute Idea, perfected and self-sufficient in spirit, must, for some unspecified reason, go over into the other of its being, nature. Given that the Absolute Idea is necessity's avatar par excellence, it is clear that it lacks the capacity of free choice. The fall of this idea into existence would thus appear to be brought on by the necessity of remaining consistent with the dialectic of opposition. This consistency of method results in a world of nature that, like Fichte's Not-I, exists only for the sake of providing logic with its oppositional other, a nature that enjoys the instrumental status of being a mere means to our (techno)logical ends. Schelling emphasizes that he can see no good reason why Hegel charts this particular course, and that indeed the movement from the world of the *Logic* to the world of nature is a jarring one at best, and one that disrupts the otherwise simple elegance of the *Logic*. This harsh transition makes it appear as if for Hegel "nature *in general* is only the agony of the concept" (I/10, 152). Hegel suggests that the Absolute Idea must "prove itself," but for whom? "[F]or itself?" As the Absolute Idea it most certainly "knows in advance that it is not going to perish in its becoming other" (I/10, 153). Schelling can only conclude that this transition occurs so that the philosopher Hegel can prove his system accounts for nature and "the world of history" (I/10, 153). But it is when Hegel comes up against this factual world of history and its chaotic lived time that his system encounters its most serious difficulties. For even when it has arrived at its logical terminus, Schelling claims that this science does not escape its status of relative truth, since in its terminus it still lacks the knowledge of the positive being of existence. Therefore, this science is the "not-yet-knowing" philosophy, and thus a negative philosophy. It is precisely this lack of being in Hegel's final idea that generates the need and motivation for the transition to a positive philosophy.

Schelling reworked the text of the Berlin lectures to demonstrate, as clearly as possible, the point that Hegel himself had not yet pushed the negative to its true terminus. His claim that his science of reason terminates in an idea that encompasses and grounds actual existence is, for Schelling, a claim that promises more than it could ever deliver. In this sense, Schelling had to intensify the strictly logical nature of Hegel's science so that its negative character could be seen for what it is, and not what it claims to be. Negative philosophy cannot make the jump into positive existence by separating itself from the concept, rather, it must listen for the demand from within its highest idea for a *real being* that, from within the structure of autonomous negation, can never be explained and accounted for.

Moreover, within a system such as Hegel's, the demand for real being falls on the deaf ears of an impersonal, machinelike necessity. For such a system has no category for need, demand, motivation, longing, or hope—the very concerns of meaning that Schelling wants philosophy to address and integrate in the expectation that it will then become more commensurate with our experience, and thus play a stronger role in society. "Can one even think" Schelling asks, "of the demand [that] the world be shown to be the consequence of the *sheer necessity of reason*...as an *original* longing" (*WMV*, 100), since how could *longing* belong to a world dictated by necessity in which the Absolute Idea enjoys a predetermined "history"? While everything moves in Hegel's system, and thus creates the illusion of a process, since there is no real *other* to the necessity of reason, there can be no real opposition and thus no real freedom. Consequently, there is no real development, that is, no real history, since there is no future in this system that is not already contained within the concept. Gesturing toward an eternally recurring circle of appearances, Schelling sees the outcome of Hegel's work in a rather dark and discomforting light, as Hegel's system ultimately leads to nothing more than the denial of history and the future:

> In the final Idea all real processes are sublated, and in this final moment idealism quite obviously, and devoid of all timidity, falls back into a subjective idealism. At the end, we stand at that point where we already stood in Spinoza. *The entire system is Spinoza's translated into idealism.*... I call the outcome a sad one, since if everything occurs as appearance, if the entire real world can be posited and grasped as a necessity of thought, then we find ourselves enclosed entirely in the sad circle of appearances, which the idea cannot breakthrough. This system leaves to neither the world nor the individual human a true future. Within this world, the only goal is the unsullied salvation of the logical concept, and in the history of the world all actions are led back merely to the logical concept. For this have all the heroes of humanity worked and bled. Everything that history exalts is simply a disguise of the absolute thought, which is the only content [of history]. (*GPP*, 235)

With this we see perhaps why Schelling's positive philosophy attracted the attention it did in Berlin in the 1840s: it offered up the hope of a "true future" both for history and for the individual human. The positive philosophy is a historical philosophy, and this means an open-ended system capable of integrating unpredictable development. A historical philosophy means a philosophy of positive experience, an "existential system," (*PO*, 125), that cannot be based on what reason expunges from its immediate immanent content, but must rather be founded in an experience transcendent to, and thus other than, reason, an experience, which more than reason's negations, is positive, that is, free, and thus capable of creating the new. Freedom, as the condition of real history, expresses the very essence of Schelling's positive philosophy, insofar as this essence itself is historical, that is, develops unpredictably.

Within the vacuum of negative philosophy's structures a type of freedom is indeed derived, but only as a logical emanation of the concept locked within the essence *qua* method. This unchanging essence predetermines, and thus limits, its actualization in being. Like the analytic implications of the laws contained within the concept of a triangle, the unfolding of the essence in existence occurs necessarily as something that is not not-to-be-thought. However, just as the order of the negative philosophy's reflexive negation inverts the true order of nature, the ecstatic "overthrow of reason" that grounds positive philosophy sets that order back in its natural arrangement.

Once set aright, reason is no longer its own self-reflexive object. As we have seen, through the inverted idea of the pure Subject ("the *unmediated* concept of reason") reason becomes "free of itself, that is, no longer its own object" (II/3, 165). Freed from reflection's hall of mirrors, reason can address and deal with reality as *Wirklichkeit*, beginning with the existing Subject καθ αὐτο: "What shall reach reality must then also proceed directly from reality, and indeed from pure actuality, thus from the actuality that precedes all possibility" (II/3, 162). For a science of reason to ever move beyond it's virtual world of thought it must begin *outside* thought, it must become ecstatic, and thus *transcendent*. And for this to happen it must begin with that which is other than thinking, with that which evaporates "before we even think it"; it must begin with the pure simple being of "the absolutely original" that demarcates "the outermost point of predication" before which nothing can be thought [*das Unvordenkliche*].[89]

This beginning is an experience that Schelling alludes to when he speaks of the sublime amazement of "the fact of the world." Following Leibniz, the very fact that there exists anything at all, rather than nothing, provokes a sublime sense of wonder.[90] As we are about to see, it is in the experience of this amazement that one realizes the ecstatic nature of existence, in that both terms, expressed in the terms *exstasis* and *existêmi*, originally indicated a "standing out of" or "being set outside oneself," indicating the emergent discontinuity of our world's unmediated and thus *actual* reality (II/2 57, 179).[91] The origin and cause of this "exuberant being" (I/10, 181), however, lies *jenseits* the outermost point of predication; this dynamic force of existence cannot be caught in reason's inverse reflections, or within any clear and static limit. It is a force of being that, when allowed into the philosophical arena, is that through "which reason is set *outside* itself" (II/3, 162). This liberation of reason from its own reflective obsession with catching a glimpse of its past self allows it to turn to reality, where it is now free to project itself out into an open future.

In Schelling's reading the unity of being and thinking exists not as the result of a self-referential negation, but because the ground of a concept's being—its *Seinsgrund*—is itself an *actus* preceded by no potency. In the same functional role as the unconscious in his *System of Transcendental Idealism* (1800), the *Seinsgrund* is that before which nothing can be thought [*das Unvordenkliche*]. To this extent, this ground, this *actus*, is a blind and contingent being, that is, it is free. Given this, existence does indeed 'stand out' of its ground, which can only be conceptualized as being freely initiated by the pure *actus*. And the only way to describe the initiation of this free act is through the metaphors of desire and will; through an incomprehensible free act which causes the "*Umsturz*" (overthrow) of reason, whereby reason, when faced with this groundless ground, becomes "paralyzed, *quasi attonita*" (II/3, 165). Reason's inability to demonstrate its own principle within itself forces the realization that it is in fact dependent on that which, as its irreducible other, it can never hope to predicate: essence is dependent on being, reflection is dependent on immediacy, negation is dependent on positing, and self-consciousness is dependent on self-awareness. The relation between these sets of terms is oppositional in the same slightly asymmetrical way that preserves oppositional difference, yet gives the slight preponderance to that member of each pair that pushes out toward further differentiation.

What such a negative philosophy seeks to ground as its truth in its *terminus*, is thus actually its *presupposition*: what it seeks as its result—*philosophia*, the desire for wisdom—is much more its ground than its result. Complementing the starting point of his negative philosophy, Schelling again locates the desire of wanting as the groundless *actus* of his positive philosophy.

ABDUCTION AS THE METHOD OF POSITIVE PHILOSOPHY

Positive philosophy begins with the absolute magnitude of pure existence, unlimited by reason's negating determinations. Only by refusing the confining force of negation can Schelling's philosophical efforts release the integrating affirmation of our existence that, for him, animates every meaningful and thus 'live' philosophical system. Beginning at this outermost point of predication, at the edge of Kant's abyss of human reason, Schelling claims to be able to tap into the sublime power of awe and wonder that, since Plato, has been the starting point of philosophy. For it is only due to this type of experience that reason is forced out of its static circuit of reflection to become ecstatic, and thus capable of further supporting philosophy in its ongoing efforts to develop the meaning of creation:

> "Only the fact of the world is object of philosophy,...that which in the world is the true fact and to communicate its inner meaning, that is the work of philosophy" (*GPP*, 272).[92]

Schelling articulates this inner meaning of the world within a Kantian frame. As we have seen, he cites the "genetic point of contact" between his work and Kant's as the latter's doctrine of the transcendental ideal, God. Consistent with the fundamental orientation of all his writings, the work of communicating the meaning of creation is ultimately the task of communicating the divinity of existence, and therewith of articulating not just the idea but, more importantly, the actual reality of this divinity. As Kant and Hegel demonstrate, an "absolutely immanent" negative philosophy leads us to the two problematic concepts of "the most supreme being" and the "necessary existence" that this being enjoys (II/3, 168). As we have seen, the sum or result of negative philosophy, the "absolutely *immanent* concept...of the most supreme being," cannot entail the "the absolutely *transcendent* concept" of reason's most "immediate concept," the *actual* being of that which necessarily exists. The fact of existence has no logical guarantee since this fact cannot be generated as the terminus of a logical process. Perched precariously on the border of the problematic, *if* existence manifests itself, then the ground for this is not the necessary and logical consequence of thought's reflective possibilities, but is rather an *actual* ground whose being lies outside reason's jurisdiction. According to Schelling, where metaphysics has always gone wrong is in not keeping these two concepts of the most supreme being and necessary existence separate and distinct. Unable to abide within its proper limits, previous metaphysics has always attempted to derive the existence of the latter from the essence of the former. Even Kant, who Schelling considered to be "so close to achieving" a "resolution" of this dilemma, "failed" due to the fact that he never explained how "both concepts must limit one another" (II/3, 168), an explanation that Schelling contends his positive philosophy provides.

Since negative philosophy is incapable of breaking out of the virtual realm of pure reason, Schelling's argues that it must hand over to positive philosophy the "task" [*Aufgabe*] of demonstrating the existence of this most supreme being; a task that begins with the inverted idea of "that which necessarily exists" as its "starting point" (II/3, 168). Schelling characterizes the execution and fulfillment of this task as the never-ending process of demonstrating God's divinity that, as the interpretation of a process freely initiated, posits an open future incapable of being reduced to the necessary unfolding of any predetermined plan. The positive philosophy is thus historical in every sense of the word, which in this context clarifies the contingent and problematic nature of the task positive philosophy must carry out.

Whereas negative philosophy remains trapped within the circular world of the regressive method, the progressive method of the positive philosophy arguably promises a more forthright and open-ended approach to the question of the meaning of existence, which for Schelling always hinges on the divinity of existence. As we have seen, the primary shortcoming of the regressive methodology employed by negative philosophy is that it must always presuppose the very thing it seeks to prove. Negative philosophy promises to deliver truth, consciousness, and God as the terminus and sum of its methodical efforts. Yet in each case, it must presuppose the ground of the very idea it wishes to prove. Citing Kant, Schelling reminds us that if we seek to prove that "there is a most supreme being in the sense that it includes existence, then the proposition that it exists is certainly nothing other than tautological" (II/3, 157). An argument that attempts to derive what is actual and existent from what is possible only as a thought will always engage in this type of a *petitio principii*.

As Schelling has argued, the only idea that negative philosophy is capable of generating that, in fact, will correspond to what is actual, is the *idea* that, just as it did for Kant, emerges as the sum and terminus of reason's self-reflexive work, namely, the inverted idea of "that which indubitably exists." This *concept* of a necessary being is that of the pure Subject, which, "free from all potency," is incapable of being doubted since doubt is only possible "wherever there are two cases, two possibilities" (II/3, 158). But in the case of that which is more than a concept, of that which "is factually [*faktisch*] the necessarily necessary existing being," we do not have the option of considering *possible* alternatives (ibid.). In this sense, the fact of the world's existence is for Schelling indisputable: creation "is factually…the necessarily necessary existing being." It is the lack of speculative possibility in this fact that stops reason dead in its tracks, initiating a discontinuous transition through which reason is pushed out of its predictable orbit of reflection. This enables the progressive method of the positive philosophy to avoid the reflexive tautology that lies at the bottom of the regressive method. Beginning with the *actual absolute* of this inverted idea, there is no circularity since one does not presuppose the very concept that one seeks to prove. In doing this Schelling makes clear that we must invert and reverse the direction of the science that will attempt to make this new type of positive demonstration:

> I cannot therefore proceed from the concept of God to prove the existence of God, but I can proceed from the concept of that which indubitably exists and conversely prove the divinity of that which indubitably exists. Now if the divinity [*Gottheit*] is the *what*, the essence, the potency, then I proceed not from potency to being, but rather conversely from being to essence: being is here *prius*, essence *posterius*. But this transition

is not possible without a reversal, without changing the entire direction of the science which proceeded from that which has the capacity to be, and to break off from it, and to start from the very beginning a new science, which is precisely the positive philosophy. (II/3, 159)

We can now see more clearly that the negative philosophy is "a *philosophia ascendens*" (ascending from below), in so far as its immanent process follows of necessity a trajectory aimed at producing the concept of the most supreme being. Likewise, the "positive philosophy is a *philosophia descendens*" (descending from above), to the extent that it starts out from "the absolutely *transcendent* concept" of reason, which is none other than the necessary existence gestured at in the inverted idea of "that before which nothing can be thought" [*das Unvordenkliche*] (II/3, 151). Schelling characterizes the methodology of this new science as "a *progressive* Empiricism," in that it argues from experience *forward*, into the future (II/3, 130, n. 1). In doing this, positive philosophy distinguishes itself from negative philosophy in that it is "not *regressive*, that is, it does not proceed backwards from experience toward that which is above experience" (II/3, 130).

In making this methodological distinction between the progressive and regressive strategies of positive and negative philosophy, Schelling again employs the architectonic of Kant's critical edifice. As we have seen, he bases his construction on Kant's *System of Cosmological Ideas*, wherein the latter presents us with his account of how the mathematical and dynamic categories of the understanding synthesize the unconditioned (A 409/B 435ff.). The regressive synthesis of the mathematical categories is only ever capable of generating a "potentially infinite," namely, a possible unconditioned. In contrast, the progressive synthesis of the dynamic categories *begins* with what is actually unconditioned, the absolute magnitude of what Kant calls "the self-subsisting whole" of nature (A 418/B 447), which Schelling calls the pure *Daß* of existence *qua* "the fact of the world." The possible unconditioned generated by Kant's regressive method corresponds to Schelling's concept of the most supreme being that is generated by negative philosophy; the actual unconditioned of the self-subsisting whole of nature synthesized by Kant's progressive method corresponds to Schelling's inverted idea of "that which just is" [*das bloß Seyende*] (II/3, 162). Kant, however, due to his interest in making his philosophy *ground* mathematics, and therewith all science, finds that "reason" has no interest whatsoever in the progressive form of totality synthesized by the dynamic categories of existence. In the first *Critique*, he writes:

> I propose to name the synthesis of a series which begins, on the side of the conditions, from the condition which stands nearest to the given appearance and so passes to the more remote conditions, the regressive

> synthesis; and that which advances, on the side of the conditioned, from the first consequence to the more distant, the progressive. The first proceeds *in antecedentia*, the second *in consequentia*. The cosmological ideas deal, therefore, with the totality of the regressive synthesis proceeding in antecedentia, not in consequentia. The problem of pure reason suggested by the *progressive form of totality is gratuitous and unnecessary*, since the raising of it is not required for the complete comprehension of what is given in appearance. For that we require to consider only the grounds, not the consequences. (A 411/B 438; my emphasis.)

Faced with the inexponible concept of simple existence, the negative and thus regressive synthesis discovers that, since this absolute magnitude contains "nothing on which to base a series [*keinen Exponenten einer Reihe haben*]," reason can find "no ground for proceeding regressively to conditions" (A 414/B 441). This is because reason, when faced with the inexponible concept of an absolute measure, could only proceed progressively, *in consequentia*, from the fact of the world to its consequences that can only be determined in a future yet to occur. Consequently, Kant considers this strategy and method "gratuitous and unnecessary," since such an approach, by definition, would fail to satisfy the goal of his first critique, which is none other than delimiting the static set of "all pure a priori knowledge" (A xv).

Once again we encounter Schelling extending Kant's architectonic to suit his own plan for what philosophy *should* be, namely, more than just a negative science of mere form and possibility. Schelling thus resolves the problem that Kant never took care of, the problem of providing an account of the transcendental ideal *qua* God as both the *sum* and *ground* of philosophy's activities. As we have seen, if one chooses to remain within the purely formal science of Kant's negative philosophy, within which the necessary concept of the most supreme being only emerges as the result of a logical process, then one must also deal with the inherently circular nature of such a regressive strategy—a point Kant never addressed. It was as if he could not connect his demolition of the ontological argument with the viability of his own attempt to provide a conceptual grounding for actual experience: in both the very conclusion to be demonstrated must "always itself be presupposed" as "its own ground of proof" (A 737/B 765). Schelling's criticism of Hegel's system repeats this charge of circularity: being that is alleged to be generated as the result of a logical method must "always itself be presupposed" as "its own ground of proof" (A 737/B 765).

In order to avoid this *petitio principii*, Schelling advances a new approach to addressing the question of being that no longer engages in such circular maneuvers. In doing this, he sees the possibility of actually moving philosophy forward from condition to consequence, changing and developing as experience itself develops, evolving into the indeterminate future. Such a progressive method would therefore involve all three tenses of time, instead of the regressive method's 'timeless now.' This fact would require philosophy to address seriously the phenomenal time of existence, in addition to the abstract, and thus eternally recurring, present of the mathematical categories. Perhaps most importantly, such a progressive method would, by addressing the future, allow for the integration of purpose and finality into the very structure of existence. The will, motivation, intent, and purpose would thereby become constitutive of the world and our existence: the "ought" of practical reason would then share its telic force with that of theoretical reason.

What Kant finds unnecessary for his formal science of concepts, Schelling believes is the key to making philosophy once again relevant to the contingent lives of human beings. Addressing "what has an attractive power for the human spirit" is essential to this process (*GPP*, 81). For Schelling this can only be the power whose essence reveals itself in our freedom and our capacity for awe and wonder at the fact of creation and existence itself, a fact of existence whose inner meaning he seeks to demonstrate as the reality of the divinity of creation. To do this, Schelling proceeds not from "the essence, the potency…to being, but rather conversely from being to essence," where "being is…*prius*, essence *posterius*" (II/3, 159). Beginning with the inverted idea of that which just is, the task of the progressive method of positive philosophy is to interpret the consequences of this groundless fact as they make themselves manifest in existence. This proposed solution to one problem, however, in turn raises a set of entirely new problems.

Confirming what he had argued when he was but twenty-five years of age, the truth of a philosophy is demonstrated by its power to provide not only "a ready solution to problems hitherto insoluble," but to also succeed in generating "entirely new problems, never before considered" (I/3, 330). In this regard Schelling succeeds famously in generating "entirely new problems" vis-à-vis the methodological soundness of his positive philosophy. For in adopting Kant's "gratuitous and unnecessary" progressive method for his positive philosophy, Schelling advances a position that could appear to have exchanged an old *petitio principii* for a new one, namely, an exchange of a regressive circularity for a progressive one. This can be seen clearly in his account of how his progressive method should demonstrate the divinity of creation:

> In the positive philosophy they are connected in such a way that one says: that which necessarily exists (that is, that which simply and necessarily exists) *is*—not necessarily, but rather it is *factually* [*faktisch*] the necessarily necessary existing being [*Wesen*] or God. This is proved *a posteriori* in the manner already indicated, namely, in that one says: if that which necessarily exists is *God*, then this and that consequence—we want to say, then *a,b,c* etc., become *possible*; but if according to our experience

a,b,c etc., really exist, then the necessary conclusion is that that which necessarily exists is *really* God. (II/3, 169)

The method of demonstration Schelling appears to be describing once again seems to be loading the dice before they are thrown: the conclusion to be demonstrated is again presupposed as its own ground of proof. That is, the conclusion that consequences a,b,c etc. are possible only if God exists, might appear to be presupposed as the ground whereby the conclusion could be proved. Yet one essential difference between Kant's and Schelling's methodology is that the latter's method is empirical, in that he makes no claim to being able to "inquire insight" into this question "merely from the concepts involved" (A 737/B 765). Only experience can confirm or refute the truth of his conclusion. But the empirical dimensions of Schelling's method do not do away with the fact that his method of demonstration is built on a hypothesis whose status is questionable. For why is God the only possible answer here, when there could always be other explanations for why a,b,c etc. do actually exist? Schelling's hypothesis would thus seem to be problematic at best.

The best possible defense of Schelling's hypothesis and method is to compare it with the *abductive form* of logical argumentation developed by perhaps Schelling's most philosophically significant American reader, C. S. Peirce.[93] The point of connection lies in how Peirce maintains that an abductive argument begins with a "problematically propounded hypothesis, in order to explain a surprising observation."[94] The application of Peirce's words to Schelling's divinity hypothesis is clear: it is a problematically propounded hypothesis that Schelling does in fact advance to explain what, for him, is a surprising—or amazing—observation, namely, the fact of the world's existence. For Peirce, the confirmation of such a hypothesis shares the same problematic nature as the hypothesis: it is incapable of generating the consciousness of necessity that Kant demands of apodeictic knowledge. The conclusion always remains problematic, since although "facts have been constrained to yield confirmation to it by bearing out a prediction based upon it," there are alternative explanations for why or how the predicated events came to be.[95]

Peirce continues to argue, however, that the "truth" of an abductive argument derives more from the believer's *decision* to believe it true, than from the empirical evidence that could conclusively verify it. With this, Peirce provides us with an account of *meaning ascription* that almost perfectly corresponds to what Schelling calls "emphatic knowing," in which the believer of such an abductive argument *freely chooses* to attach significance to its conclusion (*GPP*, 97). And the only warrant which Peirce gives for engaging in this form of reasoning is an ethical or practical one, insofar as the only justification for emphatically accepting such a position as true would be the degree to which the belief, as Schelling argues, is "commensurate to experience" (II/3, 114). Peirce writes:

> The principle is that we are always justified in presuming, for the purposes of conduct, that our sole end may be reached.... If, then, it comes to this, that a certain hypothesis must be true or there is no comprehensible truth, and if, as our ethical and esthetical discussions have shown is the case, the comprehension of the universe is the sole aim which a man can deliberately pronounce to be good, he is justified in unconditionally embracing the hypothesis which is alone consonant with the attainment of a comprehension of the truth.[96]

Peirce proceeds to suggest that the only justifiable abductive hypothesis that would satisfy his demand for "the comprehension of the universe," is "the hypothesis that the universe is governed by a self-conscious mind."[97] This is clearly a problematic hypothesis that comes very close to Schelling's hypothesis regarding the divinity of creation. One is free to believe this problematic hypothesis, but of course, no matter how much one may wish it were otherwise, it is always capable of being not only doubted, but of simply not being true at all. Schelling defends against this latter possibility by requiring that the problematic hypothesis, emphatically known, must be "commensurate to experience." His position on this count is best illustrated through the example that he repeatedly uses to justify the progressive method of his positive philosophy, namely, that of our experience of other individuals' *personalities*. In the Berlin lectures, Schelling makes the following point in the context of his attempt to expand the sphere of empiricism:

> For no one knows what exists within a person until that person expresses himself. His intellectual and moral character exists only *a posteriori*, which is to say that it is discernible only through his statements and actions. Now suppose that the discussion was about an intelligence in the world assumed to have a free will for action, then this intelligence would likewise not be knowable *a priori*, but only through its deeds that occur in experience. Although a supersensible being, it will nonetheless be something that can only be known commensurate with experience [*Erfahrungsmässigkeit*]. Empiricism as such, therefore, hardly excludes all knowledge of the supersensible as one customarily assumes, and even Hegel presupposes. (II/3, 113)

We have no direct empirical verification of another individual's character and personality, yet we accept as a problematic hypothesis the reality of another individual's powers of spontaneity and freedom. This hypothesis can be doubted, and indeed could one day be shown not to be true. Yet this hypothesis is held to be true because it is not only commensurate with experience, but also because it helps us comprehend another individual's personality and makes life less boring.

Putting the matter as simply as possible, we can see in this example several essential features of Schelling's positive philosophy, all of which cause him to title this mode of philosophy a philosophy of *revelation*. He gives the positive philosophy this provocative title because it is primarily concerned with that dimension of our experience governed by *freedom*—and thus with the wonder engendered by unpredictability, individuality, and the singular creativity revealed in the emergence of the new—and with the *conviction* required to negotiate the doubt inherent in this contingent and underdetermined realm of existence. All of these factors are informed by Schelling's understanding of what is *positive*, a term he applies to all objects of philosophical inquiry that have as their ground the *actus* of a free will: positive is that which reveals the *actus* of a directly unobservable personality. Thus, beyond the homogenizing effects of an objective method, Schelling articulates an intensely individual and creative approach to philosophy:

> "All original thinking always refers to a real object [*Gegenstand*]. Object and resistance [*Gegenstand und Widerstand*] are at bottom one and the same word: the object of philosophy is always of the sort that locks within itself what I must first extract. This wrestling thought I call positive thinking. That original thinking, actively referring to that object, is all about that object.... The true object is always something positive; only the means to arrive at that object is thinking, that is, the person must himself think out this way. The person engaged in philosophy cannot be helped in any other way. (*GPP*, 94)

Take then the object of the fact of the world, of simple existence. Accept Schelling's definition of the task of philosophy as finding the 'inner meaning' of this fact. Far from there being one method that all must follow in doing this, Schelling argues for an almost *anarchic* approach in which each individual must, for themselves, create their own account of the inner meaning of existence, while nonetheless always remaining fully aware of that fact that these meanings could be in error. The one test that determines the plausibility of these meanings is the degree to which they are "commensurate to experience."

In the absence of method and the presence of the real possibility of error, Schelling locates the distinguishing features of his positive philosophy vis-à-vis those negative philosophies modeled on the form of the quantitative sciences. What his positive philosophy is concerned with, and how it understands the task of dealing with those concerns, inhabits a region of human existence that the quantitative sciences are incapable of dealing with. This position drove Schelling to critique the belief that, as Kant himself maintained, only those disciplines may be called a science which can provide such "indubitable evidence as mathematics" (*GPP*, 95). And whereas no one debates whether mathematics should be called a science, the question of whether or not philosophy is a science is highly debatable. If one accepts the mathematical form as normative, philosophy either must give up on its claim to being a science, or it must generate itself through the pure necessity of thought as mathematics does. Highly critical of this position, Schelling argues that it has determined the "history of modern philosophy," demonstrating the degree to which mathematics "hangs before the philosopher as an exemplar of all sciences" (*GPP*, 95). For example,

> Christian Wolff, who claims to have developed the fragmentary philosophy of Leibniz into a full system,...believes to have demonstrated that philosophy is a mathematical science. From the other side Kant believes to have shown this. He as well demands for a true metaphysics evidence similar to mathematics.... The consistently recurring argument of this type of philosophy is thus: either philosophy is not a science or it must be a science according to the type of mathematics. (*GPP*, 96)

Schelling finds this argument to be unconvincing at best, and at worst downright dangerous to not only the future of philosophy and the role it plays in our lives, but to our existence in general. His substantive rebuttal of this argument springs from his understanding of human nature, and the types of knowing and truth that are best suited to cultivating and further developing that nature:

> The question here is whether, in the face of only this form of knowing, human nature can be ascribed to what it realizes from pure reason. Certainly, there can be no purer necessary thought than $A = A$. However, if we ask whether this alleged knowledge really *knows* something, then we must confess that with this we really know *nothing*. Here we would then have a non-*knowing* knowledge. But where a knowing knowledge is maintained, something must be present *in which the opposite must be possible as well*. (*GPP*, 96)

The distinction Schelling draws here is subtle yet all-important. Once again turning Descartes on his head, Schelling states that only when the possibility of doubt *is present* do we have the possibility of having "real knowledge"(*GPP*,

97). This follows from his allegiance to an understanding of a free—and thus contingent—human nature that refuses at its core to reduce the meaning of its life to the trivial certainty of a tautology. The so-called "apodeictic truths" of math derive their power from the impossibility of conceiving the truth of their opposite. That is, the possibility of doubt is precluded by *the form* of these truths, since the form of such truth precludes the possibility of more than one solution. The certainty of the *cogito* derives not from the content of its thinking, but from the simple fact of its *form*. Or as Kant put it in his *Opus Postumum*, the difference between the metaphysician and "the transcendental philosopher" is "that the latter addresses merely what is formal, the former what is material (the object, the material)."[98] For Schelling the metaphysician, the knowledge supplied by apodeictic truth "is just a knowledge in thought," since it follows only the necessary forms of thought's "possible experience," not the positive, historical and thus *meaningful* path of real experience:

> From all this it would follow that in the mathematical sciences there is no authentic knowledge, no knowledge in the narrower sense. One could oppose the so-called apagogic proofs against this; but ultimately these lead to the presentation of an impossible opposite in the very nature of the object itself. Certainly from the above it follows that knowledge in geometry is of a totally different nature than that in philosophy, if namely in the latter a knowledge occurs in the particular sense. Everyone who has reflected upon the field of mathematics knows that geometry is a science of a logical character, that between the presupposition itself and its consequences there lies nothing else in the middle save mere thought. (*GPP*, 97)

It is this something "in the middle" that, other than "mere thought," Schelling finds of capital importance to his understanding of what constitutes and informs authentic knowledge; a something in the middle that is ultimately grounded in his conception of human nature, and that cannot be made transparent through the insight of reason alone. It is the *actus* of a free person making *a decision*: "I call only that knowledge authentic which is decided, not through mere thinking, but rather by an *actus*" (*GPP*, 97). Knowledge, in this more restricted sense, can only be maintained when *the opposite* of the object under consideration is also possible, for example, whether or not I stay married to my partner, or whether or not you believe in God. This mode of knowledge can only be authentically decided through the *actus* of my will, and not by an externally imposed decision-making calculus.

This is not, however, to say that there is no such calculus followed in reaching such a decision. The point is simply that such methods are only a necessary but insufficient condition for *grounding* this positive knowledge. Schelling treats this point by noting that only with the "exclusion" of other possibilities does this real knowledge justify itself: "A can be X, but it can also be Z. But because it is not Z, I know that it is X." Accordingly, "certainty is nothing other than the positive opposite of doubt. But there is no doubt where there are not at least two options possible" (*GPP*, 97). Conversely it follows that "[a]uthentic knowledge always includes within itself the possibility of its opposite. The true, real subject in every possible assertion is that what is predicated of it could just as well be as not be" (*GPP*, 97). This authentic knowledge thus necessarily includes an *overcoming* of doubt in a judgment, an overcoming that Schelling links with the very heart of philosophy as an active *longing* for wisdom. In overcoming not knowing and the possibility of error, this deciding generates an "emphatic knowledge" in which the copula of the judgment expresses the actuality of that decision:

> Just as the "IS" can be thought with and without emphasis, so too can knowledge be thought as emphatic or not emphatic. In every proposition that is not a true judgment, the "IS" is posited devoid of all emphasis. If the "IS" should be emphatic, then the subject of the proposition must be capable of being—and also not being—what it *is*. (*GPP*, 97)

What is the scope of possible subjects for this authentic knowledge? Negatively we know that these subjects cannot include any aspect of experience that is limited exclusively to speculative thought or governed exclusively by a crude materialism. Positively defined, we know that this "historical philosophy" claims to be a *positive* science, whereby its subject is the scope of possible actions performed by people animated by a free will, both in the individual and collective arenas. In this sense, the scope of this knowledge is progressive because it is oriented towards a future that has not yet occurred.

Take for example the question of the meaning of existence: The task of meaning attribution to the fact of the world thus becomes an irreducibly creative endeavor orientated towards the future. The meaning of the fact of the world—the meaning of existence—is not some preexisting treasure waiting to be unearthed or some esoteric code waiting to be deciphered. Developing the meaning of existence is a creative project whose execution requires an individual's authentic knowledge; a project, therefore, whose uniqueness demands more complexity than the universalizing necessities the mathematical categories can offer; an act of meaning attribution that can only be guided by *reflective judgment*. Consequently, there is no predetermined essence or concept to determine this reflective form of judgment: we are in the sphere of *phronesis*, where the generation and application of ideas cannot be encoded into algorithmic form; we are engaged in a creative process, the general rules of which we are cognizant, but whose application to each individual experience we cannot determine. And as in Kant's third *Critique*, our judgment in this process can only be guided by the "absolute magnitude" delivered by the sublime wonder of the very fact of existence. For it is only in this experience that the necessities of immanent thinking (negative) become ecstatic (positive), thereby freeing the individual to envision the possibilities of a future yet to be. Positively defined, this "historical philosophy" requires the anticipatory pull of the future's possibilities to act as a telic cause of that history's further development, in other words, a temporal pressure exerted by the future wherein "every result (future occurrence) exerts" a force "on what has gone before it" (II/3 278). Far from being "gratuitous and unnecessary," the future exerts a pressure on the past and present, whereby the "yet to be" proves essential to conceptualizing the process of individuation and differentiation that characterizes historical development. This ecstatic future points to the irreducibly process nature of self, creation, and deity: none are finished or complete. Schelling discusses this fact of our existence as early as his *System of Transcendental Idealism* in 1800:

> History as a whole is a progressive, gradually self-disclosing revelation of the Absolute. Hence one can never point out in history the particular places where the mark of providence, or God Himself, is, as it were, visible. For God never *exists*, if the existent *is* that which presents itself in the objective world; if *He existed* thus, then *we* should not; but he continually *reveals* Himself. Man, through his history, provides a continuous demonstration of God's presence, a demonstration, however, which only the whole of history can render complete. (I/3, 603)

Perhaps the central goal of Schelling's historical framework is to provide humanity with a future that will help free us from our pasts, both individual and collective. Such a pragmatic history is impossible as a schematic listing of the events of the past; it requires instead an imaginative infusion of meaning and a productive use of the imagination to conceive of possible futures that are presently counterfactual. It requires the ample employment of authentic and emphatic knowing. In short, this positive history is impossible without a future as a source of *hope*.

In this Schelling adopts prophetic tones harmonious with Kant's account of the Kingdom of Ends, in which our exclusive dependence on a negative and *instrumental* reason is supplanted by an integrative reason capable of realizing our nature in its wholeness and, therewith, of reconciling our fractured self with nature. This realization discloses the structures of human consciousness not as opposed to but as complementing, and thus parallel to, the structures of nature. Humanity thereby emerges as the *autoepistemic organ* of nature's self-organizing activity: we have the ability not only to narrate the course of nature, but also to alter it by manipulating behavior through the mass media, to redirect it toward new goals by rewriting genetic code, or to severely transform it through nuclear war or global warming. We are, as Schelling writes in his *System of Transcendental Idealism*, "co-poets" [*Mitdichter*], of our history, working in collaboration with the forces of creation. Not only can we read the book of nature, but we can also edit and rewrite it. For the author of this book and writer of our drama does "not exist independently of us, but reveals and discloses himself successively only, through the very play of our own freedom, so that without this freedom even he himself *would not be*,…we are co-poets [*Mitdichter*] of the whole and have ourselves invented the particular roles we play" (I/3, 302).

TOWARDS A PHILOSOPHICAL RELIGION

Schelling fully accepts the irreparable destruction of the 'old metaphysics' wrought by Kant's critique of its ontological argument, wherein the attempt is made to derive the actual being of an *ens originarium* from the necessary idea of reason. Yet Schelling criticizes Kant mightily for extending what he had proved only of this central argument to philosophy in general, thereby "tacitly" assuming "that there is no other philosophy than the pure rational philosophy" employed by the former metaphysics and his own negative philosophy (II/3, 83). For as we have seen, left to itself, pure reason is incapable even of grounding its own employment, much less addressing the human need for *positive* meaning. Thus with his positive philosophy Schelling seeks to develop a new form of metaphysics that, like its predecessors, wants "to communicate the inner meaning of the fact of the world" by demonstrating the reality of the divine in creation.

In doing this, Schelling once again makes explicit use of Kant's own system resources to make his case. Calling upon Kant's *Doctrine of Method*, Schelling echoes Kant's call for the "dogmatic use" of reason, but with the additional qualification that we distinguish "between a dogmatic and a dogmatizing philosophy" (II/3, 82). Dogmatizing philosophy is the corrupt form of what Schelling calls a "positive rationalism," which, like Hegel's "logical dogmatism," attempts to derive positive existence from reason's immanent power of negation (II/3, 82). What makes such a strategy corrupt in Schelling's eyes is that this form of metaphysics remains blind to its inability to achieve what it seeks to prove: it does not realize that it fails in its efforts to extend reason, by means of inferences, to existence. "In this effort," writes Schelling, "reason is not dogmatic since it does not reach its goal, but rather it is simply dogmatizing" (II/3, 83). In this sense, and only in this sense, did Kant forbid metaphysics from "transcendence." But according to Schelling, Kant "forbid it [transcendence] only for dogmatizing reason, that is, for reason that of itself seeks, by means of inferences, to reach existence" (II/3, 169). Whereas the old metaphysics was, in this sense, dogmatizing, Schelling argues that "Kant's critique…did not extend to the true dogmatic philosophy, that is, to what metaphysics should be" (II/3, 82).

What metaphysics should be is what Schelling's positive philosophy is aiming at, which, as we have seen, upends the traditional ordering of essence and existence, and therewith transcendence and immanence. While Kant did forbid reason to reach out from within itself to an existence transcendent to its immanent essence, Schelling argues that Kant did not forbid transcendence when executed by the *dogmatic* use of reason, "to proceed conversely from that which *simply*, and thus infinitely exists, to the concept of the most supreme being as *posterius*" (II/3, 170). If we begin with that which simply exists, with what is "anterior to all concepts," and then move to the progressive proof that the concept of divinity applies to this being, "then I have surpassed nothing, and on the contrary, if one calls this being transcendent, and I advance within it to its concept, then I have surpassed the transcendent and in this way again become immanent" (II/3, 169). If, as Schelling argues, existence precedes reason's essence, then existence is transcendent to the immanence of reason. Far from beginning within the immanent world of pure thought and then seeking the transcendence of actual existence, positive philosophy starts from the ecstatic transcendence of simple existence, the absolute other of conceptual thought, and then in turn becomes immanent.

In this new dogmatic form of metaphysics, in this "*philosophia descendens*," (descending from above), there "is nothing that I have to exceed" (II/3, 151, 169). Schelling claims that this fact insulates him both from Kant's critique of the ontological argument and his own criticism of the blindness of a dogmatizing metaphysics that delusively believes it has proven what it has not. Since Schelling moves from the transcendent to the immanent, he averts Kant's charge, and since the demonstration his positive philosophy pursues is never-ending, and thus never conclusive, he is not subject to his own criticism. Following up on the distinction Kant makes between truth κατ ἀλήθειαν and κατ ἄνθρωπον in the dogmatic employment of reason, Schelling seeks in his own dogmatic metaphysics to generate a positive emphatic knowing, whereby "the contention is not that…assertions may not, perhaps be false, but only that no one can assert the opposite with apodeictic certainty, or even, indeed, with a greater degree of likelihood" (A 739/B 767). The "authentic knowing" Schelling situates at the heart of this new form of dogmatic metaphysics is irreducibly individual, since the only way to arrive at this knowledge is through a "wrestling thought" he calls "positive thinking," wherein "the person must himself think out th[e] way" to arrive at such knowledge (*GPP*, 94). As such, positive philosophy "requires independent thinking, to create new strategies" to understand and communicate the inner meaning of existence (ibid.).

A new strategy Schelling advances is that of what he calls a "philosophical religion" (II/1, 255). Conceding that such a philosophical religion does not yet exist, the positive and free thinking that would characterize its dynamic will distinguish it from Kant's "rational religion," which, trapped within the limits of pure reason's virtual world, is incapable of supporting the free and authentic "wrestling thought" Schelling demands. Yet this wrestling thought must also free itself from the various forms of revealed religion, including Christianity, in order to break through to a truly "free religion" (II/1, 258). To do this will require "*an expansion of philosophical consciousness*" (*GPP*, 84) that is not only capable of addressing and integrating the freedom of existence and historical phenomenon previously discussed, but is also inclusive enough to get beyond philosophy's compulsive need to forever splinter off into mutually exclusive schools of thought.

This demand for a more inclusive consciousness grows in large part out of Schelling's conviction that the opposite strategy of *exclusion* leads to one-sided truths that are ultimately false if held as comprehensive truths. Inverting this point, Schelling argues that there is no philosophical system that is unconditionally false. Rather, "[w]hat is actually false lies in the direction of exclusion. But since it [the philosophical system] is false only from the exclusive position, in itself it is not false" (*GPP*, 84). This inclusive philosophical consciousness must, of course, address religious phenomenon, becoming, as it were, a requirement for developing a "framework in which Christianity is also an essential member, but precisely only a member" (*WMV*, 84). As he says in the Berlin lectures of 1842, due to the historical reality of an emerging world culture, which includes both Eastern and Western philosophical and religious traditions, he is "compelled" to call for a wider philosophical consciousness in order get beyond the parochial nature of the European *Weltanschauung*. Citing "the virtually unrestricted expansion of world relations," he argues that "the Orient and the Occident are not merely coming into contact with one another, they are being compelled, as it were, to fuse into one and the same consciousness," a consciousness that has not yet been realized, but one that must be cultivated and "expanded into a world-consciousness!" (II/3, 4). Such an expanded consciousness will be capable, on the one hand, of breaking free of past forms of religion, yet, due to its *religious dimension*, will also be charged with preserving what is true within these historical forms. Or, as Schelling phrased it in Berlin: "That philosophical religion will be the true one that embraces the elements of all religions, and therewith is capable of seeing the truth in mythology and revelation without, however, sublating the authenticity of this truth" (*PO*, 379).

In the final analysis, the essential relation of philosophy and theology has, since his first writings, never been questionable to Schelling: "true philosophy is simultaneously theology or philosophical religion."[99] To communicate the inner truth of all religions—from the mythological, to the revealed, to the philosophical—without, however, doing injury to their unique and enduring truths is precisely the task of Schelling's positive philosophy in its greatest possible expanse. The Berlin lectures present his final iteration of the historical and theoretical justification of this positive philosophy.

TRANSLATOR'S NOTE

Over the past few decades, there has been a growing appreciation in the English-speaking world of the robust nature of German philosophy traditionally referred to as German Idealism. As the conventional story goes, this school of thought was initiated by Kant's Copernican Revolution and brought to its close in Hegel's 'absolute idealism'. One of the clearest benefits of the increased appreciation of this tradition, however, has been the realization that this period of philosophical ferment fails to be adequately circumscribed by the figures just mentioned. The scope of the work generated during this era is just too rich and complex to be subsumed under the category of German Idealism or even its rebellious sibling, Romanticism. Perhaps the one philosopher whose work demonstrates the limitations of these conventional scholarly categories is F. W. J. Schelling. This is due not only to the lengthy duration of his philosophical career (his first published work appeared in 1793, and his last lecture was in 1854) but also to the intimidating intellectual and scholarly expertise he brought to his work. An early master of six languages, Schelling began his studies of Leibniz's *Monadology* and Plato's *Timeaus*, both in their original languages, before the age of fourteen. This fact alone presents serious challenges for contemporary scholarship, particularly in regard to transcribing his journals and notes. Written in any combination of seven languages, some modern, some ancient, there is no longer any one scholar capable of tracing all the contours of Schelling's intellectual landscape. This difficulty is compounded by the fact that the subject matter Schelling wrote about was even more varied than the languages he employed in his writings. Biblical exegesis and scholarly philology; philosophy of nature and transcendental philosophy; aesthetics and the poetic arts are included in the wide spectrum of topics Schelling approached—few scholars risk an attempt at accounting for how they all may fit together.

An early star on the German philosophical firmament—appointed to lecture at Jena in 1798 at the age of twenty-three—Schelling personally knew most, if not all, of the central figures who developed post-Kantian philosophies in the decades before and after the turn of the nineteenth century. A classmate of Hölderlin and Hegel at the Tübingen Theological Seminary, it was his relationship to Hegel's work that brought Schelling to Berlin in 1841 to offer up a corrective to the former's 'panlogism.' Schelling's lectures on *The Grounding of Positive Philosophy*, translated here for the first time into English, not only offer up a penetrating critique of Hegel's absolute idealism, but they also present us with an introduction to Schelling's revolutionary effort to ground a philosophy of existence.

Like all of his later work, Schelling never published the text of these lectures. He left this task instead to his son, Karl Friedrich August Schelling, to compile and prepare them for publication in the edition of Schelling's collected works that appeared between 1856 and 1861. As the most comprehensive edition of Schelling's writings, the collected works were accepted as authoritative in terms of both the content of the texts included, as well as the chronology of their composition. Over time, however, it has become clear that Schelling's son was often quite aggressive in executing his editorial responsibilities. Faced with over forty years worth of thousands of manuscript pages, many of which were different versions of the same work, Karl Schelling inevitably made a few errors. For example, in the collected works he states that the text translated here is that of his father's inaugural lectures in Berlin in the winter semester of 1841–42. Yet according to other accounts published at that time, it would appear that text of *The Grounding of Positive Philosophy* was not read by Schelling in his first semester in Berlin, but rather one year later in the winter semester of 1842–43.[1] This confusion could easily be dispelled if we had access to the manuscripts of Schelling's lectures, but unfortunately, virtually all were destroyed during the Allied bombing of Munich in July of 1944. Nonetheless, the most important fact is that Schelling himself wrote the text translated here. Based on comparisons with his other writings on positive philosophy, and with the numerous lecture notes taken by his students, it is beyond doubt that the text of *The Grounding of Positive Philosophy* is authentic and reliable.

Translating Schelling is a difficult task. The talent and genius with which he uses language make for a text that, as he himself demanded, is as much philosophy as poetry. I have attempted to do justice to both demands by translating systematic terms consistently, yet in English that I would like to think has a natural ring and flavor. For example, Schelling builds much of his case in the following lectures on the inverted idea of *das Unvordenkliche*, a term which points to that sphere of existence that lies beyond the immanent operations of reflexive thought. A literal translation of the term often reads *the unprethinkable*. I have opted for the more liberal rendering of "that before which nothing can be thought." When compelled to insert an additional English term into the translation, I indicate this with square brackets. Ambiguous terms are followed by the original German in square brackets, while confusing terms or phrases are explained in the translator's endnotes. In his capacity as editor Karl Schelling provided a few footnotes that I have reproduced in the text using roman numerals, and which I occasionally supplement with a brief explanatory note, always indicated through the use of square brackets. To facilitate the critical reading of this translation, the standard page numbers of the collected works edition are incorporated into the text. I have also made every effort to remain true to Schelling's distinctive typographical habits, such as the frequent use of italics, the *Gedankenstrich* ('—'), and the equal sign ('='). Finally, while Schelling's sentences often cover an entire page, I have made every attempt to render them into a more concise order, making every attempt to preserve, if not their duration, then their structure and rhythm.

The full title of these lectures as it appears in the collected works is *The Introduction to the Philosophy of Revelation, or the Grounding of Positive Philosophy*. For the sake of clarity, I have decided to refer to these lectures as *The Grounding of Positive Philosophy*. I have also taken the liberty of assigning a brief title for each lecture based on the outlines Schelling's son provides for them.

The Grounding of Positive Philosophy

The Berlin Lectures

On Philosophy

It would seem neither improper nor undesirable if before the exposition of the particular subject of the lecture that I now have the occasion to give, that I put forward a general word about philosophy as such. There is perhaps not one among you who has not come here with some type of idea, or at least a presentiment, of what philosophy is. *Here*—even the beginner will say—here those questions will be answered for me for which in all other sciences there is no answer and that sooner or later, but always inevitably, disturb every upright spirit. Here that veil will be removed that until now has hidden from me—not particular objects, but this *entirety* itself, of which I feel a part, and of which the more I sought to learn of its particulars became all the more unfathomable. Here no doubt will be won those eminent convictions that maintain human consciousness aright, without which life would have no purpose and would thus be deprived of all dignity and independence.

All the sciences with which I have previously concerned myself are based on presuppositions that in themselves are not justified. The mathematical disciplines progress within themselves without significant scandal, but mathematics does not comprehend itself since it provides no account of itself or of its own possibility, and as soon as it wanted to ground itself, it would [4] with that very attempt go beyond itself and abandon the basis on which it alone can achieve its results. Besides mathematics, I have until now primarily concerned myself with the study of classical languages. I am indebted to this study for that formal exercise of the spirit that, more than any abstract logic or rhetoric, puts me in the proper state of mind to notice and to express the most subtle gradations or distinctions of any thought; I am indebted to this study for the priceless advantage of always being able to *inhale* directly from the great works of antiquity that spirit from which they are inspired, to elevate and to refresh my soul. Yet the more deeply I grasped and examined the construction of these original languages, the more I felt the need to penetrate to the very nature of this wonderful instrument itself which, when appropriately used, expresses *thoughts* with infallible certainty and, regarding *sentiment*, is delicate enough to reproduce its quietest breath yet strong enough to reproduce the raging storm of the most vehement passions. Where does language come from, how was it that it came into being for humanity? Where does this power come from, which this instrument creates not *before* its employment, but immediately *in* the employment itself? A power that I brandish not with hands or external organs, but directly with the spirit itself, within which I truly dwell, which animates me, and within which I move freely and with no resistance?— Next I directed my attention to the external objects of nature around me. I acquainted myself with the fundamental propositions of physics, acquired the elementary ideas and concepts of the most general natural phenomena. I became familiar with the laws of gravity, of pressure, of kinetics, and I observed the effects of light, of heat, of magnetism, and of electricity. I listened to explanations of these phenomena as well. Some of these phenomena, like gravity, were attributed to immaterial causes; others were attributed to, as one says, certain subtle or imponderable substances. Still, if I go so far as to grant that these substances and forces actually explain these phenomena—a position about which I hardly feel convinced in every regard—[5] there is always a question that remains: From where do these substances and forces themselves derive and for what purpose? What type of necessity do they have to exist and why are there such things? I will grant that light consists of—or is produced by—the vibration of the ether, but what of the ether itself that fills outer space, what cause do I know to ascribe for its existence? It seems to me something so contingent that I cannot even comprehend it and thus cannot accept as actually explained any phenomenon that depends on it.

I have also looked into natural history, and if this inexhaustible manifold of colors, forms, and shapes in which organic nature appears to play already aroused my youthful sensibilities, and if I then later believed that I had detected a subtle law that for once would guide my spirit through this labyrinth—showing me the path of generative nature itself—there nevertheless remained for me always an unanswered question: Why are there such beings at all? Why are there plants, why animals? One answers me: they are but steps over which nature ascends in order to arrive at humanity—thus in humanity I shall find the answer to all questions, the solution to all riddles, and for this very reason I am inclined to agree with those who for ages have claimed the sole object of the final science that answers all questions, the sole object of philosophy, is man. But if man is undoubtedly the *culmination*, and to this extent the *goal* of all creation and becoming, am I therefore entitled then and there to proclaim him to be its *ultimate purpose* as well? Would I be justified in doing this if I knew how to specify what that being [*Wesen*], which permeates every level of becoming as its efficient cause, had *intended* for him? Am I, however, capable of specifying this? I could conceive of that being perhaps as something that, initially blind, struggles through every level of becoming toward consciousness, and humanity would then arise precisely at that moment, at that point in which this previously blind nature would reach self-consciousness. But [6] this cannot be, since our self-consciousness is not at all the consciousness of that nature that permeates everything: it is just *our* consciousness and hardly encompasses within itself a science of becoming applicable to all things. This universal becoming remains just as foreign and opaque to us as if it had never had a bearing on us at all. Therefore, if this becoming has achieved any kind of purpose it is achieved only through humanity, but not *for* humanity; for the consciousness of man does not = equal the consciousness of nature. But, one answers, of course the ultimate and highest purpose does not lie in the human faculty of cognition, since if nature is impenetrable to man, conversely, man is foreign to a nature that indeed continues beyond him and his works, and thus for which he has no significance. The reason for this lies precisely in the fact that man has *separated* himself from nature and in the fact that—as experience shows—man was by no means merely destined to be the goal or culmination of a process independent of him, but was rather destined to be himself the originator and creator of a new process, of a second world that would lift itself above the first. The true purpose of man lies in what he, through the freedom of his will, should be in this different world. Man was the goal of nature only to the extent that he was destined to *sublate* [*aufzuheben*] nature within himself, to continue beyond nature, and to begin for himself a new chain of events. But far from hoping to be able to arrive at the *true* reason for the world through this deferment of the ultimate purpose, this freedom of the will—which I have conceded to man and from which I now should expect the solution of this great riddle—itself leads to a new one that indeed is the greatest of all riddles, and plunges man into an even deeper (if possible) ignorance than that in which he previously found himself with respect to only nature. For when I consider the actions and consequences of this freedom in general—and I had also taken at least a general look at history before I turned to the study of philosophy—this world of *history* presents such a dreary spectacle that I completely despair of there being no [7] purpose and therefore no true reason for the world. For if every other creature of nature, in its place or at its stage, is that which it should be and therefore fulfills its purpose, then so much the more is man—since he can become what he should be only with consciousness and freedom—as long as he remains unconscious of his purpose and is swept along by this tremendous and never-ceasing movement we call history toward a goal of which he is not aware, he is himself purposeless, and since he should be the purpose of everything else, then through him everything else again becomes purposeless. All of nature toils and is engaged in unceasing labor. Man for his part also does not rest, and it is as an old book says: although everything under the sun is so full of toil and labor, one nonetheless does not see that anything is improved or that something is truly accomplished in which one might truly believe. A generation passes away, and another arises to itself again pass away. In vain we expect that something new will happen in which this turmoil will finally find its goal; everything that happens happens only so that something else again can happen, which itself in turn becomes the past to something else. Ultimately, everything happens in vain, and there is in every deed, in all the toil and labor of man himself nothing but vanity: *everything* is vain, for vanity is everything that lacks a true purpose. Thus far from man and his endeavors making the world comprehensible, it is man himself that is the most incomprehensible and who inexorably drives me to the belief in the wretchedness of all being, a belief that makes itself known in so many bitter pronouncements from both ancient and recent times. It is precisely man that drives me to the final desperate question: Why is there anything at all? Why is there not nothing?—

That there should be a science that responds to these questions, which would snatch us from this despair, is unquestionably a compelling, indeed a necessary, longing—a longing not of this or that individual person but of human nature itself. What other science should it be that is capable of this if not [8] philosophy? For all other sciences known by man—invented or developed by him—each has its specific task and none responds to this final and most universal question. So there will be no doubt about this: philosophy is in itself and at all times the most longed for of sciences, since through it all other knowledge receives both its first highest reference and its final support. If I cannot answer this final question, then for me everything else sinks into the abyss of a bottomless void.

These questions, however, are not now advanced for the first time and the need for philosophy has not arisen only in our age. What Horace says regarding heroes, "Fuere fortes ante Agamemnon," applies to those who search for wisdom as well.[1] Philosophical spirits have wandered not only under the plane trees of the Lissus, but also under the palms along the Ganges and the Nile, even if no perceptible or definitive word, but at most a vague sound, has reached us, and even the earlier as well as the later philosophers of Greece—Pythagoras as well as Plato—were familiar with questions on account of which they deemed it worth the trouble to travel to the ends of the known world to secure their answers, as, for example, the dying Socrates challenged his students to ask even the barbarians about wisdom. And how many and what momentous centuries have in the meantime passed over the human spirit! How [this wisdom] was first transplanted through Christendom to Europe, and then in more recent times through the virtually unrestricted expansion of world relations, how the Orient and the Occident are not merely coming into contact with one another, but are being compelled as it were, to fuse into one and the same consciousness, into one consciousness that should for this reason alone be expanded into a world-consciousness! How much has the German spirit alone achieved and accomplished for philosophy from the Middle Ages until now! Yet we must nonetheless confess that there was perhaps never before now a time in which a philosophy that would actually take hold of the great issues—not merely treat them with formulas—was more urgently and universally needed and perhaps no other time when we have been driven farther away from philosophy's proper goal. [9]

If for many years human affairs have maintained a certain uniform course then they become convictions necessary for life that, quite independent of philosophy, acquire their validity precisely through their necessity—a type of sweet habit. In such times, one does not easily think of an investigation of these principles, and even if these long-held standards and doctrines have long since inevitably grown lax—and indeed have fundamentally lost their original force—precisely such a fact is handled as a mystery. For fear of destroying the cozy situation, one avoids looking this fact in the face or declaring that the moral and spiritual powers that still hold the world together, albeit in a merely habitual sense, have long since been undermined by the advance of science. Such a situation can often last so unbelievably long because precisely that which was untenable in the earlier beliefs (according to the previous concepts) is *so* obvious that the more powerful minds do not find it worth the trouble to expose this, and instead leave the business to those mostly powerless minds, incapable of doing anything on their own, to publicly declare what for every profound observer has long since ceased to be a mystery, namely, that there is no place for these truths—considered as unassailable—in the consciousness of the present age. There then arises most often a great clamor, not so much about the matter at hand—which one has long since been unable to hide and now cannot deny as well—as about the unseemly audacity with which the matter is proclaimed. The more farsighted, however, will recognize in all this only an actual need—the need to become aware in a new way of the principles that hold human life together. Not the truths but the consciousness in which, as one says, they can no longer find a place, is that which is obsolete and should therefore make room for a different, expanded consciousness. But the transition to this new consciousness *cannot* happen without a disruption, indeed without a momentary nullification [*Aufhebung*] of the earlier condition. In this general breakdown, there will be for quite some time *nothing* [10] that is secure, to which one could subscribe, and on which one could build: the beautiful and enchanted illusions of an age gone by vanish before the merciless truth. Truth—*pure* truth—is what one demands and still seeks in all relations, in all the institutions of life, and one can only rejoice when a time comes in which war is openly declared on every lie, every deception, where as a principle it is proclaimed that what is desired is truth at *any* price, even the most painful.

For more than the half century since Kant's *Critique of Pure Reason*, the German spirit in particular has embarked upon a methodical examination of the foundation of all knowledge, indeed of all the basic elements of human existence and life itself. Since then it has fought a fight the likes of which has never been fought with the same persistence, in constantly changing venues, or with such unrelenting ardor. And far from regretting this, one would like to call out to the Germans to hold out in this fight, and not let up until the great prize is won. For the more lurid one may portray the threatening phenomenon of our age, the discord, the disagreement, and dissolution, the more certain it becomes that the truly learned will see in all this the portents of a new creation, of a magnificent and enduring restoration, which of course would not be possible without the excruciating pains of labor and the ruthless destruction of all that has become corrupt, fragile, and worn out that must precede it. Nevertheless, there must be an end to this battle since there cannot be, as some imagine, an endless—that is, purposeless and meaningless—progress. Humanity does not advance on into infinity; humanity *has* a goal. There is, therefore, a point to be expected where the struggle for knowledge *achieves* its long-sought aim, where the millennia-long unrest of the human spirit comes to its rest, where man finally takes hold of the proper organism of his knowledge and learning, where the spirit of universal mediation pours forth like a balm over all the previously disparate and mutually exclusive elements of human learning, healing all the wounds [11] that the human spirit in its zealous struggle for light and truth inflects on itself and from which our age still partially bleeds.

"But this would be too much"—one could for instance object to our last remarks—"to expect of philosophy, if through it one considers a restoration of this age as possible, since on the contrary philosophy itself has fallen into contempt, and that widespread interest, that enthusiasm for philosophy which one knew in earlier times is no longer apparent." It may well be that over a long period of time, and benefited by accidental circumstances, a way of doing philosophy has made itself credible that conveyed to some honorable men a certain aversion to philosophy. And perhaps an entire class of esteemed scholars who come from such an age believe, and have made no secret of this, that they can do away with all philosophy. In this case, of course, when pure historical knowledge is not combined with a sense for the ancient classics, and instead steps in as its replacement, the lack of a more profound education will soon become perceptible. However, if I see in philosophy the means for healing the fragmentation of our time, then I do not thereby mean a feeble philosophy that is a mere artifact. I mean a robust philosophy of the type that can measure up to life and that—far from feeling powerless in the face of life and its awesome reality or being confined to the miserable business of only negation and destruction—takes its vitality from reality itself, and for this very reason brings forth something that is again efficacious and enduring.

Still, perhaps one says, "It is not at all the task of science, and thus not that of philosophy, to bring the shrill discord of this age back into harmony. Would not the healing and reconciliation of our age be expected more truly from poetry?" Yet history shows us well that an exuberant age, contented and satisfied with itself, pours itself into poetry and proclaims that poetry is as it were the natural product of an era that has appeased all its essential interests. On the other hand, however, history shows us [12] no example of an age that deeply divided, confused, and doubtful of itself has reconciled and healed itself through poetry. "Secrets," says Friedrich Schiller, "are for the happy."[2] Indeed, one could say that poetry is for the happy. Yet where are those who are happy in an age that is at odds with its past and present, that cannot find the breakthrough to a different age, into the true future? If an actual poet is found in such an age, he will be of the type that knows how to gather all the dissonance of the times into his spirit and combine them into an elaborate but supremely subjective totality, like Lord Byron; lesser spirits will have to reach for frightful and even abominable subjects so that, in contrast to reality, poetry will still appear to be something. I do not, however, really need to speak about this. From what one hears as far as poetry is concerned, the judgment of our age—or as far as Germany is concerned—has already been pronounced by another person, and, indeed, by the type who does not think much of philosophy but who expects a fresh and healthy poetry only as the result of political upheaval. Now this may well remain *his* opinion, into which I have no cause to go. I would, however, like to throw out the general question: how can one who pays no attention to such an essential element of German literature as philosophy credit himself with the ability to presage the future of German literature? For philosophy has penetrated so deeply into all the affairs of this age and into literature in particular, it has acquired such a deep and internal bearing on poetry, that from now on—or at least for the moment—the destiny of both can only be a common one. Just as in earlier times, poetry preceded philosophy—Goethe in particular had a truly prophetic relation to this—so now a revitalized philosophy is destined to bring about a new age of poetry, if only because it returns to poetry its necessary foundation, namely those momentous themes in which our age has lost faith because it has long since lost all understanding for such matters. [13]

To be sure, a decent teacher of philosophy does not first anticipate objections to the intended effects of philosophy from others. It is his duty, once he has shown the edifying side of philosophy, to reveal the dismal and offensive side of it as well so that no one deceives himself. And but a glimpse into its recent history provides adequate material for melancholy reflections on philosophy; this is because until now there has been no way to philosophize, or, as one otherwise says, none of the different philosophical systems has been able to survive over the course of time. I contend that it is also the duty of the teacher to reveal this side of philosophy, which repulses more than it attracts. For whoever considers how many people have shipwrecked on this rocky sea, how some with no vocation for philosophy have consumed the best years of their life, emptying their very soul in the fruitless and foolish pursuit of philosophy, who, without mentioning the desolate halls of prehistoric schools of wisdom, wander among the weather-beaten tombstones of former doctrinal systems-whoever notices, closer to our own age, how scholasticism, which remained throughout the entire Middle Ages in possession of an almost exclusive domination, and was still favored by the leaders and teachers of both churches in the time of the Reformation, and how in the seventeenth century, with no great resistance, it was suddenly and so completely defeated, if not in the schools then nonetheless in popular opinion by Descartes, who because his work, however, was still too immature to be called philosophy, caused one to become ungrateful to all philosophy, and it required nothing less than the entire stature of a Leibniz to partially restore philosophy's honor; — whoever considers how no less than the brilliant Leibnizian system, in the form provided it by Christian Wolff, dominated the German schools for quite some time, yet had nonetheless all but disappeared, and counted only a handful of scattered followers when Kant's *Critique of Pure Reason* systematically put an end to it, or even how it was earlier forced to capitulate to a shallow popular philosophy lacking foundational principles and a guiding star; [14] — whoever considers how again the last philosophy mentioned, the so-called Critical Philosophy, which for a long time enjoyed a nearly unlimited, one could even say tyrannical stature, and how these days it is scarcely known and still less understood by many who glorify philosophical studies and knowledge, and how it has, in particular, lost any influence on all the great questions of life; —whoever considers how the dynamic Fichte, the founder of Transcendental Idealism, whose appearance worked like a bolt of lightening, who for a moment more or less inverted the polarities of thought, but sadly, like a bolt of lightning, again disappeared, and how in the *contemporary* consciousness of the German people the site could still scarcely be found on which he then constructed his system, so that one would find it difficult to make clear to his successors the fundamental ideas of his doctrine;—whoever then notices how after a period of exhilarating activity, where the successful sublation [*Aufhebung*] of the antithesis between the real and ideal world appeared to abolish all the limitations of previous knowledge so that *one* law led through the world of nature and mind, and how in those days nature itself also appeared to adapt to this new knowledge, through a series of brilliant and illuminating discoveries that followed the first observation of Galvanism—as when, to use an expression of Goethe, a true heavenly knowledge appeared to descend— whoever then notices how after such an era a new darkness nonetheless follows, and what began great ended small;—whoever observes and considers all of this, truly, may well be filled with melancholy at the vanity of all human struggle for that highest knowledge that is demanded by philosophy. He may well find only a profound if bitter truth in those words that Goethe puts in the mouth of the negative spirit in his *Faust*:

> O believe me, who for many thousand years
> Have chewed upon this hard repast,
> That from the cradle to the grave
> No human could the old sourdough digest. [15]
> Believe me also, this whole universe
> Has only for a God been fabricated.
> He finds Himself in an eternal glory,
> But us He's brought to darkness unabated,
> And you but one brief day has allocated.[3]

This diversity, this alternation of systems not merely different from each other, but also opposed to each other, is a phenomenon that in any case indicates a quite distinctive nature of philosophy. And if we do not avoid recognizing this nature completely, precisely this phenomenon must be brought into our considerations, and, where possible, it must be comprehended from the nature of philosophy itself.

One cannot avoid this diversity of philosophical systems by somehow saying that every philosophy is nonetheless still philosophy, just as every type of fruit is fruit; and how amazing would it be if someone would reject grapes or some other type of fruit because, although he craved only fruit, he did not crave this fruit. I do not believe that the objection, which takes the diversity of systems in philosophy as proof against philosophy itself, allows itself to be repulsed with merely this simile. To begin with it, is not compelling that he who craves fruit must for that very reason accept any type. For if along these lines one offered him for example a wild pear, or so-called *Heerlinge*, he would be justified in saying that that is not fruit, since he had asked for fruit, namely, something edible. Just as one with a thirst who craves water would not be obliged to drink nitric acid, since he craves something drinkable, not something that is just physically or mechanically drinkable—a *potile*-but rather something that to his taste is drinkable, that is, a *potabile*. Second, it is just not compelling that we have a craving for philosophy *in general*. This would be like those fathers or guardians who direct their wards at the university to study philosophy—regardless of *which* kind, since after all it belongs to a proper education to also know something about philosophy, or, at the very least, to receive [16] some practice in logical and dialectical argumentation, so that, as one says, the mind will in general be put in order. Everyone, however, wants to know something about philosophy. For example, one who acts like he has contempt for philosophy would probably take no offense if one said to him that he does not know how to compose a march or Latin verse, but would nonetheless find it highly offensive if one were to tell him that he does not have a philosophical mind.

But if it be allowed for one to say such a thing, if someone did not want or intend to speak simply about philosophy in general, but to present *the* philosophy that *is*, and thus also endures, such a person would be the most inclined to let all previous developments have a just hearing, since they all must find their goal in the true philosophy. Such a person would feel the greatest reluctance to arouse the opinion that those attending his lectures should be prepared exclusively for some one system and should be intentionally left in ignorance about all the other standpoints that lie outside that position or should only be told of them in a partisan manner. Nothing could more enrage a youthful and fiery sensibility, burning for the truth, than the intention of a teacher to prepare his audience for some one special or particular system, wishing in this way to emasculate them by underhandedly removing the freedom of inquiry. Consequently, I have prefaced all my other lectures on philosophy with a genetic exposition of the systems of philosophy that have arisen since Descartes until recent times. Recently there has been a profusion of such expositions written and presented in which partisan intentions unfortunately stand out all too shrilly; for unfortunately, in some circles philosophy has gradually become a partisan issue, whereby it has nothing to do with truth, but only with the preservation of an opinion. In this lecture series I will restrict myself by beginning with Kant, or more accurately speaking, with the old metaphysics that serves as the foundation of the Kantian philosophy. This old metaphysics was not a system in the sense that one speaks of systems since Descartes. [17] But just as in Germany, for example, one speaks of a common German law, so too was the former metaphysics to a certain degree the common German philosophy predominant in the schools. This was a metaphysics that continued to hold its ground even after the appearance of these systems, since the entire system—for example, the Cartesian—was never incorporated into the common philosophy, but rather, at most, into their individual components. For this reason I will begin with the old metaphysics in order to show how, as the result of a necessary development, philosophy had to reach the point that it—just as its negative and positive facets distinguished themselves—would also realize that in the joining of these two facets it would finally discover its complete and altogether satisfying conclusion. You see this point already touched on in an earlier lecture, where it dealt with the presentation of the positive philosophy itself, which I again pick up here in order to ground it and expound on it still further. Yet, since this time the negative or rational philosophy will only be spoken of according to its general propositions, ideas, and methods without itself being explicated, I will attempt for this purpose a different derivation of this science that for some of *you* will be perhaps more comprehensible. [18]

On the Academic Study of Philosophy

Before the presentation itself, I would like to put forth a few general remarks about listening to philosophy lectures. There is nothing more common regarding philosophy lectures than to hear complaints about their unintelligibility. When this occurs, a certain injustice is done to some teachers to the extent that the blame is placed on his individual inability to express himself distinctly, or that he lacks the gift of clear analysis, whereas the blame properly lies in the subject itself. For where the subject is *in itself* unintelligible and muddled, the highest art of oratory would still be incapable of making it intelligible. Thus, if one would first strive for intelligibility in the subject itself, then that of the lecture would emerge of itself. What Goethe says is thus valid here as well:

> Understanding and good sense
> Express themselves with little art.[4]

What is true is hardly of the type that it allows itself to be found only with unnatural efforts or articulated in unnatural words and formulas. Most people spoil their first foray into philosophy through the unnatural excitement that they regard as the correct disposition with which to approach it. Some have dealt with philosophy in the same way as people who have long grown used to living only with their equals and when they [19] associate with someone above them, or should appear before one of the so-called great ones of this earth, behave clumsily, awkwardly, and unnaturally. Indeed, in philosophy one believes such behavior belongs to the subject so much so that one ultimately judges the degree of scholarly expertise according to the degree of the perverse distortions and contortions into which a philosophy deteriorates. On the contrary, however, one should remain convinced that anything that allows itself to be articulated only in a garbled and eccentric manner cannot, for that very reason, be what is true and right. What is true is easy, says an ancient; but it does not come to us without effort, for indeed to find what is simple and easy is most difficult, and for this very reason it is difficult to understand many thinkers precisely because they have not found this simplicity. Most imagine that what is true must be difficult in order to be true, but when what is true is found it always has something of the luck of Columbus about it. A consummate work of art, a painting by Raphael, looks as if it had effortlessly created itself, and everyone thinks that it could not possibly be any other way, but only the artist knows how much he was forced to discard in order to reach this point of lucid clarity and intelligibility. The difference between the mere dilettante and the genuine artist consists precisely in the fact that the former remains stuck in the mere preliminaries of art and science without ever getting to the heart of the matter, whereas the latter goes beyond this to freedom and creates a free art. You must summon courage to do philosophy. In philosophy it is not about an opinion that would be imposed on the human spirit like a burden or a heavy yoke; its burden must be easy, its yoke light.[5] Plato does not crucify himself as some philosophers of late have done. Rather, one can say of Plato what has been said of Orpheus: through the mere tones of his music he moved mountains and tamed the wildest monstrosities in philosophy.

Thus, one must first strive for *objective* intelligibility, for clarity in the subject; for, to be sure, subjective intelligibility permits of very different degrees, and if what is true can only be [20] what is in itself intelligible, conversely, it does not follow that what is intelligible—just because it is intelligible—is the truth. For what is common and everyday is of course intelligible to all, whereas in philosophy there is a clarity that brings the novice and especially the better minds to despair. For example, I know of a student to whom a well-meaning teacher, when he thought it time that the student should also engage in philosophy, put in his hands a leading book of then-popular philosophy, Feder's *Logic and Metaphysics*.[6] This book filled the student with the deepest distress because he believed that he did not understand it, for what he did understand of it seemed too trivial to him to be considered as the actual content of the book and because of the work's all-too-great clarity the student gave up ever trying to comprehend anything about philosophy. Yet when that same teacher later put in his hands Leibniz's aphorisms, known under the title *Theses in gratiam principis Eugenii* (which was written for the famous duke Eugen von Savoyen and contains the foundational principles of the Monadology), the student regained his courage and thought that perhaps he was capable of understanding something of philosophy after all.[7] Specifying a general standard of intelligibility that would be acceptable to everyone is just not possible, and those students who come here having learned how to deal with philosophy in a perverse and forced manner find what is simple and not perverse difficult, much in the same way as one who, if he had spent the entire day on a tread wheel, would find in the evening that he could no longer move in his usual and natural way. One ought to deal with such spoiled individuals as Socrates did with the students who came to him from the Sophist and Eleatic schools, who with simple questions, so to speak, he put on a limited diet, thereby attempting to reacquaint them to what is simple and wholesome. But of course, nothing has yet been provided for such a treatment in the organization of our university's curriculum.

If philosophy in general has the reputation of a certain unintelligibility, then it is perhaps even more important to consider as well the usual means of support and facilitation [21] one employs to make a lecture more intelligible. I would like to say something about this as well.

Counted among the means of support for an oral lecture are, above all, textbooks written by the lecturer or someone else, which serve as the basis for what will be presented and which he comments upon and explains. Now I cannot provide for my lectures, least of all the present one, a textbook written by another or even myself that would serve as their basis. Indeed, the content of these lectures is just not suited to the format of a typical textbook: it does not consist of a series of finished propositions that can be put forth individually. Rather its results are generated in a continuous but thoroughly free and animated progression and movement, whose moments do not allow themselves to be captured in the memory, but rather only in the spirit. Therefore, the entire series of lectures, to the extent that they are purely scientific, would have to be printed, and this will now also presumably happen.

I must leave it to you, my listeners, to determine whether after this explanation you would still like to make use of another conventional device, or perhaps now find it superfluous. I mean that widespread custom of note taking, which one primarily justifies, in that it puts one in the position to dwell by every point according to need and to recall the entire series of moments over and over again. For this reason, and since there is after all no textbook available, I have nothing against the taking of notes in this sense, but rather excuse it, particularly when it is actually a matter of summation and the entire work does not consist in simple dictation. For I cannot deny that only with restrictions and only in a very qualified sense can I approve of note taking in philosophy lectures, not on account of their improper use, of which I have here first learned, of how very, very far science is behind art regarding the protection that art and science have a right to expect. For if a piece of sculpture were exhibited in a public space in this metropolis of German culture, as I have confidently called Berlin, there would not be one individual, even in the class of the lowest rabble, [22] who would entertain the thought of defacing, sullying, or bombarding that work of art with filth, immediately after its installation. The general level of culture has to such depths long since penetrated, and it does not require a law, nor the anticipated general indignation, to prevent such an outrage. When, however, a scientific work of art is unfolded in public lectures, there, it seems, that a dirty and pandering publishing house, which mutilates and smears it, need fear neither a manifestation of indignation nor even the use of existing laws.[8] Nevertheless, as I said, it is not because of improper use of this kind, but for reasons quite independent of it that note taking in philosophy lectures, at least in itself alone, has always seemed to me to be an ambiguous means of insuring an understanding of a scientific exposition. With the mere taking of notes it is always to be feared that while one thinks only of grasping the word of the teacher, the context of the thought itself becomes lost, and afterward one attempts in vain to reconstruct it from a defective collection of notes. The renowned Greek philosopher Antisthenes, a leader of the Cynic school, was once asked by a pupil what he needed in order to attend his classes.[9] The philosopher responded that he would require a βιβλαριον καινοῦ, a γραφειου καινοῦ, and a πιναχος καινοῦ, — words that could be understood to mean a new notebook (probably for compositions), a new stylus, and a new slate (perhaps for taking notes). The pupil, if one thinks of him as the one in *Faust*, must have been quite satisfied for the moment to hear from the mouth of the philosopher his own opinion confirmed, that to understand a philosophy lecture one requires above all a new stylus and slate.[10] But the earnest cynic was a rogue like Mephistopheles and knew how to make a pun—for if one took the word καινοῦ as two words, then one may understand that he told his pupil he needs a notebook and understanding, a stylus and understanding, and a slate and understanding; that is, [23] understanding doesn't depend on anything else, the decisive element one must use is one's own self-engaged thought, one's own understanding.[11] These words resemble those of the famous General Montecucculi, who in response to the Kaiser's question of what is necessary to wage war replied that three things are necessary: first, money; second, money; and third, money.[12] The same Antisthenes replied to one of his pupils who had complained to him of having lost his lecture notes: you should have written them in your soul, not on pieces of paper. The most fruitful method of taking notes would be if one, with care and discrimination, were to record only the essential points—and particularly the transitions, which form the connective elements of the inquiry—and then according to this summary—this skiagraphy—would then attempt to work out and produce the entire lecture itself again, a possibility that is provided for in this lecture series, in that between each lecture a day will remain open. (I have found that with this arrangement more is gained for the understanding of philosophy lectures than with an uninterrupted series, which most listeners are unable to deal with.) If one attempts to reconstruct the entire lecture in this manner, then this will be a self-won content, and this effort is doubly beneficial since it will feed back into a more decisive and lucid understanding of the lecture. In this way, one learns to attach importance to that which through the progressive development of the inquiry conveys its inner connection, the inquiry's connective tissue. Still better is when more do this collectively, one helping and supplementing the other, so that through such collaboration the entirety is once again produced. Only thereby does the lesson come alive for each student, and the more deeply inspired content won through this shared effort and discussion will become at the same time the bond of a *true*, spiritual friendship. For this is the greatest appeal of the academic life, or at least it should be—this being together with others, so united in one common purpose, as in the course of life that follows people cannot be so easily united again.

Things are in order in an institution of higher learning only when many students,[24] or at least the better and more gifted ones, understand what is most worthy of being sought and desired in the sciences. It thereby cultivates a type of shared spirit of scientific inquiry and a youth imbued with character, who does not falter with ambivalence, but who decisively turns away from what is base, in whichever form it may present itself. There are among adults enough of the type that Dr. Luther calls "weathervanes," who put their finger to the air to learn which way the wind blows, wishing, in the words of Luther, to find out first whether Christ or Baal is right. It is worthy of youth to stand by that which they recognize as right and to deny the better sentiment in nothing. Even the greatest talent is first ennobled through character. But character can be cultivated only in the thrust and counter-thrust of a shared struggle for *one* goal. The true spice of academic life is the ever-changing excitement and enthusiasm for science, without which all the other joys of this way of life would soon become stale. If the German academic life maintains a lasting worth in the memory of many, if the faces of the oldest men still brighten with the recollection of the university and the life there, then this is certainly not due to the memory of sensual pleasures, but is chiefly due to a recollection tied to that consciousness of a shared, courageous struggle for intellectual development and higher knowledge. The student who has not passed time in intimate allegiance with like-minded youth in a shared striving for conviction and clarity in important matters has not enjoyed academic life.

It is becoming of noble-minded youths to concern themselves with sunshine and even mindless merriment, to which they are to a certain degree still entitled, but they are to search the darker shadows of more serious matters as well, and it is essential that such gravity does not assault the manner or the subject matter they pursue. That teacher is no friend of youth who attempts to fill them with the grief and sorrow for the ways of the world or the course of [25] politics when they must first acquire the strength of guiding convictions and beliefs. Likewise, it is most often only an abuse for ulterior motives and one's own shallowness to use youths, as one says, to demonstrate freedom of thought and teaching. I say an abuse for ulterior motives so long as one can doubt to what extent these individuals who mouth the words "freedom of thought" are themselves actually willing to admit freedom of thought, which they most often lay claim to primarily for their own incidental opinions, while considering themselves justified in assailing other opposing views by any means that stands in their power. Regarding the appeal to academic freedom, it can hardly be accepted as long as those who speak of such things somehow find it totally acceptable that someone who allows himself to be employed and supported by a church, whose foundation he covertly seeks to undermine in his lectures, nonetheless would himself concede no unlimited freedom of instruction to a teacher of theology at a Protestant seminary, for example, who with fire and spirit (as it may very well be) seeks to uphold and assert something like the necessity of a visible head of the church, of a most high and infallible judge in issues of faith, and other fundamental principles of the Roman Church—faced with such a scandal these people would hardly tolerate an appeal to academic freedom. That thought and inquiry must never be restricted, that science, that even instruction must be free (at least within the confines of what is proper and fitting), all this is so obvious that he who professes such platitudes can really only have the *intention* of conveying in a harmless way the idea that here or there freedom of thought or teaching is in danger, and thus in a cheap purchase acquire the reputation for exceptional candor. To be sure, our youth should also be enthusiastic about this priceless good, purchased at so high a price by Germany—may heaven and the good sense of our rulers always provide that this treasure is never lost through unskillful use!—but only so that they strive all the more zealously to obtain the intellectual and scientific proficiency that is necessary to put this freedom to an [26] honorable use and bring forth that which on whose account it was worth the effort to win this freedom. For what is routine and trivial requires no such freedom of thought. A total inversion of mankind's worldview, such as that provided by the Copernican astronomy, was able to impel the spiritual leaders of an earlier time to incarcerate a Galileo and force him to renounce his theory. By means of tremendous magnification, Ehrenberg's discovery first unlocked for the human eye a world of perfectly disciplined and organized animals, a world that could have appeared to an earlier and more constricted age as something sinister and dangerous, as if there was something not quite right about magnification.[13] These are discoveries through which the human mind is liberated, expanded, and actually raised to a higher level. Nevertheless, the world does not care whether one reads in a work by a Latin writer *declarabat* or *declamabat*, or whether one should begin the deduction of categories with the category of quantity (as was the custom from Aristotle until recent times, and for which there were good reasons), or with that of quality (as more recent logic prefers, perhaps only because it did not know how to deal with quantity), this is perhaps important for the schools, but not the slightest thing in the world will be changed as a result of it. One must, however, be reasonable and concede that the common masses are at the very least not completely indifferent to the output of the mind, and especially of philosophy. For if it were ever possible that a doctrine was to gain the upper hand, according to which the best and wisest things for humans should be leftover food, drink, and other goods of this type, a doctrine according to which everything metaphysical should be completely removed from human conviction: if it were ever possible that such a doctrine were to come about—something I still consider less likely than primates becoming the rulers of humankind, or that humanity would forever disappear from the face of the earth, and thereupon the primates would then become rulers of the world—but suppose that such a teaching did appear, then of course the government could do nothing other than [27] more or less look on with folded arms, in impassive resignation at its downfall.

The entire edifice of human affairs is comparable to that image the king of Babylon saw in his dream: his head was of fine gold, his breast and arms were of silver, his belly and loin of bronze, his thigh of iron, but his feet were part iron and part clay, which were then crushed and mixed together with iron, clay, bronze, silver, and gold, and became like chaff on the summer threshing floors, which the wind scattered so that one could no longer find them anywhere.[i] If one could ever extract all that is metaphysical from the state and public life, then they too would fall apart in the same way. *True metaphysics* is honor, it is virtue; true metaphysics is not only religion, but also respect for the law and love of one's land. What would be the outcome and result of a philosophy such as the one described above (if one can call something of this type philosophy)? Answer: the moral of Falstaff in the well-known monologue before the start of battle:

> Honor pricks me on. Yea, but how if honor prick me off when I come on? How then? Can honor set to a leg? No. Or to an arm? No. Or take away the grief of a wound? No. Honor hath no skill in surgery, then? What is honor? A word. What is in that word honor? What is that honor? Air; a trim reckoning! Who hath it? He that died o'Wednesday. Doth he feel it? No. Doth he hear it? T'is insensible, then? Yea, to the dead. But will it not live with the living? No. Why? Detraction will not suffer it. Therefore I'll none of it. Honor is a mere scutcheon: and so ends my catechism.[14]

With such a moral as Falstaff's would a catechism of this doctrine also have to end, if everything metaphysical were ever to be removed from the world and the faith of humanity? Human affairs do not allow themselves to be governed by mathematics, physics, natural history (I revere these sciences highly), or even poetry and art. The true understanding of the world is provided by precisely the right [28] metaphysics, which for this very reason has from time immemorial been called the royal science. For *the* very reason that some have reproached our universities for holding the young man in too great an isolation from the world—as if he did not require precisely such a setting, so that the composed, undisturbed development and cultivation of his mental powers may be sustained—for this very reason are our universities properly esteemed, worthwhile, and praiseworthy institutions. In the blessed hours of these auspicious years, great decisions are made and ideas received that later will step forth into reality: here every person must find and acknowledge the calling of his life. No one should believe that something can emerge later in life for which he did not already here lay the groundwork, or that he could attain some kind of achievement, which he may well call his life's work, that at the

---

i. Daniel 2:31–35.

very least had not already stood here before his soul as a presentiment. The dreams of youth themselves—even if they remain dreams—are not without meaning if they make what is base inaccessible for future life, if one can apply to them what Schiller allows to be said to the unhappy Don Carlos:

> Tell Him
> That he should have respect for
> The dreams of youth when he becomes a man;
> That the heart of divinity's tender flower should not
> Open to the deadly insect of vaunted better reason—
> That he should not lose his way
> When the wisdom of dust blasphemes
> Heaven's daughter, enthusiasm.[15]

May this also apply to *your* future. Do not be astonished if I speak to you this semester in a more personal manner than I have in the past; this stems from the fact that my tenure here is decided. Consequently, I have taken on the duty to be for you not merely a teacher, but to the extent I am capable, of being your friend and adviser as well. My calling for this is due just as much to the science that I teach, the only one that seizes the entire person at his very core, as to the fact that, although the years have drawn me far from *you*, [29] I did nonetheless once feel as you do now, and have still not yet forgotten how to feel how one in your years feels.

If the state of social relations under which science exists with us does not permit the teacher to teach in the manner of the philosophers of old; if the relationship of the pupil to the teacher can no longer, at least not usually, be a living relationship as in Socrates' or Plato's time, one would nevertheless like to try at the very least to work toward such a relationship, in that one would see to it that the rapport between teacher and student is not one-sided, but is rather reciprocal. No one doubts that it is beneficial for the student to speak out against the teacher, present his doubts, request clarification of what remains obscure, and through questions, make sure whether and to what extent he has grasped the teacher's thoughts. Yet the well-meaning and conscientious teacher should also not be indifferent to know *whether* he has been understood, for indeed he can only then continue with assurance to the next topic if he is convinced that the preceding material, on which the next topic depends, has been correctly and completely comprehended. The teacher is often first made aware through his listeners of a misunderstanding that he has not considered (for who could consider every possibility?), and can perhaps with one word do away with an error that would have otherwise made all that was to follow obscure and confusing. I have therefore in the past sought to make possible such an *exchange* of views through a discussion group connected with my lectures, where everyone throws out questions, presents their doubts, where the listener can also repeat what he has heard according to *his* interpretation, so it may be confirmed or, according to circumstances, be corrected and supplemented. For the time being it may well have to be as it was last winter: anyone for whom something has remained obscure or who nurtures a doubt that he cannot resolve for himself, should put it in writing on a signed piece of paper and either [30] place it on my lectern or send it to my apartment. I will reply to what comes to me in this way either when the context will not suffer too much from it, or at an appropriate point in the lecture. I assume that there is no one among my audience who after this could believe he is only here to make objections, but not, however, in order above all else to learn. Naively and as is only proper, I assume that there is no one here who does not have the honest and actual intention—be it a great deal or very little—but in any case to *learn* from me. If someone believes he understands the matters to be discussed here better than I, then he should please let me know so that I may try as quickly as possible to learn from him. Due to the nature of the subject at hand, questions, misgivings, and objections can only be considered after a topic has been thoroughly discussed and the teacher has explained himself completely on the matter. There are people lacking in upbringing who, as soon as they learn of something unheard of, feel an itch to make objections. I of course do not wish to promote a reaction of this type, and I am quite convinced that I will not have to deal with it here. Until the point at which the matter at hand is completely exhausted, a Pythagorean silence must be law for this type of pupil.

I have made my way through the different means of support for an oral lecture: textbooks, note taking, and the exchange between teacher and pupil. I would now like to mention another thing that, according to circumstances, can be one of the most powerful means of support for the study of any science, and thus also for the understanding of a philosophical presentation. I mean the *reading material*, the study of the primary works that are written in every science and denote a significant moment in its advancement or improvement.

When I spoke earlier of *primary works*, I indicated fully that I do not consider *daily lectures* to be beneficial to scientific studies—as little as the idle talk of the day that is heard today and forgotten tomorrow, without leaving behind a trace in our [31] souls. There is, however, yet another distinction between scientific works and those that are only incidentally serious: not all have flown forth from their source in the same way and not all are equally original. If the secondary works are not absolutely necessary for one to understand the primary works, one would do very well indeed to stick exclusively with the originals, so that one may thereby dedicate to them even more time and effort. To exhaust the depths and very soul of a single dialogue of Plato, such as the *Sophist* or the *Philebus*, will certainly yield each of you much more significant results than an entire army of commentaries. From the truly original works, there always comes to us a uniquely invigorating spirit that incites our own productive powers, whereas with other works it falls asleep.

Also from a moral perspective, what one reads is far less insignificant than one would think. In life, it is not always in our control to determine to whom we will allow access to our soul. All the more diligently then should one study these original works, so that one accustoms oneself early on to that which is eternal, unchanging, and enduring, and thereby learns contempt for what is here today and gone tomorrow.

If I am to designate now that which above all else is to be recommended in relation to the lecture that follows, or to the study of philosophy in general, it will be unavoidable to express the following in more specific terms than I have previously.

Ever since that great movement ushered in by Kant, it has been a question not of this or that philosophy, but rather—just as Kant's critique itself addressed this issue—it has been a question *of philosophy itself*. *De capite dimicatur*, it is a question of the essential point, that is to say, it is a matter of philosophy itself. For those emboldened by fortuitous circumstances into deluding themselves that the time has come in which their vacuous theories [asserting] the absolute negation of everything metaphysical in science and humanity may now assume the throne, it must be very upsetting to hear [32] that one must return once again to the fundamental investigations. Historically speaking then, one must once again return to Kant. Consequently, since they cannot hinder this, they will summon everything in their command to at least cast suspicion on this undertaking and will, for example, put forth the pretense that our undertaking is simply a matter of religion, that the disagreement is a religious one, that one simply wishes to establish religion in the old sense—particularly positive religion—and so on, for with this they believe to have already sufficiently discredited *this* aspiration. But this is not so. It is a question, and indeed a very serious question; once again—may it be the last time!—it is a question of the meaning of philosophy itself.

We admit for the time being no specific philosophy, neither a religious one nor one that claims to be irreligious. We leave both of these open, for one cannot speak of what is derivative before one is certain about the primary matter at hand, which is here that of philosophy itself. Since Kant's *Critique of Pure Reason*, philosophy has been engaged in a progressive development, and is perhaps now engaged in its final crisis. Even if it is already possible to analyze the necessary result of this crisis, one cannot—for the time being at least, while this result does not have widespread acceptance—do it independently of the historical process whose end it is; that is, we are compelled to traverse the entire route of philosophy from Kant until the present time. For I most definitely have to dispute the opinion that any position can be advanced that is completely removed from a connection to Kant. This could be shown alone by the fact that every attempt to nullify this connection and establish something beyond it, no matter how much effort and refinement has been applied to it, has barely won recognition even in limited circles, and certainly no widespread consideration. I would cite as an example what one calls the Herbartian philosophy.[16]

On the Academic Study of Philosophy

Philosophy, still in development even if engaged in the final stages of its becoming and the explication of its final result, [33] does not, at least for the time being, allow itself to be presented in an instructive, informative, and universally convincing manner without going back to Kant. If I were therefore to recommend some type of research at the beginning of this presentation, I would know of nothing more enlightening and useful than the study of Kant's *Critique of Pure Reason*, a work with which one should begin even more since it is also the proper source for the vast majority of the contemporary philosophical vocabulary. Whoever wishes to make philosophy their major field of study must always begin with Kant. Not all students however, are in this position; but even those who devote only part of their time to philosophy should not neglect to study at the very least the short but succinct excerpts taken from the *Critique of Pure Reason*, approved by Kant himself, and to which the publisher, Johannes Schultze, has even contributed a commentary.[17]

I have once again returned to the point, which from the outset I have designated as the beginning of our own exposition—to Kant. [34]

Metaphysics before Kant

Kant himself presupposes the old metaphysics, and his critique relates directly to it. Thus, we too will have to begin with it. It derives from scholasticism, which throughout the entire Middle Ages was, in general, the dominant philosophy. The differences that occurred within scholasticism itself were not essential differences through which its standpoint could have been altered. Since the fall of scholasticism, such a long-lasting peace in philosophy has yet to be achieved again. The true philosophy, the highest philosophical science of scholasticism, was metaphysics, a word whose origin is as doubtful and uncertain as whether the title *Metaphysics* now carried by Aristotle's book comes from the author himself. In its literal meaning, metaphysics would be the science that concerns itself with those objects that extend beyond what is physical and natural. To this extent, it could be regarded as the science that chiefly deals with what is supernatural and supersensible. In fact, these were the principal objects of the former metaphysics. The nature of God and his relationship to the world—the world itself, conceived in its totality, as a cosmos, no longer the object of *just* a physical representation or knowledge—the beginning and ultimate purpose of the world—man as the band between the physical and a higher world—the freedom of the human will— [35] the difference between good and evil and the origin of this difference; the emergence of evil itself; the immateriality of the human soul and its perpetuity after death—these of course constituted the primary content of metaphysics. Nonetheless, one could not consider these as its only objects. It was also not a hyperphysic, but rather a metaphysic, since even in the world of visible nature not everything is the object of just a physical inquiry because even material nature has its metaphysical side. In addition, even if the absolute supersensible, God, was the *goal* of all metaphysical endeavors, there was still the matter of finding the intellectual *means* for a knowledge of this supersensible. Metaphysics found these means in three different *types* of knowledge, which therefore also allow themselves to be seen as three sources of our knowledge, and with which one must become thoroughly acquainted in order to penetrate the spirit of the old metaphysics, for indeed, knowledge of God was possible only through the combination or integration of these three sources of human knowledge.

The first of these sources was the *understanding* [*Verstand*], intellectus, under which was understood the faculty of general concepts that, when applied to experience, become general principles.

Just as one can observe that in the everyday and scientific use of one's understanding, certain forms of judgment and inference are applied, as it were, by instinct, and constantly repeat themselves—forms that, when freed of the stuff of their application and presented in their purity or abstraction then become the content of the so-called everyday or formal *logic*—so it was easy to see how certain final and general concepts serve as the basis of all our judgments and inferences, and without which *every* thought, not just the philosophical, would be impossible. Whoever had no concept of substance and accident, cause and effect, could think of nothing. When the chemist proves the empirical proposition that the process of combustion consists of a combination of oxygen in the atmosphere's air and a burning body—specifically of the increase in weight of the burning body, for example, of a [36] burning metal and the corresponding decrease in weight of the air that remains left over—what does he tacitly presuppose in this, perhaps without even being aware of it himself? Nothing other than the proposition that the body's contingent manner of appearance can change without subjecting the substance itself to an increase or decrease in weight, that is, he distinguishes at least between substance of the body and its accidents—thus he distinguishes between substance and accident in general. Similarly, if some new phenomenon arouses the attention of the natural scientist, and he feels himself called on to find the cause of this phenomenon, he thereby, without justifying himself further, presupposes as something understood the concept as well as the law of cause and effect, namely, that in nature it is impossible for there to be an effect without a determining cause. Since, as a result of these general concepts and principles, all thought that extends beyond mere material representation itself is first made possible, and since *without* these concepts and principles *thought itself* would be annulled [*aufgehoben*], one thus presupposes that they have already been posited with the nature of thought itself and that they are natural to it. Or, as one later claimed, they are innate or inherent to thought, so that one need not first obtain them from experience, since experience only provides the material for their application, whereas they are already given along with the human understanding before experience, and in which respect they should then most certainly be called a priori concepts and laws.

The old metaphysics thus posited the first source of knowledge in the pure understanding, which it defined as the source or faculty of all those concepts and laws that are clothed for us in the character of generality and necessity. Nonetheless, these concepts and laws would be lacking all use if experience were not to be added.

Consequently, *experience* was viewed as the second source of the knowledge to be produced in metaphysics and was then divided again into inner and outer experience, according to how it instructs us of phenomena or conditions outside us or within our own being. Experience does not reveal to us what is universal, necessary, [37] and unchanging, but rather only what is particular, contingent, and transitory in things. Yet it is precisely what is particular and contingent in things that is the real basis of science upon which it supports itself in the *production* of knowledge and science. For this too was always presupposed as well, namely, that metaphysics is not a ready-made science that exists without our assistance, but is instead a science that must first be produced. A productive activity in no way inheres in these general concepts and laws of the understanding: on their own they would produce nothing and on their own no real knowledge inheres in them. Aristotle already says the decisive words: *scire est agere, intelligere est pati* [knowledge is active, understanding is passive]. It seems to us that we relate more passively to the necessity that these concepts and principles impose on our thought; in the same way, what we obtain directly from experience is something that we take but do not generate.

The productive activity, which can first be called philosophical and through which metaphysics first arises, has its presuppositions in each of the first two sources of knowledge: in understanding and in experience. That faculty, however, for which these presuppositions serve as its basis and by means of which they arrive at that which is neither directly provided through the pure understanding—which is in no way something concrete or real, and thus provides still less of anything that is personal—nor through experience—that which is provided neither through the pure understanding nor through experience is precisely the absolute supersensible [*das absolut Uebersinnliche*]. The faculty that puts us in the position to arrive at a knowledge of the supersensible from both of those presuppositions is a third source of knowledge in general, and is the immediate source of a freely produced knowledge (a knowledge that, as will become clear from what follows, can in any case only be a mediated knowledge). It is *ratio, reason*, understood as the capacity to deduce [*Vermögen zu Schließen*]. This capacity to deduce consists solely in the application of general principles, provided with the understanding itself, to the contingent elements present in experience. [38] Through deduction we are led to a third source, which, elevated *above* both, must simultaneously have something in common with both, or unite both, in that which is the universal *per se*, which as such is simultaneously something concrete. Both must be united in that which is absolutely concrete, which, precisely because it is this, is simultaneously that which is the universal *per se*: this power must unite both in God as the truly *universal* cause, who as universal cause is simultaneously personal, and thus an individual. Metaphysics believed that it could accomplish this solely through reason as the capacity to deduce. When I incorporate the phenomena given in experience into the world of concepts and determine these phenomena as *contingent* (which could also not be), yet existing, and when I then apply the general laws of the understanding to what exists contingently—namely, everything that comports itself as just an effect, that is, as something that could also not be (for this is the proper concept of an effect), that cannot be determined to exist without a *cause*, but only through a determinate cause—I elevate myself, on the one hand, to the *concept* of an absolute cause through which the world, that is, the complex of all special and merely relative causes and effects, is determined to be [*zum Daseyn bestimmt*], and on the other hand, to the insight into the *existence* [*Existence*] of this absolute cause, which to know was considered to be the ultimate and highest goal of all metaphysics. In general, then, the former metaphysics was based on the assumption that it is capable, through the application of general concepts and fundamental principles to what was provided in experience, of inferring that which is beyond all experience. One has disparagingly called this metaphysics in recent times a metaphysics of the understanding [*Verstandsmetaphysik*]. It would be nice indeed to wish that one could say the same of every philosophy, namely, that it incorporates understanding at all.[ii]

After the foundations of this metaphysics have now been explained, there will be no difficulty in making comprehensible in which way that moment had to arrive when it was impossible to continue with [39] this metaphysics and why it was necessary for philosophy to distance itself farther and farther from it. It is quite obvious, namely, that such metaphysics, without any further justification, simply assumes and presupposes the sources, the three capacities of experience, understanding, and reason, from which it derives its knowledge. But as time progressed it could not be avoided that these sources themselves would become objects of doubt or, at the very least, of criticism; as soon as this occurred, the shape of philosophy *had to* change. Descartes was the first to announce significant doubts against external, sensible experience, and in doing so he negated [*aufhob*] it as a *principle* of knowledge, since it now became itself an *object*. Doubt could not apply to whether we necessarily represent external things. Instead, the question was whether we are not deceived in this, for example, by a god who merely brings forth for us these representations of external things, while they do not exist beyond us, an opinion maintained by Malebranche, that all objects were to be seen by us only in God, which was later even endorsed by the famous Berkeley. Already in this doubt lay the demand to demonstrate the necessity of the thing itself.

At first, therefore, it was experience that as the certain source of knowledge was challenged and itself cast into doubt.

But even before Descartes, the famed Francis Bacon had, on the contrary, advanced sensible experience as the only genuine, original source of all knowledge. Worn out by the syllogisms of scholastic metaphysics, he aroused the most widespread distrust toward this entire manner and method of operation and the entire genus of general concepts and the conclusions that built upon them. Induction, combination, and analogy should be the means to

---

ii. Compare the parallel exposition about the method of the former metaphysics in the *Introduction to the Philosophy of Mythology*, I/5, pages 261-62.

arrive at that which in all phenomena is in agreement, equivalent, and identical, and in this way finally to reach out beyond individual phenomena to arrive at their general characteristics. The expansion of material human knowledge was due to this assignment of immediate experience as the exclusive source of science, in contrast to which metaphysic's tedious and artificial propositions—won with syllogistic methods—seem trivial and wanting. [40] Everything turned toward this immediate source of knowledge and away from the source that in metaphysics had been regarded as special and independent, the pure understanding. Until through John Locke, and later David Hume, that second source, the *intellectus purus*, which, although it had never been dependent on experience, completely lost significance and authority when Locke, by means of a reflection on experience, derived those general concepts and fundamental propositions from experience alone. Consequently, these general concepts and fundamental propositions are really only subjective principles that are just dressed in the character of generality and necessity. As the power and the (independent of all experience) reputation of these a priori concepts and fundamental principles was shattered, the nerve of metaphysics proper was severed as well. Leibniz sensed this acutely, and for this very reason, from then on the question of whether there are within us innate concepts independent of experience became one of the central questions for philosophy. Leibniz's major work against Locke was his *Essai sur l'entendement humain*, which, save for Germany, had as little effect in arresting the ubiquitous and incessant spread of empiricism as did any of his other efforts.[18] —From this point on then there were no longer two different foundations for metaphysics, but just a single homogenous one—experience; for even those concepts and laws that had been earlier regarded as necessary and inherent in the understanding a priori had become simply the result of either a relentless, habitual routine, or of an experience intensified through reflection. But nothing more can be inferred from a simple homogeneity: a and a yield no possibility of a syllogism. What had earlier been regarded as generally valid in itself—namely independent of all experience—lost this character and became that which is singular, particular, or enjoys a doubtful generality. But even the principle of logic *ex puris particularibus nihil sequitur* [nothing follows as a consequence from pure particulars] shows that a syllogistic philosophy in this manner was no longer possible. The former metaphysics then, which for quite some time had enjoyed virtually nothing but a conventional acceptance (it still survived in the schools [41] really only by virtue of an unspoken agreement), had in fact already collapsed before Kant, and the real business of Kant was merely to give it a thoroughly formal hearing, artfully executed in every respect. If one were only to consider the succession of systems that have followed since the downfall of the old metaphysics, and the troubles thereby brought about in all the sciences—particularly in academic studies—one might very well regret how that state of completeness in which philosophy earlier found itself had been abolished [*aufgehoben*]. There was, however, no way to maintain that state if one did not wish to bring the human spirit itself to an absolute standstill. Over time, this spirit could not content itself with that philosophical method of knowing for the very reason that the knowledge so produced was simply artificial, since the coherency it achieved was merely a coherency in our thoughts, but not in the matter itself. The path of this merely syllogistic knowing only arrived at a proposition that asserted a specific content, but not that this content itself was realized [*eingesehen*] as a necessary content. Of course the conclusion can be drawn from the principle of substantiality that the phenomena and emotions of our inner life have as their base a substance that one calls the soul. (*In general* the old metaphysics took its objects from experience or everyday beliefs, for example, the concept of the human soul; the objects were *given*, and it was merely a question of finding the right predicates for them.) Knowledge regarding the human soul consisted simply in that one considered it as a substance, which should then be further defined through new syllogisms as an incorporeal and immaterial—and therefore as an immutable or indestructible—being. To this extent, one could believe himself to be in possession of a general truth: there *are* immaterial, incorporeal beings—that is, souls—which are indestructible. To the question *why* there are such entities, however, there was no answer; the necessity of the existence of such beings [*Wesen*] was not realized. The great turnaround of more recent times [42] consisted precisely because of the fact that one no longer aims for the predicates, but that one demands to become certain of the *thing* [*Gegenstände*] itself. Even today, some come to philosophy with the notion that it deals with certain propositions or assertions, which one could carry away from it like some kind of treasure. Yet this is no longer the case. Contemporary philosophy involves the derivation of the things themselves, which in the earlier metaphysics were quite simply assumed from mere experience or the general consciousness. That is why this content always remained external to reason. Accepting as given even being, the nature or essence of the thing was incomprehensible to reason, with the result that one understood nothing about being. One could perhaps believe the *proposition* is proved: because of the manifest, purposive arrangement of the world, it is necessary to presuppose an intelligent and freely acting creator of it. But with this the nature, the essence of this intelligent creator of the world was not realized [*eingesehen*]; he too remained something merely external to philosophy, the connection between him and the world was merely a *nominal* one (in which basically nothing could be thought), not a real one with which a real insight [*Einsicht*] could have been combined. For if I do not *realize* in what way a being [*Wesen*], thought of as external to, and exalted over the world, could bring forth a world distinct from and posited *outside* itself, then perhaps I can divine a faith in this assumption and it can have an influence on my life, but my insight has won nothing other than mere words lacking understanding. For there would not even be a real concept of *man* and the insight that he is a being capable of free will and action, if there were not, coupled with this thought in our idea, simultaneously an awareness [*Kenntniß*] of the means and the instrument of his free actions, an awareness of the physical *possibility* of his actions. This manner of knowing must sooner or later appear to the human mind as insufficient: either he must abandon metaphysics altogether, that is, all knowledge of that which lies outside and beyond experience, or he must search for another way to arrive at it. [43]

The bridge over which metaphysics thought it possible to cross from the sensible world to the supersensible was that of the general rational principles, particularly the principle of causality. Once these were removed as generally and absolutely valid principles, that bridge vanished, and with it the highest and ultimate orientation of metaphysics was eliminated: if it is unable to go out beyond just the sensible world, then that which alone gives metaphysics its value and significance vanishes. Thus particularly David Hume's attack (his writings have been translated into German more than once) must have once again summoned the spirit of the old metaphysics in *Kant*, just as Locke had awakened it in Leibniz. No less, therefore, did it also lie in the interest of experience and the empirical sciences that the character of the universal laws of the understanding—of their validity that, independent of experience, first conditions experience itself—be preserved, especially the law of cause and effect. For if the universal laws of the understanding, on which every connection in experience and every possibility of an empirical science are based, are merely the consequence of chance habit, then the demise of every empirical science is at hand. This in fact was the central, motivating thought in Kant: he wanted to save at least empirical *science*. Since he could not hide the fact that, even though these principles can be applied with the greatest of certainty to the objects of experience, and thus within the world of experience, the *syllogistic* application of these same principles yields only a very uncertain and fragile connection to the objects that lie beyond all experience. In fact, the uncertainty of such inferences was felt even regarding objects not because of their nature, but only incidentally, since previously they have been outside our direct experience. Thus before the discovery of Uranus one believed to have cause to infer the existence of a planet beyond Saturn, and later still to infer the existence of a planet between Mars and Jupiter on account of there being an open space between them that was too great. But as much as one believed—particularly in the latter case—to support this position through a mathematical progression one wished to have found in the reciprocal [44] withdrawal of the planets from each other, one was just as glad when experience showed not just one planet but, surpassing the claims of science, four planets in that space (four planets that of course had to be considered the equivalent of one).[19] Even less could one conceal this regarding objects that lie outside experience. In this respect it is understandable that Kant defended the authority, independent of all sensory impression, of the universal laws of the understanding for the realm of experience, but only for this one realm. A realm over which metaphysics in its former expanse, in so far as it made a claim on objects that lay beyond all experience as well, enjoyed no advantage, whereas Kant believed to have shown a priori the possibility of a real experience, of an objective knowledge of sensible things.

To pursue the matter further, we must now consider Kant from two perspectives: first, his position toward the earlier metaphysics, and second, his position toward philosophy in general, that is, to what extent did his critique relate not to the material of the earlier philosophy but primarily to the foundation of the former metaphysics? This could not occur, however, unless he himself simultaneously advanced his own theory of human knowledge, through which he then became the founder of an entirely new turn in philosophy.

Regarding Kant's critical position, he advanced it above all against the immediately preceding Leibnizian-Wolffian philosophy. He himself came from this philosophy, and in this respect, his critique could not have a widespread effect, insofar as that type of philosophy had never found widespread credibility and was valid least of all for the type of philosophy with which the existence of metaphysics either stands or falls. On the other hand, insofar as it related to the final result of all metaphysics, to that being on whose account there was truly a metaphysics at all, to this extent Kant's critique was decisive for the entire future [45] of metaphysics.

As is well known, the former metaphysics was composed of four different sciences. The first was ontology, which drew its name from the fact that it should encompass the first and most general determinations of being: all those concepts that allow themselves to be derived from the most supreme concept of *being as such* (of the *Ens*). In the vocabulary introduced by Kant it was the science of the general concepts of the understanding or categories. Ontology was followed by rational cosmology and psychology; but the crown of these different sciences was the so-called natural or rational theology, which—although it simply incorporated the *concept* of God from experience or tradition—did, on the other hand, set as its principal undertaking the task of proving the *existence* of God. One cannot maintain that Kant really hit the mark in his critique of the so-called proof of the existence of God. In particular, he did not even uncover what in my judgment is the real error of inference in the so-called ontological argument (which will be extensively discussed in what follows). Nonetheless, the positive results of Kant's critique of rational theology overall are more important than the negative. The positive result was that God is not the contingent but the *necessary* content of the final, highest idea of reason. This was not a claim of the immediately preceding metaphysics, at least, or of metaphysics in general, that is, if we do not go back to Plato and Aristotle, for whom God likewise was the necessary end [*Ende*]. The concept of God in more recent metaphysics was at bottom just as contingent as any other concept. The positive result, though, agreed with the negative, namely, that reason cannot know the real being [*Seyn*] of God: God is merely the highest idea and precisely because of this must always remain the end that can never become the *beginning* and, thus, can never become the principle of a science. Or, as Kant expressed the matter, this idea always has only a regulative—

never a constitutive—function, that is, reason has the function of necessarily striving toward God and seeking to lead everything on into this highest idea—which lies precisely in the concept of a regulative principle—but can *begin* nothing with this [46] idea, and can never make this idea into the beginning of any knowing. Theoretically, with this negative result all real religion was basically negated [*aufgehoben*] since all real religion can only relate to a real God, and indeed to him only as the lord of reality [*Herrn der Wirklichkeit*] and because a being that is not this can never become the object of a religion, much less the object of a superstition. This, however, could never be the case according to the negative result of the Kantian critique: for if God as *lord* of reality was knowable then there would be a science for which he was the *principle*, and from which reality could be derived. But Kant denied this. Still less did there remain a possible relation of natural theology to *revealed* religion. Revealed religion presupposes a God who reveals himself, thus an active and real God. From the God whose existence is proved, which the old metaphysics believed it had, a transition was possible to one who reveals himself. Of the God who is just the highest idea of reason, it could only be said that he reveals himself to consciousness in a very improper sense, completely different from that in which those who believe in revelation speak of revelation.

Yet as Kant destroyed the old metaphysics, he simultaneously became the founder of a completely new science, since under the modest name of a critique of pure reason he claimed to have put forward a complete and exhaustive theory of the human faculty of knowing.

Kant begins his theory of knowledge (in which the different faculties are taken only from experience, as contingent) with sensibility [*Sinnlichkeit*] that, as he says, supplies the initial material of all our representations, which refer either to things outside ourselves or to processes within us and within our own consciousness. The former we perceive through the outer sense, the latter through the inner. The sensible representations, however, disclose two forms, which as *conditions* of all sensible intuition cannot first be obtained from just this intuition. Thus, as a result of an [47] initial arrangement of our faculty of knowing, these forms must be as it were preformed in us a priori, before the real intuition, although they first come into use with the real intuition. These two forms are, for the external senses, space and, for the internal, time. Everything outside ourselves we perceive in space, everything that occurs within us, for example, the *representation* of external objects themselves, occurs in time.

Kant continues from sensibility to the second source of knowledge, the understanding [*Verstand*], which relates to sensibility as spontaneity relates to receptivity. Through the first source (as he expresses it), an object is *given* to us, through the second it is *thought*—indeed, according to concepts that refer a priori to the objects and that we have not simply derived from the objects themselves. However, the remark cannot be repressed that it is quite impossible for the *object* to be given to us through only receptivity. For no matter how general and undetermined we may think the concept 'object,' there are already determinations of the understanding to be encountered in it; indeed, there is at least the *determination* that it is something that is a being [*ein Seyendes*], something that is real. Yet Kant himself first classifies this concept among the categories; what should appear as an object therefore cannot be a given provided solely through receptivity. The object *as such*, according to Kant's own theory, presupposes that the categories have already been applied, at least that of the most general, namely, that of being. What is provided through sensibility can therefore not yet be the object, but can only be just the *sensible impression*. Admittedly, the transition from the sensation, from the sensible impression, to the representation of an object in our consciousness is so quick and immediate that one could believe that the latter is already provided with the former, the sensible impression. That this is not the case, however, *shows* itself when I determine an object not specifically, but rather only as an object in general. When I bump into something in the dark, I say, "Here is something, that is, a being, an object in general." A being in general, however, cannot now, nor ever, be provided through sensation: this is obviously a [48] concept and can only be thought in the understanding. Thus, that Kant allows the object to be provided through sensation or receptivity is at the very least an imprecise expression. For Kant does recognize, in the most definite manner, that the sensible impression is first elevated to a representation and to objective knowledge through those concepts that he assumes, a priori, independent of the sensible impression, to be a result of just the *nature* of our faculty of knowledge *present* within us. I will say nothing of the manner in which Kant obtains these concepts and nothing about how he believed to have secured their complete enumeration. For ten to twenty years, the Kantian table of twelve categories has maintained a reputation in German philosophy scarcely less than that of the tables of the Ten Commandments, and everyone has believed that they must deal with everything according to this table; however, upon closer examination they may very well be subject to a significant reduction. This alone would be the topic of a special evaluation of the Kantian theory, in which not its particular content, but rather its *general* significance would come up for discussion.

To the extent that Kant assigns the general concepts of the understanding a basis in the faculty of knowledge that is independent of and precedes *real* knowledge, he admittedly eliminates the simple a posteriori origin of these concepts ascribed to them by Locke, Hume, and the entire empirical school that had developed from the two. Kant eliminates it, though not without simultaneously reducing them to mere subjective forms of the faculty of knowledge, which, to be sure, correspond to something in the objects, insofar as they are objects of our experience but do not, however, correspond to the objects *in themselves*, independent of experience. If, however, we assume that there are necessary, innate concepts already present in the faculty of knowledge, through whose application the simple sensible impression is elevated for us to real experience and to objective knowledge, then in this theory the things that occur in real experience are composed of two elements. We must distinguish in everything the determinations of the faculty of knowledge: [49] the general determination is indeed that this is precisely a thing, an object, that is, a being at all, and thus something real (this it must be even independent of the categories). A more precise determination is that it is in time and space (according to Kant, this determination is also derived, not from the understanding, but rather from the faculty of knowledge), and then further, that the object is a substance or accident, a cause or effect. Thus, in every thing known by us there is both that which the faculty of knowledge contributes to the object and that which remains in the object *independent of the faculty of knowledge*. This, however, is what is unknown, equivalent to the mathematical x, as Kant himself calls it, which is present in the impression, from which we in fact must, willingly or not, *derive* this impression, and which we are not capable of eliminating. Still, just how could this x, which we indeed necessarily think of in a causal connection with the impression, be something that precedes all categories and is incapable of being determined by them? For we must think of it, willingly or not, as a being, as what is real, and, consequently, we must think of it subsumed under a category, for we in fact have no other concept for this other than precisely that of something which exists [*des Existirenden*]. Even when we strip away all other determinations, *this* at least remains: it must at the very least be something that exists. How could this unknown, to which we willingly or not apply the concept of cause, be void of all determinations? Here is an obvious contradiction. For on the one hand, this unknown x should precede the application of the categories (it must come beforehand, since it first conveys or induces their application to the sensible impression). On the other hand, however, we cannot avoid giving this unknown something a connection to the faculty of knowledge, in order to determine, for example, the something as the cause of the sensible impression. We must apply the categories of being [*Seyenden*], of causality, and so on to that which according to the presupposition is external to all categories, to what Kant himself calls the thing in itself, which designates it as the thing that precedes and is external to the faculty of knowledge.

You now see: this theory just quite simply does not work. One does not even need to raise the question of how that [50] thing, which in itself is not in space and time and can be determined through none of the categories, slips in through the back door into our faculty of representation and submits to its forms, taking on the determinations of our faculty of knowledge, which have their foundation solely in our subjectivity. The central question always remains: what is this thing in itself in its own right? Only when I have known *this*, will I presume to know that which is really worth knowing. This thing in itself was therefore the point of departure beyond which Kant's *Critique of Pure Reason* could never move, and because of which it *had to* fail as an independent science. Right from the outset one urged it to either altogether discard this thing in itself, that is, to declare itself an outright idealism that transforms the entire world into one of just the necessary idea or to confess that thought proceeds from this point and that these different elements just do not allow themselves to be thought together. Even Kant appeared ambivalent, since there are various statements that can only be united with a perfect idealism (I refer you to a synopsis which you can find in Jacobi's *David Hume*, or *A Discussion about Idealism and Realism*).[20] Yet of course these statements are contradicted by others in which the thing in itself was gotten hold of; indeed, Kant even included in the second edition to his *Critique* an explicit refutation of idealism. Kant, therefore, remained bogged down in what was for him an insurmountable contradiction. It is clear, however, that scientific progress could not remain bogged down in this theory as well. Kant maintained that there is an a priori knowledge of things, but he removed from this a priori knowledge that which is precisely the most important thing, namely, that which exists [*Existirende*], the 'in itself' [*An sich*], the being [*Wesen*] of the thing, that which *really is* in it. For that which appears in things by virtue of the supposed determinations of our faculty of knowledge is not really in them. But then ultimately what is it that is within them independent of the determinations of our faculty of knowledge? Kant has no answer to this. The unavoidable next step was therefore the [51] insight that if there is a knowledge at all of things a priori, and even if that *which exists itself* can be known a priori, then the matter and form of things must be derived together and from the same source. This thought came to fruition in the work of Fichte, whose greatest, most unforgettable service will always remain to have first grasped within his spirit the idea of a *completely* a priori science. Even though he did not carry out this idea in reality, he nonetheless bequeathed a great legacy for philosophy, namely, the concept of an absolute philosophy that presupposes nothing, in which nothing is assumed from *any other source* as a *given*, but rather everything is to be derived, in intelligible succession, from one general *prius*, from that which alone is to be immediately posited. Because Kant made the critique of the faculty of knowledge the sole content of philosophy, he thereby set philosophy in general on a trajectory toward the subject. Fichte located this one general *prius*, which was entirely natural considering this trajectory, in the 'I,' and indeed in the 'I' of human consciousness. His system was *complete* idealism, a system for which the entire so-called objective world has no real objective subsistence, but is rather there only in the necessary ideas of the I. With the transcendental, that is, super-empirical, *actus*, whose expression is the '*I am*,' with this self-consciousness an entire system of existence is posited for every human being. The source and first foundation of all existence is in the I or, more properly speaking, the I am. In this timeless act, through which every single rational being comes to consciousness, the entire system of external existences is posited as in one fell swoop for this individual. Thus, as Fichte expresses it in one of his later popular writings, only the human species exists, everything else is only there in the necessary ideas of the I.

It would have, of course, been valid to derive from the nature of the I such a system of necessary ideas that corresponded to the objective [52] world existing in experience. Fichte considered himself liberated by the subjective or individual energy with which he maintained that everything is only through the I and for the I, and the contradictions in which Kant entangled himself with the thing in itself seemed to him a sufficient justification. For him, nature in particular is not something that is self-subsisting but is rather something that exists only as the limit of the I. If the I were to vanish, then nature would have absolutely no meaning. It is there only to limit the I, not something in its own right similar to the I and just as substantial, but rather precisely as something that is pure 'Not-I,' which really is in its own right a nonbeing. The I, in the primal act of posting itself, sets this nonbeing in an incomprehensible manner in opposition to itself, but only so that it has something that it can progressively negate [*aufhebe*], against which it can advance, against which it or its consciousness can progressively expand. Consequently, Fichte first comes around to speaking about nature in his practical philosophy, specifically in his consideration of natural law, where he is required to think of several I's in interaction with each other. He deduces that every rational being must posit or intuit itself and other rational beings with a body, of which he furthermore knows must consist of a tough and modifiable material. In this context two means or media through which the rational beings may associate among themselves are, among other things, also deduced as the conditions of the coexistence of rational beings and so indirectly of the individual self-consciousness. One medium is the air, by virtue of which they can hear and have rational discourse with each other, while the other is light, so that while speaking they can simultaneously see each other: he knows of no other meaning to assign to these remarkable elements of nature. It is easy to see that a philosophical science of nature, if he even had such a thing in mind, could have been for him at most a teleological deduction of nature, in which he deduced all of nature and its determinations as being only the conditions of the self-consciousness of the rational individual. Only in this manner did he succeed in linking nature to self-consciousness, and indeed as its presupposition, [53] but not so that any kind of real connection, a bond other than that which occurs through the necessary idea, occurs between nature as presupposition and self-consciousness as a *goal* or purpose. He had basically only proved that the I must conceive such a world with such conditions and gradations.

Whoever wishes to become acquainted with Fichte, with the energy of his mind in its entirety, must refer to his principal work, the *Wissenschaftslehre* (philosophy was for him a science of knowing, and thus philosophy was properly speaking the science of all sciences, a determination whose importance will become apparent in what follows).[21] Of course, even one who exclusively busies himself with the study of the most recent developments of philosophy cannot find his way through the course of this work these days without conscious effort. In its time, however, this *science of knowing* did not lack for enthusiasts, who wished to see in it a *ne plus ultra* of the dialectical art, an unsurpassable masterpiece, in the same way as later occurred with a different and, not to mention, far less ingenious and much more mechanical philosophy. For a considerable portion of Germany had worked itself into such a pedantic fuss that it, to use a simile of J. Möser's, no longer asked for flour, but rather contented itself with, and took pleasure in, the mere clatter of the mill house. In later writings such as, for example, the lectures held here in Berlin under the title *The Way toward the Blessed Life*[22]—a work that perhaps some of you should reach for because it is more comprehensible—and even in the subsequent expositions that followed the 1794/95 publication of the *Wissenschaftslehre*, Fichte worked his ideas more and more into a popular form, as he then published a monograph under the title, *A Crystal Clear Report to the General Public Concerning the Actual Essence of the Newest Philosophy: An Attempt to Force the Reader to Understand*.[23] Here, of course, the matter became intelligible enough, but only to the same degree in which what earlier had been recognized in the *Wissenschaftslehre* as something sublime here became unfit for consumption. In still later writings, he attempted to connect certain ideas, foreign to him at first, with some of his original ideas. [54] Yet how was it possible to bring the absolute divine being [*göttlichen Seyn*], of which he now taught as the only *real substance*, into a connection with that idealism whose foundation, on the contrary, had been that every individual I is the only substance? Fichte would in fact have done much better to have remained true to himself, for with that syncretism his philosophy, from being full of the character through which it was at first distinguished, just lost itself in obscurities and a total absence of character.

Fichte's true significance is to have been the antithesis of Spinoza, insofar as the absolute substance was, for Spinoza, a merely dead and motionless object. This step, to have determined the infinite substance as the I, and consequently as the subject-object (for the I is only that which is subject and object of itself), is so significant in its own right that one forgets what became of it in Fichte's own hands. Within the I is provided the principle of a *necessary* (substantial) movement; the I is not inactive, but rather progressively defines itself of necessity. Fichte, however, made no use of this. The I does not propel Fichte through all levels of the necessary process through which it reaches self-consciousness, passes through nature, or by which nature first becomes truly posited in the I. The I itself does not propel Fichte. On the contrary, everything is just externally linked to the I through subjective reflection—through the reflection of the philosopher and not through the inner evolution of the I, and, thus, not through the movement of the object itself. Moreover, this subjective linkage to the principle occurs through a simple reasoning of such arbitrariness and contingency that one, as was said, is hard pressed to recognize the thread that runs through the entirety. [55]

KANT, FICHTE, AND A SCIENCE OF REASON

Fichte was determinative for all subsequent schools of philosophy in two respects. First, he was determinative in the limited form that he gave to the principle—limited insofar as it was expressed *only* as the I, and indeed as the I of human consciousness. In this limited form, nonetheless, was found the true starting point, according to its matter or essence, for that a priori science that through Kant had become an unavoidable demand. As I will demonstrate in more detail in what follows, it required only the sublation [*Aufhebung*] of that limited form according to which the I was but the I of human consciousness to arrive at the true *universal prius*. Secondly, it was precisely through Fichte's demand for an *absolute prius* that the way to continue beyond Kant was shown. Kant posited a tripartite a priori, which included that of sensible intuition, or time and space; that of the pure concepts of the understanding; and that of concepts that he termed the special concepts of reason, or ideas in a stricter sense. To the ideas of reason he ascribed only an a priori regulative meaning and not, as with the categories of the understanding, a constitutive meaning. Yet *above* all these various a priori forms lay a higher one that was itself again the common *prius* of sensibility, of the understanding, and of reason. That which stood above all these particular forms of knowledge could only be the faculty of knowledge or reason itself in the most general and highest sense in [56] which Kant himself called his critique of the faculty of knowledge a critique of *reason* (although he then determined reason again as the particular faculty of knowledge, namely as the special faculty which relates to the supersensible). The basis for Kant's belief that reason must specialize as the faculty of the supersensible ideas lay in the fact that reason, as soon as it goes on into the supersensible, no longer has experience on its side, and thus stands there in its *simplicity*, or on its own, lacking experience. Here reason appears as reason, whereas in sensible nature it appears mediated by sensibility.

Yet, because of this, should that which is a priori—which in the transcendental forms determines every sensible intuition of space and time—should that which is a priori in these forms—in which absolutely nothing empirical or sensible is mixed—be anything other than precisely the a priori of reason, only in a particular employment? Or from where should what is necessary and universal, which via mathematics is made to stand out in these forms, originate, if not from reason? Certainly not from sensibility as such, which Kant explains as mere receptivity. What Kant terms transcendental sensibility is thus nothing other than reason itself in the particular relationship with what is sensible. Likewise, from where should the invariable universality and continuous necessity of the concepts of reason derive, if not from reason? For it appears in the formation and employment of these concepts, but again in a particular function, in that it seeks to integrate the phenomenon provided through the forms of space and time into the unity of consciousness, into a real experience. Thirdly, it can no longer be mistaken that what is truly the a priori of reason lies in what Kant expressly terms reason, since here reason is, as it were, alone with itself, abandoned by experience, and thus beyond every relationship to anything beyond itself. Thus arose the necessity, as articulated by Fichte, of a common derivation of all a priori knowledge from one principle. This necessity had to lead to absolute reason, to reason in that absolute sense that I have just now attempted to explain. [57] It had to lead to the concept of an unconditioned *science of reason* [*Vernunftswissenschaft*] in which no longer the *philosopher*, but rather reason itself, knows reason—where reason stands opposed only to itself and is the knower as well as the known and precisely because of this, according to its matter and form, earns the title of a *science of reason*. Only then is it elevated to a wholly independent and autonomous science that is a *Critique of Pure Reason*. For reason did not reach its autonomy in this critique precisely because it related to what was simply given. And even if, as Kant claimed, the entire faculty of knowledge was correctly appraised and its entire apparatus (as Kant used to express it, as if he were dealing with a machine) examined, even with all this insight the faculty of knowledge or reason nonetheless remained opaque and incomprehensible to itself, since this so-called apparatus was again not grasped from within reason *itself*, but was instead something given to it from without.

If in this manner the concept of a pure science of reason is advanced, which from within itself reaches out to all being and no longer assimilates anything just from experience, then it is natural to raise the question whether experience—the other source of knowledge of equal birth with reason—should be completely set aside and fully excluded. I answer, "Nothing less." However, it is excluded only as a *source* of knowledge. —You will understand what type of relationship a science of reason has to experience when I proceed to the following.

Reason, as soon as it directs itself to itself, becomes an object to itself, finds within itself the *prius* or the subject of *all* being [*Seyns*]—which is the same thing—and in this it also possesses the means, or rather the principle, of an a priori knowledge of everything that is [*alles Seyenden*]. But now the question becomes *what* is it that in this way—namely, a priori—is to be known in everything that is. Is it the essence [*Wesen*], the matter of what is, or *that* it is? Here we should note that in everything that is real there are two things to be known: it is two entirely different things to know what a being [58] is, *quid sit*, and that it is, *quod sit*. The former—the answer to the question *what* it is—accords me insight into the *essence* of the thing, or it provides that I understand the thing, that I have an understanding or a concept of it, or have it *itself* within the concept. The other insight however, *that* it is, does not accord me just the concept, but rather something that goes beyond just the concept, which is existence [*Existenz*]. This is *a cognition* [*ein Erkennen*] whereby it is readily clear that while there can be a concept without a real cognition, it is not possible for there to be a cognition without a concept. For in cognition what I take cognizance of as existing is precisely the *whatness* [*das Was*], the *quid*, that is, the concept of the thing. Most cognition is, properly speaking, a recognition—for example, if I take cognizance of a plant and know what type it is, then I again take cognizance of the concept that I previously had of it, that is, in what exists. In cognition there must always be, as the Latin *cognitio* says, two elements that come together.

Even here (immediately after this distinction) it will probably become muddled for us that, insofar as the question is of the *whatness* of a thing, this question directs itself to *reason*, whereas—*that* something is, even if it is something realized by reason from itself, *that* this is—that is, *that* it exists—can only be taught by experience. To prove *that* something exists cannot be an issue for reason, due to the simple fact that, by far, the most of what reason takes cognizance of from itself [*von sich aus*] *occurs* in experience and what is a matter of experience requires no proof that it exists precisely because it is already determined as something that actually exists. Thus, at least regarding everything that occurs in experience, it cannot be an issue for a science of reason to prove *that* it exists; to do so would be superfluous. *What* exists, or more precisely, what will exist (for the being derived from the *prius* relates to the prius as a being yet to come; from the standpoint of this *prius*, therefore, I can ask what will be, what will exist, if anything at all exists) is the task of the science of reason, which allows itself to be realized a priori. But *that* it exists does not follow from this, [59] for there could very well be nothing at all that exists. That something exists at all, and, particularly, that this determinate thing exists in the world, can never be realized a priori and claimed by reason without experience.

As I first presented this distinction, I fully anticipated what would happen. There have been some who have shown themselves to be quite astonished by this simple, absolutely unmistakable, and—for precisely that reason—extremely important distinction, since in a preceding philosophy they had heard of a wrongly understood identity of thought and being. I will certainly not contest this identity, correctly understood, for it derives from my own writings, but the misunderstanding, and the philosophy that derives from that misunderstanding, I *must* indeed contest.

One need not read very far into Hegel's *Encyclopedia of the Philosophical Sciences* to find repeatedly in the first pages the dictum that reason concerns itself with the 'in itself' [*An sich*] of things. Now you may well ask what the in itself of these things is. Is it, perhaps, the fact that they exist; is it their being [*Seyn*]? Not at all, for the in itself, the essence [*Wesen*], the concept—for example, the nature of man—remains the same even if there were no people at all on the earth, just as the in itself of a geometrical figure remains the same whether or not it exists.

That a plant in general exists is nothing contingent if anything in general exists: it is not contingent that there are plants in general, but there are no plants that exist in general, since there exists only this determinate plant at this point in space and in this moment of time. If I then also realize—and perhaps it is to be realized a priori—that in the cycle of existence in general plants must occur, with this insight I have still not moved beyond the concept of the plant. This plant is still not the real plant, but rather just the concept of the plant. Further—and I certainly do not want to assume that somebody thinks he can prove a priori or through reason that this determinate plant exists here or now—someone will, however much he may accomplish, still have only [60] proved that there are, in general, plants.

If one wants to honor a philosopher, then one must grasp him here, in his fundamental thought, where he has not yet gone on to the consequences. For against his own intentions he can go astray in the subsequent development and nothing is easier than to go astray in philosophy, where every false step has infinite consequences and where one on the whole finds himself on a path surrounded by an abyss on all sides. The *true* thought of a philosopher is precisely his fundamental thought from which he proceeds. The fundamental thought of Hegel is that reason relates to the in itself, the essence of things, from which immediately follows that philosophy, to the extent that it is a science of reason, occupies itself only with the whatness [*Was*], or the essence, of things.

One has construed this distinction as if philosophy or reason did not deal at all with being [*Seyende*], and it would admittedly be a pathetic reason, which had nothing to do with being, thus only concerning itself with a chimera. But the distinction has not been thus expressed. Reason is, properly speaking, concerned with nothing other than just being and with being according to its *matter* and *content* (exactly this is being in its in itself). Nevertheless, reason does not have to show *that* it is since this is no longer a matter of reason, but rather of experience. Admittedly, if I have grasped the essence, the *whatness* of something, for example, of a plant, then I have grasped something that is real, for the plant is not something that does not exist, a chimera, but is rather something that does exist [*etwas Existirendes*]. In this sense, it is true that what is real does not stand in opposition to our thinking as something foreign, inaccessible, and unreachable, but that the concept and the being are one: that the being does not have the concept outside itself, but rather has it within itself. Nonetheless, in all this the discussion was only about the *content* of what is real, but regarding this content, the fact *that* it exists is something purely contingent: the circumstance of whether it exists or not does not change my concept of the content in the least. Likewise, if one maintains the opposite: [61] things exist as a consequence of a necessary and immanent conceptual movement, of a logical necessity, by virtue of which the things themselves are rational and thus present a rational nexus. If one, however, wanted to conclude further from this that their existence, or *that* they exist, is therefore also a necessity, one would have to respond in the following way: of course there is a logical necessity in things and of course this is nothing contingent. To this insight, science has so far advanced, for example, that, first, the cosmic principle enters the world and organizes it, then particular nature appears—initially as inorganic nature—then the organic kingdom of vegetation elevates itself above the former, and then the animal kingdom rises above the latter—all this allows itself to be realized a priori. Yet in all this one sees that the discussion is only about the *content* of what exists: *if* there are things that exist, then they will be of this kind, and will come to be in this sequence and no other—this is the meaning. But that they exist I do not know in this way and must convince myself of this from somewhere else, namely, from experience. Conversely, reality does nothing to the whatness [*dem Was*] and the necessity that is independent of all reality. Thus, for example, the indivisibility of space is not a matter of real space, and what is in real space—order, symmetry, and definition—is all of a logical origin.iii In this way one may comprehend the importance of that distinction. Reason provides the content for everything that occurs in experience; it comprehends what is *real* [*Wirkliche*], but not, therefore, *reality* [*Wirklichkeit*]. This is an important difference. The science of reason does not provide what really exists in nature and its *particular* forms. To this extent, experience, through which we know what really exists, is a source of knowing independent of reason and, thus, travels right alongside it. And *here* is precisely the point where the relationship of the science of reason to experience allows itself to be positively determined: the science of reason, contrary to excluding experience, requires it. For precisely because what [62] the science of reason comprehends a priori—or construes is being—it is vital for it to have a control through which it can demonstrate that what it has found a priori is *not* a chimera. This control is experience. For only experience, and not reason, can say that *that* which has been construed really exists.

The science of reason, therefore, does not have experience as its *source*, as the former metaphysics had it in part, but it does indeed have experience as its escort. In this way, German philosophy has incorporated Empiricism—which for the past century has been exclusively embraced by every other European nation—within itself, without thereby becoming Empiricism. Nonetheless, there of course comes a point where that relationship ceases, since experience as such ceases. According to Kant God is the final, all-conclusive concept of reason—thus, of its own accord, reason will always find this concept not as its contingent, but rather as its *necessary* terminus. *That* God exists, though—

---

iii. Perhaps there is something analogous to this thought in the alleged Platonic distinction between ἀριθμιῶν εἰδητιχῶν and μαθηματιχῶν. [Schelling refers to what Aristotle writes in his Metaphysics regarding Xenocrates' distinction between ideal numbers and mathematical numbers (cf. *Metaphysics* 1086a5f).]

about this, reason cannot refer to experience as it does with all the other concepts it realizes a priori. What philosophy will conclude as soon as it arrives at this point, however, cannot yet be explained. First, I must clarify *how* the science of reason arrives at this point.

If the philosophy that proceeded indirectly from Kant, and directly from Fichte, was no longer a mere critique in the Kantian sense, but was rather the science of *reason*—the science in which reason should discover of itself, that is, from within its own original content, the content of all being—then the question now arises, what is the original and, thus, the sole *immediate* content of reason, that at the same time is constituted in such a manner that it can reach out of itself—hence indirectly—and arrive at *all* of being. According to Kant, reason is nothing other than the faculty of knowledge as such, so that what is posited within us becomes, from the standpoint of philosophy, an object for us—so that reason itself considered entirely objective is the *infinite potential of cognition* (for reason remains this even apart from its subjective position, apart from its being in [63] any one subject). *Potency* is the Latin *potentia*—power—and is opposed to the *actus*. In the conventional use of language, one says, "The plant in its seed is the plant in its mere potency, *in pure potentia*, whereas the real mature or developed plant is the plant *in actu*." Here, potency is considered merely as a *potentia passiva*, as a passive possibility; the seed is not necessarily the potential of the plant; there must be other external factors—fertile soil, rain, sunshine, and so on, added to it so that this potency becomes *actus*. As the *faculty* of knowledge, reason also appears as a *potentia passiva*, insofar as it is a faculty that is capable of development and, in this respect, is admittedly also dependent on external factors. Here, however, reason is not the faculty of knowledge subjectively considered, rather that standpoint has already been assumed from which reason itself is its object. Considered as an object, where the limitations of the subject are removed through abstraction, it can be nothing other than the infinite potency of cognition. Reason in its own and original content, without being dependent on anything else, has the compulsion to go forth into all being because only the *all* of being (the entire fullness of being) can correspond to its *infinite* potency. The question, therefore, becomes what this original content is. It appears to be an actual cognition, but one that is incapable of having the pure, infinite potency of cognition. Reason, though, must have such an original content, only that—and this can be pointed out in advance—it must be a content that is not yet a cognition, which it has through no cause of its own, with no *actus* from the side of reason. Were it otherwise, reason would cease to be the *pure* potency of cognition. It must be reason's innate and inborn content, one that is posited with reason itself (as one says of gifts and talents that we do not ourselves acquire), a content that all real cognition presupposes and that reason thus also possesses before all real cognition. A content that we could, therefore, call its a priori content, which from this point on—after *this* explanation—should not be difficult [64] to determine more precisely. Since every cognition corresponds to a being—a real cognition to a real being—then nothing other than the *infinite potential of being* can correspond to the infinite potential for cognition, and this is then the innate and inborn content of reason. Philosophy, or reason, would be directed, above all, to this immediate content of reason insofar as reason acts as the subject in philosophy. In the activity of turning toward its content, reason is thinking—thinking κατ' ἐξοχήν—namely, philosophical thinking. But this thinking, as soon as it turns toward the content, immediately discovers therein its own thoroughly mobile nature and, with this, a principle of movement is provided, which requires that a real science should arise.

Through the mobility of its highest concept, contemporary philosophy distinguishes itself from scholasticism, which could appear to have had a similar starting point. The scholastics held that the infinite *potency* of being corresponds to the *Ens omnimodo indeterminatum* from which it proceeds: they understood this not as something that somehow already exists, but rather, as they said, as that which exists as such. This *Ens* of the scholastics was something quite dead—from which, for this very reason, only a *nominal* progression was possible from the highest conceptual genus, *Ens in genere*, to the genus and species of being, to the *Ente composito, simplici*, and on to the particular classes of essence that would be further determined. In the Wolffian philosophy, the *Ens* defined by the scholastics as the *aptitudo ad existendum* was even defined as a mere *non repugnantia ad existendum*, through which the immediate potency is completely reduced and diminished to a mere passive possibility, with which again nothing can be started. But the infinite *potency* of being—or that immediate content of reason that has the *infinite capacity to be* [*das unendliche Seynkönnen*] is not just the ability to exist, it is also the immediate *prius*, the immediate *concept* of being itself. In this way it subsists in accordance with its nature—hence always—and in an eternal manner (*modo aeterno* in the logical sense). It must, as soon as it is thought in the [65] concept pass over into being, since it is nothing other than the concept of being. It is, therefore, that which is not to be held back from being, and, therefore, that which immediately *passes over* from thinking into being. Because of this necessary transition, thinking cannot remain as that which has the capacity to be (therein lies the justification for all progress in philosophy).

Here, however, it cannot be avoided that some people will primarily think of a real transition, and imagine that the real becoming of *things* should now be explained. But this would completely miss the point. What a science of reason derives is of course, among other things, precisely that which occurs in experience and under its conditions in space and time as individual entities, and so on. However, the science of reason itself moves forward in mere thought, although the contents of the thought or concept are not, as in the Hegelian logic, once again mere concepts. In the fact that a science of reason derives the content of real being, thereby ignoring experience, lies what is for many the illusion that they have not just grasped *what is real*, but have also grasped reality, or that they have grasped how what is real *arises* in this way, so that this merely logical process is also the process of real becoming. In this alone nothing else occurs save thinking; it is not a real process that develops here, but rather just a logical one; the being into which the potency passes over is a being that itself belongs to the concept and, thus, is only a being in the concept, not outside it. The transition is *simpliciter*, a becoming other: in the place of the pure potency, which as such is nonbeing, there appears a being. But the determination 'a being' is itself here a mere *quidditative*, not a *quodditative* (scholastic expressions, but expedient designations). I am here only concerned with the *quid*, not with the *quod*. A being or something is just as good a concept as *being* or potency is a concept. A being [*ein Seyendes*] is no longer being [*das Seyendes*]—it is something other than this, but only *essentially*, that is, according to its concept, but not *actu*, something different. The plant is not being, but is rather already a being. But it is a being even [66] if it never really existed. It is, therefore, only a logical world in which we move in a science of reason; to imagine that a real chain of events is intended here, or to claim that this chain of events took place during the original generation of things would not only be contrary to our meaning, but also would be an absurdity in itself. Since the infinite potency comports itself as the *prius* of what it generates in thinking through its transition into being, and since it corresponds to nothing less than *all* being, so then is reason, due to the fact that it possesses this potency from which everything real for it can emerge—and, indeed, possesses it as what has grown together with it and is thus its inseparable content—set into an a priori position vis-à-vis all being. One grasps, to this extent, how there is an a priori science, a science that determines a priori all of *what* is (not *that* it is). In this way, reason of itself, without somehow calling on experience for assistance, is put in the position to arrive at the *content* of everything that exists, and consequently to the content of all real being; not that it takes cognizance a priori of whether this or that thing really exists (for this is an entirely different matter), but rather that it only knows a priori what is or what can be, if something is, and determines a priori the concepts of every being. Reason arrives at what can be or will be when the potency is thought of as self-moving only in concepts, and, thus, again, only as *a possibility* in contrast to real being. These things are only the particular possibilities established in the infinite, that is, in the universal potency.

But what cause does thinking have to pursue the potency in its becoming other? Well, consider the following. Reason wants nothing other than its original content. This original content, however, possesses in its immediacy something contingent, which is and is not the immediate capacity to be; likewise, being—the essence—as it immediately presents itself in reason, *is* and is not being. It is not being as soon as it moves, since it then transforms itself into a contingent being. Therefore, to speak the truth, [67] even if I *had* being in the first concept, but not in such a way that it could not withdraw [*entwerden*] and become something other for me, then I also did not have it. Yet I want it, and in fact it is only *this*, which I really want. Yet I want *true* being that can no longer become something different. But the capacity to become something different cannot be excluded from the first and immediate concept. I must, therefore, allow it to emerge out of being [*Wesen*], and eliminate it from itself [*sich selbst ausschließen*]. It eliminates itself in that it passes over into contingent being [*Seyn*]. I must first allow what is contingent in the original content of reason to remove itself so that I may arrive at what is essential and so, finally, to what is true. The immediate content of reason is not yet what is true or unchanging, for otherwise there would be no movement at all and, thus, no necessity for going forward, that is, no science. In this science, however, everything that is contingent, that is, everything that is not true, is removed, or, rather, it removes itself. For the infinite potency, as it is the *immediate* content of reason, passes over according to its nature into what is different, and comports itself in this way as the *prius* of everything that is external to reason (what exists).

The *immediate* content of reason is, thus, nothing absolutely certain and unchanging. What is really unchanging in this content must first be drawn out. This happens when what is contingent is eliminated. This original entwinement of being (itself) and of nonbeing (contingencies) will not be clear to everyone. There is, however, a very obvious comparison. Fortunately, the highest speculative concepts are always simultaneously the most profound ethical concepts that are much closer to everyone; consequently, I cannot resist this comparison in order to make clear a distinction that is important for all of what follows. The human will is also relatively (i.e., within the sphere accorded humanity in general) an *infinite* potency: there is nothing at all in which the concepts *actus* and potency express themselves more definitely than in the sphere of the will. The will is in fact not only a *potentia passiva*, but is also that which introduces into the realm of experience the most decisive *potentia activa* that is intimately related to the pure capacity to be. [68] In some people, of course, the will is also a *potentia passiva*—it requires stimulation to become active—but in people who are capable of freely deciding and are able to start something on their own accord, to become the originator of a course of action, the will shows itself quite decisively as a *potentia activa*. Will [*Wille*] alone, the will in its repose—in not willing—is an infinite potency. Wanting [*Wollen*] itself is nothing other than the transition *a potentia ad actum*, and, indeed, the purest example of this transition. The individual who is aware of this infinite potency of the will in himself can assume that this potency is given to him so that he may *want* unconditionally and in every manner possible. He then fixes his will on a multitude of things that, in fact, are not worthy of the will, and not only on these but also on things that only make his will confused, troubled, and enslaved. In a manner of speaking, he only wants in order to want, to show his wanting. Or the individual can also be so disposed that not the wanting, but rather the *will itself* (thus the potency) is for him the true good, that he esteems this will too high and holy to waste it on what is second best, and thus finds his heaven more in the reposed will than in wanting. This is similar to that infinite potency of being, which reason finds as its immediate content. If the potency itself is being (as in the aforementioned case of the will itself instead of the wanting—precisely the will itself is already *being*), then it is that which Is [*Ist*], but if it is not itself being, then it comports itself necessarily as nonbeing. This amphibole cannot be excluded from the concept of infinite potency, and, thus, from the immediate content of reason: it is this amphibole that rouses and sets reason into action, that is, that calls upon reason to become a science. Indeed, as you see right here, reason is above all called upon to become a science that removes and eliminates the mere contingencies of that immediate content, that is, to become a critical science (every elimination is a critique), or, because it removes, to become a negative science. Such a science shows itself from the very start as a descendant of the so-called critical philosophy, as the consequence of the [69] standpoint philosophy obtains through Kant's critique of reason. Without this amphibole of its immediate content, thought would not be compelled to depart from it and advance to that in which this amphibole is totally sublated [*aufgehoben*], and of which one can first say *that* it Is.

Reason finds itself called upon to follow that which has the capacity to go beyond itself to being in two respects. First, reason knows that it will thereby come into an a priori relationship to everything that is externally present to it, and in this way (namely, when it follows the potency into being) it will comprehend a priori everything that is externally present to it. I say everything different that is present to it *externally* because, in doing this, that which has the capacity to go beyond itself to being also continues beyond reason and produces precisely that being which in fact occurs a priori as possibility—not as reality in reason, but rather as reality only in experience.

But the call for reason to follow that which has the capacity to be in its procession beyond itself does not lie in this alone; rather, it has yet a different and higher interest. Reason wants really nothing other than its original content, but this content, as has been shown, has in its immediacy something that is intrinsically contingent. The potency that moves within being, to the extent that it has not moved, is still the subject of being; it is still equal to that *which Is*, but it has only the appearance of being, for it presents itself as that which is not as soon as it becomes something different. Indeed, for becoming in general, for the very reason that it *becomes*, is not that which *Is*. It—the immediate potency—is thus only materially, only essentially, that is, only contingently, being so that it can also not be that which *Is*. As long as it does not move it is, so to speak, only *provisionally* being, but as soon as it steps out of its capacity [*Können*] it also steps out of the sphere of that which *Is* into the sphere of becoming and, therefore, is and is not being. Provisionally, or a priori, it is being, but after the fact it is not being. But precisely because it is and is not being [70] it is not being itself, αὐτὸ τὸ Ὄν, for this is only that which is not what *is* and not is, but rather what *Is*, the ὄντως Ὄν, as the Greeks very significantly named it, and who indeed had a reason to distinguish mere Ὄν from ὄντως Ὄν. Put in this situation, reason indeed wants being itself since, because it is unchanging, it considers only this as its true content. But it can attain to *being itself*—that which being itself is, not that which merely has the semblance thereof and can become something different, which can pass over into that which is alien to reason, into nature, experience, and so on; it can attain to being itself only through the exclusion of what is other, which is not being itself. Yet, in the first immediate thought, this otherness is not to be separated from that which is being itself: the former is unavoidably assimilated simultaneously *with* the latter in the first thought. How else then can it exclude that otherness, which is what reason does not really want, which is not really posited, but is rather only what is not not to be posited, which it is incapable of excluding only in the first thought? How else can reason exclude it other than by allowing it to emerge and really pass over into its alterity in order to liberate in this manner true being, the ὄντως ῎Ον, and present it in its purity? Any other way than this will not bring forth what it wants. For reason—and this is of great importance and our next result—reason has none other than a *negative* concept of that which being itself is. Even if the final goal and objective of reason is solely the being that *Is*, it can nonetheless determine nothing else: it has no concept for the being that Is other than that of what is not nonbeing, of that which does not pass over into otherness, that is, a negative concept. With this is then also provided the concept of a negative science, whose duty is precisely this: to produce in this manner the *concept* of what being itself is through the successive elimination of everything that is not being and that lies *implicit* or *potentia* in the general and indeterminate concept of being. This science can lead no further than [71] to the aforementioned negative concept; thus, in general, only to the *concept* of being itself. Only at its end does the question then arise whether the concept—which is the result achieved through that negative science and its simple *via exclusionis*—again becomes or can become the object of a different, positive science.

In that I determine my standpoint in such a way that for me only that which is being itself is true *being* and everything else is just apparent being, it becomes self-evident—and at last perfectly clear—that this otherness can only have meaning as what is merely *possible*, and therefore—as already shown—it is not deduced as something real (according to its reality). Moreover, this distinction between merely apparent being, which is only a capacity to be, and true being, which I, as was said, know [*erkenne*] only in being itself, is of the utmost importance. As I follow the capacity to be in thought, that which is being itself naturally remains for me outside this movement. It is itself not drawn into this movement—in which I occupy myself exclusively with the capacity to be, with what may possibly be (not merely nature, but also with the world of the spirit— that raises itself above nature belongs to what is possible; for this reason the a priori science is necessarily a philosophy of nature and a philosophy of the spirit). In that I distinguish being itself and the capacity to be, and go on from there, it is quite natural when I follow the capacity to be that I do not draw being itself into this movement as well: being itself remains for me outside this movement and first appears at its end as the result of this elimination. In this entire movement, I have only to deal with the capacity to be, with what is possible. Whether what I find in this way is from a different standpoint, namely that of experience, something real, is for me of no concern in this context; from the height that I look out at it a priori, it is merely what is possible.

The confusion into which philosophy has fallen in recent times springs chiefly from the fact that this distinction [72] is not made, that that which *being itself* is, is drawn into the process instead of it being only the result achieved through this process of eliminating that which is not being itself. I say "only the result," and thus only the end which—as one has assumed in an inversely absurd manner—cannot simultaneously also be the beginning. However, as little as being itself enters into this process (through which, on the contrary, everything that is not being itself should be eliminated), it is still necessary from the other side to allow it into this process, because only by doing so can we logically—in thought—realize the idea of being itself, which subsists through its remaining-into-itself, through its not-becoming-an-other. Thus, in order to obtain *in its own right* that which remains into itself and is absolutely equal to itself, we must first eliminate from within indeterminate being everything that is possibly of the (transitive) capacity to be. We cannot do this, however, if, to begin with, we consider being as that which proceeds out of itself, that is, as that which also has the capacity to be external to itself. Only in this way can we discover and make evident all of the transitive capacity to be (which can thus pass over into being) that is within being in order to arrive at that which does not exist as something that passes over into being, but rather what is, pure *ipseity* [*was Ist, rein Ist*].

Kant had determined God as the final concept *necessary* for the consummation of human knowledge. However, he had taken even this highest idea really only from experience, from tradition, from the widespread belief of humanity, in short, only as a given idea: he did not progress to this thought in a methodical manner. But when the other philosophy, by virtue of an objective method, really arrived at this as the highest concept, this provided it with the semblance of a *cognition*, yet this cognition limited itself to discerning that this was the highest and final concept, and not as with Kant when it was merely *assumed* or *presupposed*. This brought about the illusion of a result opposed to that of the Kantian critique, whereas when correctly understood the result was *entirely the same*. In this philosophy, every consequence was justified by what had preceded it, [73] but it was justified only as a mere *concept*. It was from beginning to end an *immanent* philosophy, that is, it progressed in mere thought and was by no means a *transcendent* philosophy. In the end therefore, whereas it had only demonstrated God as a necessary idea of reason, which of course was already *secured* by Kant, the necessary consequence of it laying claim to a knowledge of God was to rob God of all transcendence and draw him into this logical thinking, into a merely logical concept, into an *idea itself*. And because the concept of *God* was once inseparably connected with the notion of existence and indeed that of the most dynamic, there thus arose those wrongful and improper expressions of a *self-movement* of the idea, words through which the idea was personified and ascribed an existence that it did not and could not have. This in turn was connected with the other misunderstanding. This philosophy advanced incrementally from that which was determined as nonbeing since it was something capable of being cognized [*erkennbar Bestimmten*]—to that which only *subsisted* as something capable of being thought [*seyend Denkbaren*]. In the same course of advancement, that is in the same science, it was determined as something no longer capable of being cognized [*nicht mehr als erkennbar zu Bestimmenden*], which means something *transcendent*, since it stood out beyond this science. Yet precisely this advance from relative nonbeing to being, to that which according to its nature or *concept* is being, was viewed as a successive realization of the concept of being, as the successive self-actualization of the idea. This advance, however, was in fact merely a successive elevation or intensification of the concept, which in its highest potency remained just a concept, without there ever being provided a transition to *real* being [*wirklichen Daseyn*], to existence. [74]

The Difference Between Negative and Positive Philosophy

I have been asked in writing how we arrive at the infinite potency of cognition when there is, however, no such infinite object of which we are aware. *Object* would hardly be the proper expression to employ in this context—nonetheless we are aware of an immediate content in reason, which of course is not an object, that is, already a being, but is rather only the infinite potency of being. One cannot invert this relationship and say, "Produce for me an infinite object of cognition, and then I will grant you an infinite potency of cognition." To do this would be nothing other than to expect us immediately to step beyond reason, when, on the contrary, it was our intention to immerse ourselves within it completely and recognize nothing other than that which discloses itself therein. The questioner seems to believe there could be no infinite potency of cognition before there is an infinite object of cognition. The question, however, is not at all whether there is an infinite potency of cognition—since this would be the same as to ask whether there *is* reason [*eine Vernunft*], something that has yet to occur to anyone to ask, since everyone presupposes that there is reason. And that this infinite, that is, free toward all or prepossessed of nothing, potency of cognition exists, one must concede as well: prepossessed of nothing, I said, namely, of nothing that is real [*Wirklichen*]. (There are well-known theologians and philosophers who make God out to be the immediate [75] content of reason; this is contradicted here, since, by God, we must think of something that is real.) On the other hand, reason is of course prepossessed by the sheer potency of being, which, however—precisely because it is sheer potency—is in a certain sense equal to = nothing; it is that which is open toward everything, equal to everything (*omnibus aequa*), and excludes nothing—and only that which excludes nothing is the pure potency. Even what is feminine in this word, or that we say 'reason' [*die Vernunft*], points to its quality as potency, while what is masculine in the understanding [*der Verstand*] shows that understanding is the *actus*; as Lessing said, the German language is born for philosophy.

It is natural for those who believe to possess the exposition of the real chain of events in the pure science of reason, of the real generation of things, to be disinclined toward this word 'potency.' For this word 'potency' reminds us that in the science of reason, or, what is the same thing, the pure a priori science, only the possibility of things, not the reality, is comprehended. Reason, however, is the infinite potency of cognition and, as such, has nothing but the infinite *potency* of being as its content. Precisely because of this it can, from this content, arrive at nothing but what is possible a priori. This, of course, is also what is real and occurs in experience, but reason arrives at it not as something real, but as what is merely possible a priori. At some point and time in its development the human spirit will feel the need, to express myself in such a manner, to get to the bottom of being—this is a vulgar expression, which I nonetheless help myself to gladly and intentionally, for such expressions are illustrative—one would very much like, as one says, to get to the bottom of an issue. But what is here, at 'the bottom of the issue'? Not being, for this, on the contrary, is what lies on the surface of the issue, that which immediately comes to mind, and, thus, what is already presupposed in all this: if I want to get to the bottom of an issue, for example, an event, then the issue—in this instance, the event—must already be given. At the bottom of this issue is, therefore, not being, [76] but the essence, the potency, the cause (properly speaking these are all just synonymous concepts). Thus, at the highest point of its development, the propensity to understand that is so deeply embedded and insurmountable in humanity will also demand to get to the bottom of not merely this or that issue but to the bottom of being in general [*das Seyn überhaupt*]. Not to see what is above being, for this is an entirely different concept, but to see what lies *on the other side* of being [*jenseits des Seyns*]. In this way, it comes to the point where man must liberate himself not merely from revelation but from *everything* that has reality in order to flee into a complete wasteland devoid of all being, where nothing is to be encountered but only the infinite potency of all being, the sole immediate content of thought in which it moves only within itself as within its own ether. Yet in precisely this content, reason also possesses what provides it with the fully a priori position toward all being, such that from this content it can take cognizance not only of a being in general but of the entirety of being in all of its gradations. For in the infinite, that is, still undetermined potency, reason immediately discloses, not as contingent but, rather, as necessary, that *inner organism* of successive potencies through which it possesses the key to all being, and which is the inner organism of reason itself. To disclose this organism is the task of the rational philosophy.

The oldest and, when properly understood, most appropriate explanation of philosophy is this: it is the science of being, ἐπιστήμη τοῦ ὄντος. But to find what being is [*Seyende*], that is, what true being is—*hoc opus, hic labor est* [this is really work, this is really labor][24]—this must first be established by the science itself, and, indeed, for the following reason: as it manifests itself in the immediate content of reason (or the infinite capacity to be), being is just as much *It*self as well as the matter of a different being [*Seyn*]. The potency (the immediate content of reason) is indeterminateness *per se* (τὸ ἀόριστον),[25] insofar as it can be potency, subject, matter (since these are synonymous expressions), or even being [*das Seyende*]. Consequently, one does not have being itself as long [77] as one has not excluded from it what is material or simply potential (that which can be), which is the matter of a different being [*Seyn*]. To be capable of doing this, however, thought first of all must delve into this immediate content of reason, to unlock it and ask: what is that being [*Seyende*] that is the immediate content of reason; what belongs to it such that it is being? For this is not self-evident. The concept of being must, therefore, be *produced*.

Clearly, to this being [*Seyenden*] belongs first and foremost that it is the *subject* of being [*Seyn*]. With this, however, that it is just the *subject* of being, that is, just that of which being can be predicated, it would not yet be being (in the pregnant sense which we are using here, where it means the cause of all being [*Ursache alles Seyns*]. Initially, being [*Seyende*] must be the subject of being [*Seyn*]—that which can be—and to this extent it is the potency of being [*Seyn*]. But it is not the potency of something that it *not yet is* because then it would not even be being [*nicht das Seyende*], but it is rather the potency of that *which it already Is*, of that which it is immediately and without transition. Once again, the being [*Seyende*] we seek is immediately and in the first thought the potency of being [*Seyn*]. It is subject, but subject that immediately contains within itself its fulfillment (the subject is in itself a void that must be first filled by the predicate). Being, therefore, is immediately just as much being as it is the capacity to be. Indeed, it is *pure* being, entirely and completely objective being, in which there is just as little of a capacity as there is something of a being [*Seyn*] in the subject. And since in the subject = or potency = being there is immediately also an *object*, a complete concept of being [*Seyende*] must also incorporate this (the third element), which is a subject and object thought as one inseparable subject = object, so that this must still be distinguished as a third determination.

You see that what we have comprehended here under the name of being [*Seyende*] is nothing other than the subject = object of the philosophy that Fichte advanced. Thus, if this subject = object was determined in the first thought as *indifference of subject and object*, [78] this expression would be completely synonymous with the other one: the immediate content of reason is the infinite potency of being. (Fichte, however, *posited* the subject = object only in human consciousness; the philosophy that proceeded from his sublated [*aufgehoben*] this limitation, and posited in the place of the subject = object in human consciousness, the universal and unconditional subject = object.) The subject = object, however, cannot really be thought without distinguishing three moments: (1) subject, (2) object, or (3) subject = object. Immediately, that is, presupposing nothing, nothing other than the subject can be thought. Indeed, the word subject means nothing other than supposition. The only thing that presupposes *itself*, that is, allows nothing to presuppose it, is precisely the subject (in the former philosophical language *subjectum* and *suppositum* are synonymous): nothing can *immediately* be an object, for nothing is an object save in relationship to a subject, and for precisely this reason nothing can also be an immediate subject = object. This last element presupposes the other two: (1) that which lacking all supposition has the capacity to be—the subject—and (2) the object. Only with the third, however, can *precisely that* which was the subject and the object become subject = object.

Now we must promptly add that not the subject, object, and also not the third or the subject = object, none of these (if we indicate them with numbers, not 1, not 2, not 3, is, in its own right, *being*; being itself is only when 1+2+3 are combined.[iv] Thus, in order to reach being itself (and this is the matter currently at hand), in order to arrive in our thought at being itself, we must first remove the 1, 2, and 3—which in their original unity are equal to being itself—that is, we must make *them* unequal, so that together they are no longer being, but each one in its own right a being. This occurs when we allow what in being [*Seyende*] is the subject, thus, the potency of being [*Seyn*], [79] to be a potency *for itself*, that is, to be the potency of its *own* being. We then think of it as passing over into being [*Seyn*], whereby, however, it ceases to be a subject and becomes an object. In contrast, that which was an object in being must then cease to be an object and must itself become a subject in exactly the same manner as that which was subject = object is similarly excluded and posited as a being in its own right. The possibility of this procedure is provided for by the fact that that which is the subject (which of course is also the potency of a being = for = itself —and also the capacity to be in the *transitive* sense), becomes a subject *for itself*, and thus becomes the potency of its *own* being, instead of turning to the object posited within being [*Seyende*] and becoming the subject of the object. Considered in this manner, 1, 2, and 3 are, in their unity, indeed, being; they make, though, a unity that also has the capacity not to be, that is, they are that which is contingent in being, which must be removed to arrive at being itself in its purity, at being that is exalted beyond all doubt. These elements are identical, but they are not what is absolutely identical with itself.

The science that accomplishes this elimination of what is contingent in the first concepts of being—and with this frees being itself—is critical, is of the negative type, and possesses in its result what we have called being itself [*das Seyende selbst*], yet still only in thought. But to know in its own purity, through the exclusion of contingent being [*Seyn*], that this being itself *exists above* that being: this can no longer be a task of that negative science, but of a

---

iv. Compare this and the following argument with the twelfth and thirteenth lectures of the *Introduction to the Philosophy of Mythology*, especially I/5, pages 291, 313, 319, and 320. See also pages 365 and 387.—ED.

The Difference between Negative and Positive Philosophy 145

different one, which in contrast is to be called a positive science, and for which that negative science first sought the proper and highest object.

I have again led you to the point where philosophy—as far as it now seeks its final and highest object, yet brings itself only so far as the logically mediated concept in thought—is incapable of demonstrating it in its own existence, and to where philosophy, as far as it now consorts directly with this object, stands face to face with being exalted beyond all doubt. [80]

Here in the indistinction between the negative and positive philosophy, and with a philosophy that, correctly understood, could only have a negative meaning, one sought to achieve what is possible only for the positive philosophy—herein lies, as was said, the cause of the confusion and of the wild, deserted essence [*Wesen*] into which one fell when one attempted to present God as engaged in a necessary process, after which however, because this strategy could go no further, one took refuge in a brazen atheism. This confusion has in fact prevented this distinction from being so much as even understood.

Only the correctly understood negative philosophy leads to the positive philosophy; conversely, the positive philosophy is first possible only in contrast to the correctly understood negative. Only the latter's withdrawal back into its limits makes the former discernable and then, not only possible, but also necessary.

When through my public lectures something of the positive philosophy was first disclosed there were many who believed they must take up the negative against me, believing that I thought the negative should be entirely abolished, since I had certainly spoken of the Hegelian philosophy in such a way. This occurred, however, not because I considered the Hegelian philosophy to be the negative. I am not able to inflict this honor upon it, nor can I even concede that it is the negative, since, on the contrary, its fundamental error consists precisely in that it wants to be positive. The difference between Hegel and myself is no smaller in regards to the negative than to the positive philosophy. The philosophy that Hegel presented is the negative driven beyond its limits: it does not exclude the positive, but thinks it has subdued it within itself. The great slogan repeatedly used by his pupils was, "The full and real knowledge of divine existence that Kant had denied human reason is upheld by Hegel's philosophy" (even the Christian dogmas were but a trifle for this philosophy). I have contested this philosophy (which puffs itself up to be the positive, whereas according to its final rationale it can only be negative) in my public lectures not just here, but long before, and will continue to contest it as long as [81] it appears necessary to do so. Meanwhile, I will expound the true negative philosophy, which, aware of itself, in noble abstinence completes itself within its limits as the greatest benefit—at least for the moment—that can be accorded the human spirit. For through such a philosophy, reason enters into and employs that which is its most fitting and unrestricted right: to comprehend and to exhibit the essence, the *In-itself* of things. In this way, reason is stilled and completely satisfied in all its legitimate claims; no longer feeling the temptation to break into the territory of the positive, just as conversely, from its own perspective, reason is once and for all free from the constant disruption and interruption from the side of the positive. Not one philosophy since Kant has appeared in Germany against which the followers of the positive did not immediately arise with the accusation of atheism (primarily against Kant himself). But a philosophy that sincerely and genuinely contents itself to propose the concept of God as the final, highest, and necessary idea of reason, without claiming to prove the existence of God, is no longer subject to the danger of such disruption and interruption from the positive, but can and will calmly perfect itself within itself.

It often occurs even now that the partially schooled suggest I declared the former philosophy negative in order to put the positive *in its place*. It might, then, be worthwhile to speak of even a change of mind. But if a matter requires two elements, A and B, and I find myself at first only in possession of one, A, then the fact that B is added to A, or that I now no longer have merely A, but possess rather A + B, does not in fact *change* A. What is only prevented is that I believe through the mere possession of A to already possess or to be able to attain what is only first possible through the addition of B. Such is the relationship of the negative and positive philosophies. No alteration occurs to the first when the second is added to it. On the contrary, through the addition of the latter, the former engages its true essence so that it can no longer be tempted to surge over its borders, that is, to become positive itself. [82] Not long after Kant's *Critique of Pure Reason* became dominant, one started to speak of a *critical philosophy*. Soon, however, one asked whether this critical philosophy is all there is, whether beyond this there is nothing more of philosophy. Regarding my position, I allow myself to point out that soon after a thorough study of the Kantian philosophy it became clear to me that it was impossible for this so-called critical philosophy to be all there is. I even doubted whether it could be the true philosophy. Convinced of this, I maintained already in 1795, in the *Letters on Dogmatism and Criticism*, that—not without turning to Fichte's momentary and obvious contradiction—in opposition to this criticism (and thus was the critical philosophy labeled as a system), there will someday appear an entirely different, far more adroit dogmatism than that of the mistaken and halfhearted former metaphysics.[26] Since Kant of course, the word 'dogmatism' has acquired such a nasty ring to it, and even more so as a consequence of that logical dogmatism that Hegel later wanted to ground solely in the abstract concept (which is the most repugnant form of any dogmatism, since it is the most miserly, whereas the dogmatism of the old metaphysics always had something magnificent about it). Yet even regarding the old metaphysics we must distinguish between a dogmatic and a dogmatizing philosophy. The old metaphysics was a dogmatizing philosophy and, through Kant, this form is irreparably destroyed. Kant's critique, however, did not extend to the true dogmatic philosophy, that is, to what metaphysics actually should be, and not merely what it wanted to be, as in the old metaphysics, which, accordingly, I simply call the dogmatizing philosophy. The old metaphysics believed it could rationally prove, and had proved, the existence of God. It was to this extent a rational dogmatism as Kant expressed it or, conversely, as I would like to express it, a positive rationalism. This positive rationalism was so thoroughly undermined by Kant that it henceforth appeared as impossible so that, nowadays, even those theologians who gladly grab at anything to go on no longer look for help in the old metaphysics. But when that positive rationalism was undermined a purer rationalism came into view—a purer rationalism that, however, we will not [83] call a negative rationalism, since this would presuppose the positive as a possible rationalism; also, since Kant there has not been a positive rationalism. Rationalism can only be negative philosophy, and both concepts are completely synonymous. According to its subject matter, that *pure* rationalism was already contained within Kant's critique. As was said, Kant leaves to reason only the *concept* of God, and because he rejects the so-called ontological argument, which wanted to infer God's existence from his concept, he makes for the concept of God no exception to the rule that the *concept* of a thing contains only the pure *whatness* [*Was*] of the concept, but nothing of its *thatness* [*Daß*], of its existence. Kant shows in general how futile it is for reason to attempt through inferences to reach beyond itself to existence (in this effort, however, reason is not dogmatic, since it does not reach its goal, but, rather, is simply dogmatizing). Kant thus leaves nothing other to reason than the science that encompasses within itself the pure whatness of the thing and his clearly stated position is that this pure rationalism is all that remains standing of the edifice of the old metaphysics. Kant, of course, extended what he had proved only of *reason* to *philosophy*, and tacitly assumed that there is no other philosophy than pure rational philosophy. But he had hardly proved this last point. The question, therefore, had to arise whether after the breakdown of the old metaphysics the *other* positive element is completely destroyed or whether—on the contrary—after the negative philosophy had been beaten down into a pure rationalism the positive philosophy, now free and independent from the negative, must configure itself into its own science.

A science that is in a crisis, however, does not advance in such a hasty manner. For sheer caprice does not rule in scientific movements. Rather, the deeper and more extensive such movements are, the more they are ruled by a necessity that allows for no such leaps of thought, the more they oppressively demand that first the next step be completed and the immediate task at hand be solved before one goes on to more remote matters. This pure rationalism, [84] which had to be the necessary result of the Kantian critique, was only indirectly contained within that critique and was combined with too many contingent elements. It was therefore first necessary to separate these from it, to work Kant's critique itself into a formal science, into a real philosophy. The first of those called to present this *pure* rationalism must have imagined this as their *goal*. They must have been so occupied with it that they could think of nothing else: they must have thought they had incorporated everything into it, and as long as they were occupied with *it* they could not think of anything that went beyond it. To this extent, of course, there was then not yet any discussion of a positive philosophy and because of this the negative philosophy had also yet to be recognized and declared *as such*. In order for this philosophy to pull itself entirely back within the limits of the negative, of *just* the logical, and to confess itself *as* a negative philosophy, it would have *to exclude the positive philosophy emphatically*. This could happen in two ways: it could posit the positive outside itself or it could deny it outright and completely abandon or abolish it. The latter option was too extreme a demand. Even Kant himself, after he had completely eliminated the positive from the theoretical philosophy, introduced it again through the back door of the practical. Kant's philosophy, which admittedly stood on a higher level of scientific proficiency, could not grab hold of this positive message. But to exclude the positive from the negative in the other way, so that it posits the positive *outside* itself as the object of a different science—for this the *positive philosophy* would by all means have to be created. Yet this philosophy was not created and through Kant there was simply no possibility provided for this. Kant had put philosophy on a course where it would culminate and conclude as a negative or a purely rational philosophy and had provided absolutely no means for a positive philosophy.

Now we see in organic nature, however, that an earlier organism decides to become negative, or to declare *itself* as negative, at precisely that moment in which the positive arises outside of it. It was thus impossible that that philosophy could resolve itself to the pure negativity [85] demanded of it *before* the positive philosophy was discovered and actually present. Contributing to this was the fact that this philosophy developed in a very positive era that demanded knowledge loud and clear; to renounce all positive knowledge in the face of this was perhaps a prohibition that was too difficult for vigorous and aspiring minds. Among others, this philosophy stood in opposition to those who had their standpoint *only* in the positive and those who, although they renounced all scientific philosophy in order to, as it were, recover from this humiliation, only wanted all the more to ground the greater claims of all higher convictions entirely in a blind feeling, in faith, or even in revelation. One of these was Jacobi, who proclaimed as his fundamental principle that every scientific philosophy leads to atheism. This person did not shrink from treating the Kantian proposition that reason is not capable of proving the existence of God as being thoroughly identical with his own even though, between the two, there is indeed a sizable and significant difference. Yet because Kant wanted to know neither of a blind faith nor of mere feeling in philosophy, his negative outcome found itself in the position of appearing to Jacobi as atheism, and Jacobi scarcely restrained himself from pronouncing this. Aside from these men, for whom it was all just a matter of finding confirmation of their proposition that all scientific philosophy leads to atheism, and who consequently saw atheism everywhere—where it was and where it was not—aside from these, Spinoza continued to have a powerful influence,

The Difference between Negative and Positive Philosophy 149

for he first brought this confusion of the positive and the negative into philosophy in that he made that which necessarily *exists* into his *principle* (beginning), but from which he then just *logically* derived *real* things.

It was to be expected that precisely at that moment when the negative and the positive should have become forever divorced—thus at the moment of the formation of the purely negative philosophy—that the positive had to appear even more forcefully and establish its own legitimacy. And if earlier I had had the clear presentiment that on the other side of this *Critique*, which had destroyed [86] the dogmatizing philosophy, a different one must arise, and, indeed, a dogmatic philosophy that would not be touched by it, then it is easy to imagine how when that rational system, prepared by Kant and now brought to its full manifestation and liberated from all contingencies, stood before my eyes as a real system, that this same sight must have weighed on my heart all the more heavily. The more purely the negative philosophy was put forth, the more forcefully the positive had to rise up in contrast to it, and it seemed as if nothing had been done as long as this had not been discovered as well. Perhaps this will explain how, almost immediately after the first presentation of that system that had developed out of the *Critique*, this philosophy was more or less abandoned by its founder and left for the time being to those who stood ready to appropriate it, who, as Plato would say, were drawn by the brilliance of the vacated position to pounce on it with zeal.[27] For myself, this philosophy had really only been a transition. In truth, I had attempted in this philosophy nothing other than the next possible thing after Kant, and was inwardly quite removed from accepting it—no one will be able to cite an assertion contrary to this—as the *whole* of philosophy in the sense in which this later occurred. And if I allowed the positive philosophy, even after it was discovered, to be known, at most, through intimations, through the well-known paradoxes of a polemical essay against Jacobi, then I believe that even this restraint was to be praised more than rebuked.[28] For with this I left plenty of time for a school of thought, with which I wanted to have nothing in common, to develop and express itself, so that now no one can any longer be doubtful about that school of thought and my relationship to it, whereas I would otherwise probably have never freed myself of it. The only action that I took against this school of thought was to leave it to its own devices, whereby I was completely convinced that it would, with rapid strides, head straight for corruption and decay.

The *true* improvement to my philosophy could partly have been to have restricted it precisely to only a logical meaning. Hegel, however, made much more specific [87] claims than his predecessor did to have comprehended the positive as well. In general, one has made altogether false concepts about the relationship between these two thinkers. One believes that the former was angry with the latter for having gone beyond him. But exactly the opposite is the case. The first, who still had much to overcome (about which one nowadays no longer knows anything) and had to master all the material that the latter found already subdued in the concept, could certainly put up with being corrected by the latter. Even if those elements of Hegel's overall approach that were particularly hostile to all that is meaningful and inspired could not be hidden from me, I nonetheless also saw how that same approach opposed with vigor, and for the true benefit of rigorous thinking and science, much of what he found before him in that time that was spuriously brilliant, really weak— yes, even childish—and that misled through an ostensible conviviality. While others just floundered about, he at least held tight to the method as such, and the energy with which he carried out a false system—although mistaken, it was nonetheless a system—had it been turned to what is correct could have contributed a priceless largess to science. As I saw then, it is precisely this aspect that mostly accounts for his influence, in that those who praised him most fervently always removed a few platitudes and slogans, rarely spoke of specifics, but always emphasized that his philosophy is a *system*, and indeed a complete system. On the one hand, this unconditional demand for a system expresses the heights to which the philosophical science has been elevated in our time; one is convinced that nothing more can be known in its singularity, but rather only in its context and as part of a great, all-encompassing totality. On the other hand, there are many who want to be finished at any cost and feel childishly delighted to subscribe to a system, thereby elevating their own importance; primarily because of this, it is always such a deplorable affair when the labels of party or sect come into use or are again accepted as valid. For I have had the opportunity to see some whom on their own meant nothing, but when they called themselves a liberal or a monarchist sympathizer [88] fancied both themselves and others to actually be something.

Not everyone, by the way, is called upon to be the creator of a system. It requires an artistic sensibility to remain within the borders of what is natural and to keep oneself from being carried away by the pursuit of closure to absurd or bizarre conclusions. Hegel, who in the details is so sharp, was abandoned by this artistic sensibility by nothing so badly as when he moved on into the whole [*das Ganze*], for otherwise he would have detected the interruption of movement that takes place for him between the *Logic* and the *Philosophy of Nature*; from the manner alone, in which the latter was pieced onto the former, he should have seen that he was not on the correct path. I do not belong to those who look for the source of philosophy exclusively in feeling [*Gefühl*], but for philosophical thinking and invention, as for the poetic or artistic, feeling must be the voice that warns of the unnatural and indistinct, and many a path that leads to error will be spared those who listen to it for the very reason that this sensibility shuns that which is artificial and can only be achieved through laborious and unclear compositions. The philosopher who really wants a completed system must see far out into the distance, not just stare myopically at details and what lies nearby.

The earlier philosophy could not present itself as an *unconditional* system in the sense of Hegel's, but one could not, for this reason, reproach it for not being a system at all. It did not first need *to be* systematized, since it was born a system; its peculiarity consisted precisely in the fact that it is to be a system. Whether the external presentation was held to be more or less academic could appear as inconsequential: the system resided in the *subject matter* [*Sache*], and whoever had the subject matter had for precisely this reason the system as well. Yet it could not achieve closure [*sich abschließen*] as an absolute system that leaves nothing outside itself, and as long as the positive philosophy had not been created, it could do just as little to prevent another thinker from advancing this system as philosophy *per se*. At first, Hegel seemed to realize the *purely logical* nature of this science. Yet if he were serious about its purely logical meaning, then logic for him could not be just a *component*. This entire philosophy, [89] even those philosophies of spirit and nature undertaken by his predecessor, had to be logical for him, that is, they had to be logic, and yet what he specifically proposed as logic must not be something so misguided as it is in his hands. Instead of using the true and real logic as a foundation from which one could have advanced, he hypostatized the concept with the intent of providing the logical movement—which, however independent one takes it to be of everything subjective, can nonetheless always exist only in *thought*—with the significance of an objective movement, nay, what is more, of a *process*. So little had he freed himself from what is real, and which had impeded his predecessor, that he in fact *affected* what is real with expressions taken from that predecessor, which were in no way made for his standpoint. In the transition to the philosophy of nature, which can occur only hypothetically in a philosophy that remains purely negative (whereby even nature is preserved in its sheer possibility, with no attempt to explain it as a reality, a task which must be reserved for an entirely different facet of philosophy), he helps himself to such expressions—for example, the idea *resolves* itself [*entschließt sich*]; nature is a *fall* [*Abfall*] from the idea—that either say nothing, or, according to his intent, should be *explanatory* and thus include something real, an actual process, a happening. Thus, if the error of the first presentation was not to have placed what is positive *outside* itself, so this was surpassed by the ensuing (Hegelian) presentation, but only through the perfection of that error.

I return to the opinion that some have formed as they heard from afar of the positive philosophy, namely that it should take the *place* of the negative entirely, and should thereby supplant and nullify [*aufheben*] the latter. Thus was it never intended, and so easily will a creation like that of this philosophy never surrender, a philosophy that since then has determined itself for me as the negative. It was a beautiful time in which this philosophy arose, when through Kant and Fichte the human spirit released itself to a real freedom toward all being and justifiably saw to ask not what is but what *can* be, and when Goethe also shone forth as the sublime paradigm of artistic perfection. The positive philosophy, however, could not have been discovered and [90] developed without a corresponding advance in the negative, which is now capable of an entirely different presentation than forty years ago. Although I know that this simple, easy, and nonetheless magnificent architectonic, insofar as with the very first thought it crossed over into nature, and, thus, proceeding from the broadest basis, culminated in a peak that soared up into the heavens—I know that this architectonic, in its *perfect* execution, particularly in the countless details of which it is capable and, indeed, even demands, all of this is only comparable to the works of the old German architecture, which cannot be the work of one person, of one individual, and, for that matter, not even of one epoch. Yet even the Gothic cathedrals, left uncompleted in an earlier age, were taken up again by a later progeny and constructed according to their principle. Although aware of this, I nonetheless hope not to withdraw from this world, without having also consolidated the system of the negative philosophy in its true foundation, and as far as it is now possible for me, to have further developed it.

From what has been said, it becomes immediately clear how superfluous it was to want to defend the rational or negative philosophy against me or bring it to bear upon me, as if I no longer wanted to know anything about a philosophy of pure reason. Those people, incidentally, who believed themselves called to do this and, in particular, those who believed they must undertake a defense of the Hegelian philosophy against me in this regard, did this, at least in part, not to somehow oppose the positive philosophy, but, on the contrary, they themselves *also wanted* something of the sort. Only they were of the opinion that this positive philosophy must be constructed on the basis of the Hegelian system and can be constructed on no other. Moreover, they thought that the Hegelian system lacked nothing more than for *them* to carry it on into the positive, and this, they thought, can happen in a continuous advance, without interruption and devoid of any setbacks. They proved through this that, firstly, they had never had a correct concept of the preceding philosophy, otherwise they would have known that this philosophy was in itself a closed and fully consummated system. A totality that had a *true* [91] end [*Ende*], that is, an end beyond which one could not, according to circumstances or conditions, again move, but rather one that must remain the end. Secondly, they proved that they did not even know about the philosophy that they wanted to improve and expand, the Hegelian, since this philosophy had no need to be extended by them to the positive because it had, on the contrary, already done that on its own. Its error consisted precisely in this; it wanted to be something that, according to its nature and heritage, it could by no means be, namely, to be a dogmatic philosophy. In particular, it was their opinion (probably derived from dubious hearsay) that the positive philosophy begins with the personal God, and the personal God was that which they thought to acquire through the advancement of the Hegelian philosophy as the *necessary* content of reason. They did not know, therefore, that Kant along with the philosophy that followed from him already had God as the *necessary* content of reason: about this there was no quarrel and no doubt, for it was no longer a question of *content*. As far as Hegel is concerned, yes, he indeed boasted that

The Difference between Negative and Positive Philosophy 153

he had God at the end of philosophy as absolute *spirit*. But can one think of an absolute spirit that would not simultaneously be an absolute personality, a consciousness absolutely aware of himself? Perhaps they meant this absolute spirit is just not a freely acting personality, the freely acting creator of the world, or any such thing. This of course could not be the spirit who first comes at the end, *post festum*, after everything has been done, and who has nothing other to do than take up into himself all those extant moments of the process that are before and independent of him. And yet it was precisely this that even Hegel had finally sensed, and in later addendums he allowed this absolute spirit to freely decide to create a world, to externalize itself with freedom into a world. Yet these addendums came too late even in this respect. They could not say that at the creation of the world the Hegelian philosophy is an impossible thought, since after all they wanted to achieve the same thing with precisely this philosophy. Their imagined improvement of the Hegelian philosophy was thus quite actually, as one says, *moutarde apres diner*, and one would now truly have reason to assume that Hegel would be against his students. [92] One must have been no less inclined to defend him against the insult that was done to him, when others with melodramatic phrases—those sentimental, pietistic phrases capable of arousing only disgust in that powerful thinker—sought to make his philosophy accessible to a portion of the public by forcing ideas taken from elsewhere into a narrow vessel, which always failed to hold them.

The main argument of those defenders of Hegel, who at the same time want to be his reformers, is this: a rational philosophy is something intrinsically necessary and particularly indispensable to the *foundation* of a positive philosophy. Against this, one might now say that the negative as well as the positive is necessary for the *consummation* of philosophy. The positive is necessary not in *that* sense that they imagine it, however, in which the negative founds it; also, it would not be just a continuation of the negative, since in the positive there occurs an *entirely* different *modus progrediendi* as that in the negative, in that, here, even the form of the development is completely reversed. That the negative should found the positive philosophy would only be necessary if the negative philosophy handed over to the positive its object as something that is already cognized, with which it could only then begin its operations. But such is not the case. That which will be the proper object of the positive remains stuck in the preceding philosophy as that which is no longer capable of being known [*das nicht mehr Erkennbare*]. For in the negative philosophy everything is knowable only to the extent that it has a *prius*, yet this final object does not have a *prius* in the sense of everything else, since here the matter is turned on its head: that which in the purely rational philosophy was the *prius* here becomes the *posterius*. In its culmination, the negative philosophy itself contains the demand for the positive, and the philosophy that is aware of itself, and understands itself completely, certainly *has* the need to posit the positive outside itself. In this sense, one could say that, from its perspective, the negative grounds the positive but could not say that the converse is true, however, that the positive likewise has the need to be grounded by the negative. The foundation that we of course recognize from the *perspective* of the negative (but not of the positive) [93] philosophy is not to be understood as though the end of the negative philosophy would be the beginning of the positive. This is not so. The former hands over its final concept to the positive only as a demand [*Aufgabe*], not as a *principle*. Yet, one will say, then it is nonetheless grounded by the negative to the extent it receives this demand from it. Quite right, but the positive philosophy must, entirely on its own, supply the means to satisfy this demand. If the negative arrives at the demand for the positive, this occurs only in its *own* interest that it completes itself—but not as if the positive had the *need* to receive this demand from it or to be grounded by it. For the positive can begin purely of itself with even the simple words: I want that which is *above* being [*über dem Seyn*], that which is not merely being [*das bloße Seyende*], but rather what is more than this, the Lord of Being [*Herr des Seyns*]. Since it begins with a wanting [*Wollen*], it is already justified as philosophy, that is, as a science that itself freely determines its object, a philosophy that in itself, and even according to its name, is a wanting. It can therefore also receive this demand *solely* from itself, and, likewise, it can provide itself with its own actual beginning. For this beginning is of the type that requires no foundation: it is that which through itself is the certain and absolute beginning. [94]

History of Negative and Positive Philosophy

The main objection to distinguishing between a negative and a positive philosophy is, no doubt, that philosophy must be of one piece, that there cannot be two different kinds of philosophy. Before one can make this objection, however, one must first know whether the negative and positive are in fact two different philosophies, or whether perhaps they are only two sides of the same philosophy in two different, yet necessarily interrelated, sciences. This will now be decided through the following considerations. Let us note for the moment, however, that the antithesis that lies at the bottom of this distinction has been present for some time, and indeed even *within* the rational systems that have attempted to unite what cannot be united. We have not, therefore, just created this antithesis and, on the contrary, by means of strict separation we intend to sublate it forever.

From where else, indeed, if not from these two sides of what is nevertheless perhaps one philosophy, has one from time immemorial found it so difficult, or even impossible, to provide a sufficient definition of philosophy, a definition that also expresses the process of philosophy, its *modus procedendi*? If one, for example, explains it as a science that withdraws itself into pure, that is, necessary, thought, then this is a perfectly admissible [95] definition of the negative philosophy; if one, however, takes this definition as absolute, what is the necessary result? Since philosophy in general cannot refuse to also provide an exposition and explanation of the real *existence* of nature and the world, not merely concerning itself with the essence of things, the result will be—if one is consistent—that one also must assert that in reality everything is merely a logical nexus and that freedom and action mean nothing. But the extralogical nature of existence rebels so decisively against this that even those who, consistent with their concepts, explain the world and even their own existence as the mere logical consequence of some kind of original necessity do not have the words they want and must rather, forsaking the standpoint of pure thought, reach for expressions that are entirely unsuitable, and indeed impossible, from their standpoint.

The question here is thus properly seen in this way: both philosophies are demanded—a science that grasps the essence of things and the content of all being and a science that explains the actual existence of things. Once this antithesis is present, one cannot get around it by somehow suppressing one of the two demands any more than by mixing both demands, whereby only more contradictions and confusion will arise. There remains, therefore, nothing else to do than to assume that each of these demands must be put forth and considered in its own right, that is, in a particular science. This of course does not prevent one from maintaining the association and perhaps even the unity of the two. For should it really surprise us if such a double-sided nature of philosophy presents itself, since (and this is an essential point, on which I intend to dwell at length) it can be shown that both directions have been present in philosophy—the one right alongside the other—since time immemorial, and that when they have come into conflict, the one has nonetheless always held its own against the other.

To begin with antiquity, Aristotle, who is the principal source for ancient philosophy, spoke more than once of a class of philosophers whom he calls the *theologians*. If we now [96] also assume that by this term he understood those philosophers of antiquity who still stood under the inspiration of mythology or those who, in addition to the facts of nature and the use of the human understanding, also considered religious facts, namely, the mythological traditions such as that of the so-called Orphics, or the founder of that παλαιῶν λόγων who is occasionally mentioned in Plato, then Aristotle speaks in a passage from the *Metaphysics* of philosophers in *his time* as well whom he designates with the same name (the discussion is about θεολόγων τῶν νῦν τισι), and by which he can mean none other than those who trace the world back to God.ᵛ These are dogmatic philosophers, from whom the other philosophers can then only be distinguished by the fact that they sought to explain everything naturally or through reason.

The Ionic physicists certainly belonged to this latter group, particularly Heraclitus—whose doctrine that nothing ever *is*, that nothing ever endures, but rather that everything only flows or moves like a river—τὰ ὄντα ἰέναι τε χαὶ μένειν οὐδέν, as Plato expressed the doctrine, or ὅτι πάντα χωρεῖ, that everything yields or makes room for something else—basically describes nothing other than the science of reason that also abides by nothing.²⁹ What is first determined as subject is transformed in the next moment into an object; thus, the subject *surrenders* to and provides room for something different, which again is determined not to endure but to surrender to yet another and higher subject until that point is reached where the subject relates to nothing more than nonbeing [*das Nichtseyende*], and, thus, to what can no longer surrender.

---

v. Lib. XIII, p. 300 (ed. Brandis). [The reference is to the Berlin Academy's edition of Aristotles works, edited by Bekker and Brandis (Berlin: 1827). Schelling first refers to Plato's "old saying" mentioned in his *Gorgias* (499c), and then to Aristotle's account of the "mythologists" in his *Metaphysics* (cf. 1091a30).]

History of Negative and Positive Philosophy 157

The Eleatic philosophers in particular belonged to this group of rational philosophers, whom Aristotle primarily criticized because, although their science was only logic, they nevertheless sought with it to *explain* logic itself.[30] In this context, he announces that the Eleatic philosophy can arouse only bewilderment and is of no help, since movement only in thought excludes all real events. When this merely logical movement nonetheless wishes to advance itself as explanatory, [97] in doing so it never seems to leave its starting point (*since* logical movement cannot be a real progression of events—rather, everything happens only in thought—it seems that when a logical account is accepted as a real explanation that it never leaves its starting point). Precisely because of this it induces this bewilderment just as any circular movement that revolves around one point.[vi] Socrates himself used a highly developed dialectic that, far from being something positive or something that possessed a significance in its own right, for *him* had only the significance of a tool of destruction. He directed this dialectic not only against the Sophists, that is, against a subjective = logical pseudoknowledge, but also against the rational pseudoknowledge of the Eleatic school and its claim to objectivity. Moreover, one has correctly understood Plato only when one realizes how closely and inwardly related for him the Sophists and the Eleatics are; his dialectic was equally applicable to the lightness and banality of the Sophists as it was to the bombast of the Eleatic philosophers. In this context, Plutarch said that, in philosophy, Socrates employed bombast and pomposity (τῦφον) as a type of smoke (ὥσπερ τινὰ χαπνὸν φιλοσοφιᾶς) to be blown in the face of his opponents.[31] For Plato, the means to this were his questions that, while they appear to *us* as the simple questions of a child, which on occasion are even boring, nonetheless had the purpose of making those students who had become 'puffed up' by the pseudo-knowledge of the Sophists or the bombast of the Eleatics once again receptive to true knowledge through this diet of simple questioning. This is like a clever doctor who, when he intends to work on a sick body with strong medicine, first employs purifying agents so that he does not affect the preserving and *revivifying* principle of the organism, but rather the cause of the sickness itself, and intensifies this cause in its efficacy so that it strengthens the organism instead of weakening it.

Socrates primarily speaks out against this pseudo-knowledge and the difference between him and the others is that, while these truly knew nothing as well, they nonetheless [98] believed that they knew something; he, however, was the better for it since he knew that he knew nothing. Above all, it should be noted that in this famous discussion Socrates does not deny *all* knowledge [*Wissen*], but rather only that knowledge of which the others boasted; he himself ascribed to this knowledge as well, only he added that he is aware that this knowledge is no real knowledge. Thus, right from the outset this discussion

---

vi. We cannot count the Pythagoreans among the theologians or particularly the rationalists, but must rather assume that they attempted to unite both, even if it is not easy to say how they did so.

looks quite different from that of some recent philosophers, who, also wishing to present the look of Socratic unknowing, *begin* with the confession of unknowing [*Unwissenheit*], seeking right from the start to calm themselves with ignorance [*Nichtwissen*].

The Socratic ignorance must be preceded by a profound and even exceptional knowledge: a knowledge of which it is worth the trouble of saying that it *is* not knowledge, or that nothing is known with it. Ignorance must be a *docta ignorantie*, an *ignorance savante*, as Pascal has expressed it.[32] Without a profound knowledge that precedes it, the pronouncement that one knows nothing is merely ridiculous; for if one who is actually ignorant asserts that he knows nothing, then what is so strange about that? On the contrary, what would be strange would be if he knew anything at all; that he knows nothing, one believes in any case, he does not need to worry about. Among jurists it is said: "*Quilibet praesumitur bonus, donec probetur contrarium*" [All things are presumed to be done legitimately, until the contrary is proved]. Among scholars, the opposite is true: "*Nemo praesumitur doctus...*" [*No one is presumed wise...*]. If, however, the knowledgeable individual says that he knows nothing, it follows that such an assertion here has an entirely different rhyme and reason.

Socrates presupposes a knowledge in this explanation of ignorance. The question must now be what type of knowledge *it is* that he, just as the other philosophers, ascribes to. For him, though, it is a not-knowing of the type with which he *knows* not to know. We will attempt first to transform this negative determination of an ignorant knowledge into a positive one. *Thought* is still by no means knowledge. To this extent, we can call this ignorant knowledge a *thinking* knowledge, and the non-knowing science a mere *science of thought* [*Denkwissenschaft*]. Such a science includes geometry, which, no doubt for this reason, Plato, in the famous genealogy of the sciences (*Republ.VI*), counts not as an [99] ἐπιστήμη, but only as a διάνοια.[33] Thus, the knowledge that, according to Socrates' claim, has something in common with the other forms of knowing, but which *he* regarded as ignorance, may very well be the pure science of reason; a science he knew as well as or even better than the Eleatics, and from which he distinguished himself precisely through the fact that, whereas *they* wanted to make their logical knowledge into a *knowing* knowledge, in Socrates' opinion it could only be maintained as an ignorant knowing.

We now proceed a step farther. *Since* he explains the science that occurs *solely* in thought as an ignorant science, he thereby posits *external* to this one—at least as an idea—a science that must be a knowing, that is, a positive science. In this context, the confession of his ignorance now assumes a positive meaning, in that one can confess ignorance either in reference to a science that actually exists, of which one simply says that it in fact offers no real knowledge, or in reference to a science that one does not yet possess and which, as it were, still stands before us. For Socrates, evidently, both are the case. In reference to the purely logical knowledge, he explains himself in the first sense. But by doing this he presupposes a different knowledge and if he confesses his ignorance in the face of this different knowledge, it follows that this ignorance once *again* has an entirely different meaning than one customarily expects. For the one is unknowing or ignorant due to a lack of science, whereas the other is an ignorance caused by the exuberant nature [*Ueberschwenglichkeit*] of what is to be known. Indeed, the ignorance of a *Socrates* in this sense should be praised; however, it is clear that not everyone is suited to emulate Socrates in this manner.

Evidently, Socrates presupposes a knowledge to which the mere science of reason relates as ignorant [*Nichtwissen*]. Here, of course, is not the place to demonstrate fully the real desire of this most unique and individual man, who has, for good reason, incurred the hate and aversion of Sophists in all times up to the most recent. A veil still lays over his inner glory that has not yet been fully lifted. Various details, however, do survive from which it can be concluded that his spirit lingered precisely on the boundary of the merely logical and the positive. An undeniable [100] sign of this is not just the mythical, that is, historical, expression that he used to give to everything in his work that is a *doctrine* [*Lehre*], or which deserved the name of a doctrine (for example, life after death); averse to vulgar mythology, he sought instead of this a *higher* historical context, as if only in *this* context there was real knowledge.[vii] The most convincing evidence of this is that the most brilliant of his pupils, Plato (whose entire series of extant works are thoroughly dialectical, nevertheless, at the climax and transfiguring points of them all. Schleiermacher takes at least the *Timaeus* as an example of this—or was it perhaps a work in which youthful impetuousness carried away the poetic philosopher? However that may be, in the *Timaeus* Plato becomes historical and breaks through, albeit violently, into the positive, with the result that the trace of a scientific transition is barely or hardly to be detected since it is more a cessation of what has preceded (namely of the dialectic) than a transition to the positive. Socrates and Plato both relate to this positive as something of the future: they relate to it prophetically. In Aristotle, philosophy for the first time cleansed itself of all that is prophetic and mythical, and yet in doing this, Aristotle appears as the pupil of both, in that he turned away completely from the *merely* logical toward the positive that was accessible to him—to the empirical in the widest sense of the word, in which the *thatness* (that it exists) is first, and the *whatness* (what something is) then becomes second and, thus, subsidiary.

Aristotle turns away from the logical insofar as it seeks to be *explanatory* and therefore positive: λογικῶς, διαλεκτικῶς and κενῶς ('empty') are, for him, synonymous expressions in this context; he admonishes all those who, while they remain merely in the logical (ἐν τοῖς λόγοις), nonetheless seek to comprehend reality.[34] He even extends this to include Plato's *Timaeus*, as well as, in particular, the doctrine of μέθεξις ('the participation of things in the

---

vii. Compare *Introduction to the Philosophy of Mythology*, I/5, p. 284.—ED.

ideas'). This doctrine yields a correct meaning if it is logically understood so that what is beautiful, what is good (what only occurs in experience), is not the good or [101] the beautiful itself, but is rather only beautiful and good through participation in the good and the beautiful itself. If, however, μέθεξις is made into an explanation of becoming, of the actual coming into being of things, or is regarded or used as if it were sufficient for this, then of course the error arises that a real explanation is attempted with something that only has a logical meaning. In this sense, Aristotle was correct when he reproached Plato, saying that he could bring forth no intelligible words about how the ideas mediated concrete things. Only in the context of an *explanation* that attempted and yet was incapable of showing how the ideas mediated concrete things did Aristotle call this entire Platonic doctrine of μέθεξις empty, even using the word κενολογεῖν to describe it.[35] *In general*, however, he opposed the logical philosophers, arguing that there is an unbridgeable chasm between logical necessity and reality. He reproached the same philosophers for the confusion that arises when the logical order is confused with the order of *being*, after which the actual causes of being will be inevitably confused with the merely formal principles of the *science*. For precisely this reason, however, we must now say that as differently as the path of Aristotle's is from that of negative philosophy, in the essence of its results nothing so agrees with the properly understood negative philosophy as precisely the meaning of Aristotle. How this is possible will become evident through a discussion of both methods, which cannot fail to cast our previous deliberations in yet a new light.

I would like to point out, therefore, that that rationalism or negative philosophy, as much as it is in practice purely a priori, is not a logical philosophy in *the sense* that Aristotle would attach to the word. For the a priori is not, as Hegel understood it, something empty, logical, a thinking that again has as its content only thinking, and in which real thought ceases, just as poetry about poetry ceases to be poetry. The *truly* logical, the logical in real thought, has in itself a necessary relationship to being: it becomes the content of being and necessarily passes over [102] into the empirical. The negative philosophy as an a priori philosophy is therefore not in *this* sense a merely logical philosophy that would exclude being. Being is indeed the content of pure thought, but only as potency. But what potency is, according to its nature, is, so to speak, a leaping toward being. Thus, through the nature of its very content thought is drawn outside itself. For what has passed over into being is no longer the content of just thought—it has become the object of a knowledge—empirical knowledge—that exceeds thought. At every point, thought proceeds to its correspondence with what is present in experience. Consequently, at every point, thought takes leave of what has passed over into being, since it has only served thought as a step to a higher level. The same process occurs again at this higher level: being emerges from thought (which secures and comprehends its *content*), but what is comprehended is again abandoned by thought and handed over to a different knowledge, to that of the empirical. In this entire movement, therefore, thought *of itself* truly possesses nothing in its own right, but allocates everything to a foreign knowledge, namely, that of experience, until it arrives at that which no longer has the capacity to be external to thought, to that which remains abiding within thought. With this, thought arrives at that which is simultaneously itself, namely, at a thought that has escaped from its *necessary* movement and now freely sees itself, and with which precisely for this reason, a science of free thinking begins, no longer beginning as in the negative philosophy with a thought that has surrendered to a necessary movement. According to the subject matter at hand, rational philosophy is so little opposed to experience that instead, just as Kant had taught of reason, it does not even extend *beyond* experience, and where experience has its end, reason recognizes its *own* boundary as well, leaving this final concept standing there as something unknowable. According to its subject matter, even rational philosophy is an empiricism, but only an a priori empiricism.

As we have seen, as little as the a priori excludes the empirical, to which it rather has a necessary relationship, just as little is the empirical free from the a priori, [103] having rather a significant amount of the same in itself. This is so much so that I say it stands with one foot entirely in the a priori, not only to the extent that there are general and necessary forms, which means a priori forms, in everything empirical, but also in that *nothing* less than the *essence*, the proper *whatness* of everything, is something a priori, and only as something that really exists does it belong to the empirical. Its essence is, in the consummation of this science, something to be comprehended a priori, but that it exists, that it is empirical, is only to be realized a posteriori.

Yet for this very reason, just as there is a path from the logical to the empirical, there is also a path from the empirical to the logical that arrives at the innate and indwelling logic of nature. Aristotle entered upon this path—indeed, in the most expansive breadth possible for his time—in that he dealt not merely with the whole of nature, to the extent it was accessible to him, nor merely with the ethical and political relations of the human race and of his time, but in that he also treated the general categories and concepts, not just in their abstract conception, but in their application—in the actual employment of the understanding—treating nothing less than the entire history of philosophy until his time as the subject matter of his analytic investigations. In this way he ascended, step by step, to the final goal of the first science, the πρώτη ἐπιστήμη, or the first philosophy. While on this path, however, and particularly at its terminus, Aristotle also had to encounter the negative philosophy. If one follows him to the deepest depths from which he starts out, he begins his ascending progression with the *potency* (corresponding to the beginning) in which every antithesis is still enfolded. This progression ends in the *actus*, which subsists above every antithesis, even above every potency—and which is therefore pure entelechy; for entelechy is for Aristotle what *actus* is for us: the antithesis of δύναμις. Out of the womb of the indeterminacy and infinitude of potency, of what is possible, nature elevates itself step by step toward its end from which, as Aristotle says, it is attracted [*angezogen*]. As he says, within every increment its antecedent subsists only [104] as potency, as nonbeing, just as in the philosophy of nature, for example, matter relates to light only as object, but both relate to the organic principle again as nonbeing. Aristotle maintains that the antecedent always subsists in the corollary according to its potency, or as potency—ἀεὶ γὰρ ἐν τῷ ἐφεξῆς ὑπάρχει δυνάμει τὸ πρότερον.³⁶ Any point, any arbitrary limit of the series is the goal of the preceding series; every member of the series is, in its own position, just as much a final cause as the last member is the final cause of everything. Since the series cannot lose itself in infinity, and since the ascending movement of nature does not drift off into emptiness, there must be an ultimate goal of this path, which continues *a potentia ad actum*, that is, in the sense that just as the beginning is pure potency, so too is the end pure *actus*. In relationship to the approach to the end, being rules over nonbeing, the *actus* over the potency; all ὕλη (synonymous with potency) will be incrementally removed. The final telos is thus no longer potency, but is rather τὸ ἐνεργείᾳ ὄν, potency fixed entirely as *actus*. This final telos itself does not again become a member of the series like everything else, but is rather that being which exists in its own right above and independent of the entire series. Of course Aristotle employs this as that which actually exists [*das wirklich Existirende*] (not merely as an idea as in the negative philosophy)—and here lies the distinction—but he employs that which actually exists as the final telos only because it grounds his entire science in experience. He thereby incorporates this entire world, which the rational philosophy has in thought, as the existing world. Nonetheless, it is not a question of existence, for existence is, as it were, the contingent element in all this, and has worth for him only as far as it is that from which he can extract the whatness of things. Existence is the mere presupposition; it is only the point of departure. His real goal is the essence, the whatness of things and so, for him, the final telos—which is the same as that which actually exists according to its *nature* (and this is the real issue at hand)—is pure *actus*, and precisely this being, which according to its nature is *actus*, is the final telos of rational or negative philosophy.

Because of this, Aristotle also *makes no use* of the final telos—of God—or [105] of the actually existent, but expressly rejects these, in that he always determines it only as the final cause (as αἴτιον τελικόν not ποιητικόν). Consequently, since he now has this final telos as that which actually exists, he does not then attempt to make it somehow into an efficacious beginning as well. It remains for him the *end*, he does not think of making it again into the beginning, into the principle of an explanation. The entire movement of becoming is only a movement toward this end, not proceeding *from* it as from a *beginning*. *If* he uses this final telos as the basis of explaining reality, for example, of the movement of the heavens, he explains this movement not through an impetus or an effect of that ἐνεργείᾳ ὄν, but through a tug, a desire, ὄρεξις, which the subordinate nature of the stars feel toward what is most supreme.37 If for him God is to this extent only the cause of movement, then God is nevertheless only a ὡς τέλος, αὐτὸς ἀκίνητος to this movement, so that in being the cause of this God himself remains unmoved.38 Until recently, this "αὐτὸς ἀκίνητος" has been understood to mean only that God is not moved *by something other than himself*. This is not, however, how it was intended. Rather, what was meant was that even as God himself does not move and does not act, that even as efficacious he nonetheless remains unmoved; he acts but without being moved because he acts only as the final cause, as that *toward which* everything on its own accord strives. In so doing God comports himself as the object of a longing, ὡς (as Aristotle says explicitly) ἐρώμενον,39 as something that is craved by us, toward which we move or grasp, which moves us without itself being moved. Separated as this immobile God is for him, and capable of no externally directed effect (ἄπρακτοσ τὰς ἔξω πράξεις), he can only perpetually think and only think himself: he is ἑαυτὸν νοῶν.40 So thorough is Aristotle's identification of the final telos with the *actus* that he really no longer separates the νοῦς from the νόησις (from actual thought) in God and no longer holds that he is the sheer potency of thought. For Aristotle, God is the pure incessant *actus* of thought (but of no thought without content). As it is difficult for him to say what he thinks (since it is inadmissible even for us humans to think of some things, [106] just as it is better for us not to see than to see some things (βέλτιον ἔνια μὴ ὁρᾶν), so then is it even more so with God. Consequently, he decides that God perpetually thinks only himself. This should only show that this *actus* is an *infinite actus*, that is, that onward into infinity there resides within him nothing that is foreign to him (no limiting object). For this reason he speaks of a νοήσεως νόησις, which is solely the content of God himself.viii [107]

The philosophy of Aristotle is a logical philosophy, but one that starts out from a presupposed existing being; to this extent, it begins with experience. Its beginning is experience and its end is pure thought: that which is logical in

---

viii. On the other hand, it is difficult to assume that according to Aristotle the blessedness of God consists in his perpetually philosophizing in Hegelian fashion. In the middle of the preceding century, after Lessing and Klopstock had revolted, the Germans rejoiced that they too now had their own literature. Soon more critics and poets joined together in assorted genres, and then historiography and philosophy also stepped forward in generally recognized works (for in the strict sense, the literature of a people encompasses above all poetry and the criticism of literature, historiography, and, finally, philosophy). Accordingly, under these circumstances the comparisons began and soon the Germans were no longer lacking a Homer, a Tyrtaeus, a Theocritus, a German Thucydides, or, finally, some number of Platos (for the public, the German Plato was first Herder, and then Jacobi). Where then was the German Pythagoras, the German Heraclitus—should the former be perhaps Leibniz, the later J. Böhme?. Where is the German Aristotle? No one had a greater right to be so named than Kant. All this notwithstanding, a later philosophy reserved the right to be regarded as Aristotelian. This philosophy spoke of a *cycle* of the divine life in which God unceasingly descends to the deepest and unconscious being; there he is indeed still the absolute, but yet only an imprisoned God, that is, a blind and deaf absolute. But God climbs forever

(*Continued on next page*)

the highest sense of the word. Its totality, however, is one prepared in the fires of the purest analysis, of a spirit extracted from all the elements of nature and the human mind.

It was the Neoplatonists who, belonging to the transition into a newer age and aroused either by the approaching or already present Christianity, sought to revive those sentiments of a positive philosophy found especially in Plato, but which had been suppressed by Aristotle. Aristotle could not tolerate a positive philosophy, which in Plato had been a mere anticipation and to which not even he had found a scientific transition. In the absence of a positive philosophy to reach a God that *really* exists, Aristotle's path would still be, even today, the only way to proceed from the empirical, from what iof teeth or clawss given in experience and insofar exists, to the logical, to the content of being. If we merely wished to content ourselves with the God concocted by Aristotle then we would also have to be capable of that Aristotelian renunciation, to remain with God *as terminus*, and not to want him again as a generative cause. Such a God, however, would not correspond to the demands of our consciousness, before which a world lies uncovered with which Aristotle had no acquaintance. I do not mean by this Christianity alone. For Aristotle also considered the mythological religions to have the mere significance of an incomplete phenomenon; he could see nothing original in mythology and nothing that would have been acceptable to his considerations or that could have qualified as a source of knowledge.[ix]

The question was long ago raised as to why King Charlemagne conceded or wished that the books of Aristotle—who one can only regard as an atheist [108]—be introduced and analyzed at length in the academies he founded. The answer becomes clear in what was just noted: Aristotle certainly knew no other God than one that could be used as a principle from which to explain the world. At most, his God could be the ideal creator *to* which—but not *through* which—everything has come to be. Moreover, providence in the Aristotelian system as well extends only to the extent that everything aims toward this end and nothing can happen that had not been determined by this final goal of the movement, and thus only to this extent determined by God as the final cause. In contrast, however, one says that the Platonic philosophy, which is by far more closely related to Christianity, is to be excluded from

---

(*Note viii continued*) downwards only in order to, in the same way, climb unceasingly upwards through ever higher levels until human consciousness is finally reached where he works off and sheds his subjectivity and becomes absolute spirit, that is, where he first properly becomes God. I confess that among all philosophers who have distinguished themselves, those who have maintained such a cycle of the divine life seem to me the most anti-Aristotelian. Similarly, I doubt that any rational person could see in such a teaching—which ended with this entirely peculiar combination of the logical with the actual—the last word of German philosophy, in the same sense as in Aristotle the climax of classical philosophy was achieved. (Compare to this the discussion of Aristotle's theology in *Introduction to the Philosophy of Mythology*, I/5, p. 559n1.—ED.

ix. Cf. *Introduction to the Philosophy of Mythology*, I/5, p. 256.—ED.

History of Negative and Positive Philosophy 165

consideration. An author of the seventeenth century offers to this question a naive answer: the theologians are quite right when they have had something to object to or to rebuke in philosophy, since if the philosophers were to succeed in cobbling together complete agreement between the teachings of Christianity and philosophy, some could, through the temptation of the devil, hit upon the idea that Christianity itself is nothing other than a human invention, a work either of the thinking or slyly ingenious faculty of reason. In fact, however, it was nothing less than a pure Aristotelian philosophy that was taught in the Christian schools. The Christian theology, and thus also the Christian schools, required a God with which they could begin something, that allows God to be conceived as the founder of the world, and particularly of revelation. Just as the negative philosophy was incapable of incorporating Christianity—at least incapable without altering itself completely—the pure Aristotelian philosophy itself was also incapable of surviving in the Christian schools. Its place, therefore, was taken over by scholastic metaphysics, which has already been characterized insofar as it has been called a rational dogmatism or positive rationalism.

One already sees in the manner how this philosophy *began* in a rational way to arrive at a positive result, that is, to an existing God. (The essential vehicle for this was, as we saw earlier, the syllogism, the inference, that analyzed on the one hand what is given in experience, and on the other, the κοιναὶ ἔννοιαι, [109] the universals, with both presenting themselves as necessary concepts and principles.) Moreover, one sees that rationalism enjoyed only a formal function in this philosophy in the manner in which it sought to infer the *existence* of God from the thorough analysis of experience and the innate concepts of the understanding. The material that these inferences would analyze was taken, on the one hand, from experience, for example, from the purposive arrangement of nature in detail and in general, and so on, and, on the other, from the rational component of these inferences of metaphysics, which constituted the general principles—for example, cause and effect, and, particularly, that cause and effect must be proportional or that a purposive whole presupposes an intelligent cause—whose application to experience should then make possible an inference to that which is *beyond* experience. As a consequence of combining these elements, neither the rationalist nor the empiricist component in this metaphysics could come to the fore, pure and free. This artificial composition qua artificial could not endure; fundamentally, only the power of the church held it together for *so long*. After the Reformation and its consequences, this brand of metaphysics could no longer sustain itself and so there arose that movement in philosophy, which inevitably brought about the earlier described breakdown of dogmatic rationalism. Out of this breakdown there could only emerge on the one hand a *pure* rationalism and on the other a *pure* empiricism.

For the moment, let us still consider in general terms empiricism's relationship to pure rationalism. Pure rationalism, correctly understood, can crave nothing other than at its end to correspond with reality as it is given in experience. Conversely, even the most limited empiricism can admit no other goal for its endeavors than this: to find *reason* in every individual phenomenon as well as in the interrelatedness of all phenomena—to disclose and bring forth into the light of day the reason presupposed in individual as well as in the entirety of phenomena. An empiricism [110] that would renounce this goal would have to confess itself as irrational. Empiricism is, therefore, not to be directly opposed to a correctly understood rationalism (that is, how it has been cultivated since Kant), as it is, more properly speaking, a phenomenon parallel to rationalism. This empiricism has an entirely *different* relationship to the dogmatizing rationalism of the earlier metaphysics, an entirely different relationship to the pure rationalism that emerged out of the breakdown of that dogmatizing rationalism that, until now, has been our German philosophy. If one follows this empiricism—to which for quite some time all of Europe, with the exception of Germany, had surrendered to as the only true method in philosophy—if one goes back to its beginning and its source (in Francis Bacon)[x] and, following this other side, traces its path and sees to what extent, for what purpose, and how it developed, then one must become convinced that something else lies at the heart of this work, other than what appears at first glance as nothing less than a mere *aggregate* of facts. Whoever considers the zeal with which the announcement of *brute* facts is made in the natural sciences has to recognize in it something higher, if even only active on an instinctual level, a thought that stands in the background, a drive that goes beyond the immediate goal. For how else should one account for the importance placed on facts, even those that in themselves are the most trivial, particularly in natural history, for example, the number and form of teeth or claws—or how else should one account for the religious conscientiousness with which empiricism undertakes these investigations, the perseverance with which it pursues under hardships, privations of all types and often even in life threatening situations—how else should one account for this than through an indistinct awareness that in all these facts it is a question of something still more than the data itself? How should one account for this enthusiasm of the true natural scientist without recourse to an indistinct feeling that says to him that this empiricism, extended to its final boundaries [111] and gradually purged through its own actions of banal hypotheses, must finally converge with a higher system that, united with it, will form an unshakable totality, that will present itself as the fully equal result of both experience and of pure thought? How should one account for this without the still so distant presentiment that this empiricism will ultimately reveal in nature that which dwells within it, as that reason, as that system of an innate logic, to take possession of which in thought is the

---

[x]. It is in any case notable that this general zeal for empirical research or experience had at first been effected through a change in philosophy, and thus originated in philosophy itself.

History of Negative and Positive Philosophy

highest task of rational philosophy? That there is a point at which all the potencies of human knowledge, where thought and experience, which at first sight and even now still appear to lie or be so far removed from each other, will completely permeate each other and together form one insurmountable totality? This was unquestionably the final thought of Bacon, whom the thoughtless, workman-like empiricists freely invoke as their commander. Until now of course, the true philosophers of France and England have been their great natural scientists.[xi] Nevertheless, if the French and English natural scientists or philosophers learned to understand this position of German philosophy toward empiricism, they would learn that it is indeed empiricism, but an a priori empiricism. Once they have comprehended the meaning and understanding of German rationalism they will no longer demand that we allow empirical—approximately psychological—facts to precede this one true ontology, the science of necessary thought, which begins with itself, advances into itself, and yet simultaneously realizes itself immediately in experience. And would that they [112] ponder, in contrast, how through restricting their philosophical empiricism to the observation and analysis of psychological facts, they exclude themselves from that great circle of true empiricism that rules out *nothing* that is in nature or present in the great history of the human race and its development—how they cut themselves off from this magnificent empiricism that excludes nothing, which encompasses all of nature, as well as the great facts of history, and with which to coalesce and, in the end, actually become one with, is the true aspiration of a pure rationalism.

If this is the position of philosophical empiricism toward pure rationalism then we must now speak of a previously intimated second relationship, namely of the question how the positive philosophy, posited by us in opposition to rationalism, relates to philosophical empiricism. For in fact, if pure rationalism is an a priori philosophy, there seems nothing else left for *positive philosophy* to be but empiricism. Yet as I have already shown, since pure rationalism does not exclude empiricism, the positive philosophy can hardly be just empiricism in the sense as it is most often conceived and, consequently, the discussion would not at all be about something a priori. Yet some type of relationship must nonetheless occur between positive philosophy and empiricism. It is not my intention to deny this. On the contrary, I would like to point out that the concept connected to the word empiricism in the standard explanation is much too limited. When the talk is of philosophy, one customarily understands by 'experience' only the certainty that we obtain through our

---

xi. That in England philosophy (though usually not without the composite *Natural-Philosophy*) for a well-known reason means physics (because in English physician means a doctor, as in German forensic specialists are called *physci*) does not need to be proved by the titles of the most recent journals of chemistry or newspaper advertisement for hair tonic. More to the point would be to refer to the most famous periodical of England, the two-hundred-year-old Philosophical Transactions, in whose numerous volumes one would search in vain for something similar to what we in Germany call philosophy.

external senses of external objects, of the existence of an external world altogether, or the certainty that we obtain through the so-called *inner* sense of the emotions and the changes that take place within ourselves (a sense that still very much needs a critique). Here it is assumed that *everything* commensurate with experience can only be detected in the outer or inner realms of sense. [113] If empiricism becomes thoroughly exclusive, then it denies the reality of the universal and necessary concepts; it can go as far as to view even legal and ethical concepts as things that have become a part of our nature through sheer habit and upbringing—a view that is indeed the lowest level of narrow mindedness to which it can sink. But it is incorrect to view all this as necessarily connected with the concept of empiricism as Hegel does in his *Encyclopedia of the Philosophical Sciences*,[xii] when he declares as a necessary consequence of empiricism that legal and ethical determinations as well as laws must appear as something contingent whose objectivity is given up on.

It is incorrect to reduce empiricism in general to *mere sensation* as if it had only this as its object, since an intelligence of free will and action, of which each and every one of us is, does not *as such* fall under the purview of the senses and yet this is something empirical and indeed something that can *only* be known empirically. For no one knows what exists within a person until that person expresses himself. His intellectual and moral character exists only a posteriori, which is to say that it is discernible only through his statements and actions. Now suppose that the discussion was about an intelligence in the world, assumed to have a free will for action—this intelligence would likewise not be knowable a priori, but only through its deeds that occur in experience. Although a supersensible being, it will nonetheless be something that can only be known commensurate with experience. Empiricism as such, therefore, hardly excludes all knowledge of the supersensible, as one customarily assumes, and even Hegel presupposes.

One must distinguish between that which is the object of *actual* experience and that which according to its *nature* is commensurate with experience. Within nature itself there is much that has never been the object of an actual experience and yet for this reason does not at all lie outside the sphere of possible sensible experience. For beyond this sphere does everything commensurate with experience, as one imagines, cease all at once? Suppose [114] it does cease; one would nevertheless not assume that *everything* ceases, that on the other side of this boundary all movement ceases. For with movement science itself would also cease, since science is essentially movement. But, one says, the movement presupposed to occur on that other side can still be merely a movement discernible in *pure* thought, which means (if one is consequent) a movement from which every free action is excluded. For a free action is something more than what allows itself to be discerned in mere *thought*.

---

xii. Second edition, p. 213. [*Encyklopädie der philosophischen Wissenschaften im Grundrisse*, 2nd ed. (Heidelberg, 1827).]

Opposed to this view however, stands everything that is an actual *happening* [*Geschehen*], that is resolve [*Entschluß*] and action, and that extends beyond the sensible world. This is easy to realize: only resolve and action can *ground* an actual experience. If in geometry experience has no place this is precisely because in this case everything can be accomplished through pure thought, because in this case there is no *happening* to be presupposed. Conversely, everything that is not to be secured through pure thought, that is, where I admit *experience*, must be something that is grounded in free action. The opinion that what is the cause of everything commensurate to experience could itself no longer be of the same type but could only be something abstract, simply to be posited in pure thought, was the principle motive [behind the concept of] God, as far as he is thought of as the last cause of all empirical being and as far as it is possible to think of everything empirical, for example, of everything human.

Thus, there is also a metaphysical empiricism as we would like to name it for the time being; for this reason there are still other systems to be subsumed under the *general* concept of philosophical empiricism, systems other than the sensualist that limits all knowledge to sensory perception or even denies the existence of everything supersensible. The different doctrines of *this* type must now be subjected to an even more extensive exposition than the types that, regarding their goal, agree with the positive philosophy that seeks to take cognizance of precisely that which in (actual) experience cannot occur, and thus must be that which is beyond experience. [115]

Metaphysical Empiricism

The lowest level of empiricism is one in which all knowledge is limited to experience through the senses, in which everything supersensible is either denied as such or as a possible object of knowledge. If one accepts philosophical empiricism in this sense, then it does not even share positive philosophy's opposition to rationalism. For positive philosophy merely denies that the supersensible is knowable *only* in a rational manner, whereas empiricism maintains that it is not knowable in this or any other way, and that ultimately it does not even exist.

A higher level of philosophical empiricism, however, is one that maintains that the supersensible can become an actual object of experience, whereby it goes without saying that this experience cannot be of the merely sensuous type but must have something about it that is inherently mysterious, mystical, and for which reason we can call the doctrines of this type doctrines of a *mystical empiricism*. To be found among these doctrines, again at the lowest level, is that doctrine that allows us to become certain of the existence of the supersensible only through a divine revelation, which is conceived thereby as an *external* datum. The next higher level is a philosophy that goes beyond all external facts but nevertheless relies on the inner fact of an irresistible *feeling* to convince us of the existence of God while holding that reason inevitably [116] leads to atheism, fatalism, and, thus, to a blind system of necessity. As is well known, this was the earlier teaching of Jacobi, which was widely attacked because of this type of mysticism. He later sought to make peace with rationalism, and in a very unique way indeed, in that he installed reason in the place of the earlier feeling (itself provided merely for the individual) and then proposed something quite peculiar: that reason in itself—in a substantive manner, devoid of all *actus* and, thus, even before all science—is that which posits and knows God. This was a position he believed to be able to prove through a very popular argument—in a formal syllogism—which reads: "Only man knows of God, the animal does not know of God. The only characteristic that distinguishes man from animal is reason. Thus, it is reason that immediately reveals God, or it is that faculty with whose mere presence a knowledge of God is posited within us." —The proposition that reason possesses an immediate knowledge of God, and thus a knowledge of God that is not *mediated* through science, or that reason *by its very nature* posits God—this proposition found such approval from those who would gladly dismiss all science that it is more than worth the trouble to submit to a closer critique the manner in which Jacobi sought to prove, through the aforementioned syllogism, this immediate positing of God by reason.

We would like to clarify first only the major premise of this argument: "Only man knows of God, the animal does not know of God." Germans have an old proverb: "What I do not know does not affect me, that is, it moves me neither for nor against it, neither to affirm nor to deny it." Now, if in the first clause of the major premise ("Only the human knows of God") there is such an *indifferent* knowledge, a knowledge that is still neither affirmative nor negative, but permits both responses—if this is the type of knowledge implied by the major premise, then according to the rule that there should be no more in the conclusion than there is in the premise, in the conclusion, reason cannot be that which reveals God, that is, reason cannot, as the intent of the inference suggests, be that which *affirms* God. To [117] avoid this, the major premise ("Only the human...") would have to imply an affirmative knowledge. Yet if one assumes this, then the word knowledge in the major premise is used in two different senses; for "the human knows of God" means the human affirms God, and "the animal does not know of God" means the animal neither affirms nor denies God. This equivocation is again a formal error. Moreover, the first clause of the major premise would then be false. For the knowledge or the affirmation of God should be a generic character of humans, just as reason is. But this generality contradicts Jacobi's own assertion that all philosophy leads to atheism, according to which there are only those who accidentally affirm God, whereas necessarily—as a result of science—there are only deniers of God. To be materially true, the major premise would then have to read: "Only man either affirms or denies God, the animal neither affirms nor denies God." Consequently, the conclusion could then only read: "That which distinguishes man from animal (reason) is that which puts him in the position, gives him the possibility, to either affirm or deny God." Reason, however, gives man this possibility regarding *every other* object as well; formally considered reason is nothing other than the *facultas, quidlibet de qualibet re siva affirmandi sive negandi* [faculty of affirming or denying anything about anything]. Thus, nothing can follow from this that would prove a *special* God-positing power of reason.

The minor premise of the syllogism, to examine this as well, reads: "The only characteristic that distinguishes man from animal is reason." This proposition is obviously taken from the common use of language or way of speaking, where, under reason, one understands the complex of all the intellectual attributes of man. The discussion in this context is not about reason in specie, as it is in the conclusion, where Jacobi clearly means reason, but is rather about reason in contrast to the understanding. Jacobi seeks to support this proposition as well through the simple appeal to the common use of language when he says: "One has never spoken of an [118] animal's reason, yet we know and name an animal's understanding." Even in an age that truly suffered from no less an evil than an abundance of understanding, one had no cause to bestow it so generously upon animals as well. What is more, since Jacobi only appeals to *what is said*, and not—and this concerns a fact—to what everyone can judge according to his own experience, I would only like to point out, for example, that I have often heard of a rational horse in contrast to an irrational one that puzzles over every trifle and gallops always to the side; furthermore, one also speaks of a madness or of an insanity that is ascribed to animals, for example, to the horse that comes down with the staggers, from which it follows that one calls animals in healthy condition rational. One must respond to such insipid assertions not with profound discourse but with the simple facts as taught by the common use of language. Now, regarding the philosophical meaning, I have heard that one has termed the instinct of animals an analogue of *reason* but not that instinct is an analogue of the understanding. In addition, I have heard that one has explained an animal's instinct for learning as a type of reason active within them—a reason, however, that *they* do not possess, but from which they are possessed as by a foreign spirit. Furthermore, I understand very well how one can see reason in instinctive behavior, since reason is something essential and potential, something universal and impersonal, just as instinct in animals is also something that is not individual, but something universal and identical in all members of a species. How one can thus see reason in the actions of instinct, I can comprehend, at the very least, analogically. Yet in no way can I comprehend how one can see *understanding* in such actions, since understanding is always something actual, personal, something that belongs to that individual just as, in order not to be insulting, I must grant *every* person reason but not understanding as well. Besides, it is odd to hear *someone* appealing to the use of language—and indeed specifically regarding expressions such as *reason* and *understanding*—who in reference to these words has shown either such [119] superficial knowledge or such meager respect for linguistic usage that what he termed understanding in the *1780s* he began to call reason after *1800*, and vice versa, so that within twenty years both terms had completely exchanged roles. What he had earlier blamed on reason he later burdened the understanding with, and for what he had earlier praised the understanding he later attributed exclusively to reason.

In a third type of empiricism, the supersensible is made into an object of actual experience *through which* a possible ecstasy of the human essence in God is assumed, the consequence of which is a necessary, infallible vision not merely into the divine essence, but into the essence of creation and every phase of that process as well. This type of empiricism is theosophy, which is predominately a speculative or theoretical mysticism. I reserve the right to speak extensively about this type of empiricism. For the time being, it should be noted that doctrines and systems that were *all* in opposition to the dogmatizing rationalism of the earlier metaphysics will now become apparent, so that the latter never exclusively prevailed but always had these systems alongside it, systems that I have already designated with the common name as doctrines of a mystical empiricism. For the origin of revelation, as well as of an individual and inexplicable feeling, has something mystical about it. This system formed, at the very least, a powerful *opposition* to rationalism—a system that at no time, and even now, has ever *really* been overcome. This could only have happened if a true philosophy had been put in opposition to it. For the demand [*Forderung*] that announces itself in these systems cannot be dismissed by simply treating them as unscientific. They are of course unscientific, but with this [concession], the demand that lies at the core of such systems is not fulfilled. In any case, the continued existence of such mystical teachings (that throughout the entire Middle Ages ran parallel to the scholastic philosophy, approved in the schools and ordained by the church, that held its ground until the era of [120] the Reformation, after which it again arose and found its zenith in Jacob Böhme) testifies to the fact that until now philosophy has not been able to achieve in a scientific and *universally* enlightening manner, convincing of reason itself, what these teachings in an openly unscientific manner sought to achieve or feigned to achieve (in the case of theosophy, most often in an incomprehensible manner and not without falling to some degree back into mythology). For precisely this reason that they themselves have not satisfied, these teachings themselves *contain* the demand for a positive philosophy. These teachings are those which in recent times have represented the position of this second philosophy (δευτέρα φιλοσοφία), and they testify to the fact, to return to my initial assertion, that until now these two strains of philosophy have at least, according to their demand or their *potentia*, always been present alongside each other.

It is, thus, all the more necessary to provide at least a provisional idea of how this positive philosophy we advance relates to these mystical teachings. For surely it cannot be identical with any of them since it claims to be a philosophy, and, thus, a science, whereas the others, if they have not dispensed with all speculative content, have nevertheless done so with all scientific form and method. A detailed discussion about the relation of positive philosophy to revelation will emerge of itself as a result of this development, but we will no longer return to theosophy. Accordingly, I would like to provide now my explanation of the relationship of positive philosophy to *theosophy*, although, in what follows, the development of the method of the positive philosophy will itself show that it can have just as little in common with theosophy as it can with the rational systems. The positive philosophy is a new creation that can be particularly troublesome to claims of having consummated philosophy. Under such conditions, it is the normal custom to look around in the history of literature for some title or some notorious category, under which one can subsume [121] the new phenomenon, thereby hoping to lift oneself above all the trouble of a rebuttal.

However, have I myself not provided the impetus to bring positive philosophy into contact with theosophy? It was indeed claimed that the former seeks the same thing for which the later strives; the difference is only that the former seeks to arrive at its goal in a scientific manner, the later in an unscientific and nonmethodical fashion. This is how the relationship has been determined. Yet by the same right, any ignorant person could then belittle the science of astronomy since it has replaced astrology or the science of chemistry since it has replaced alchemy. What lies at the heart of theosophy, wherever it achieves, at the very least, a substantive scientific or speculative significance—which in particular lies at the heart of Jacob Böhme's theosophy—is the inherently laudable aspiration to comprehend the emergence of things from God as an *actual* chain of events. Jacob Böhme however, does not know of any other way to bring this about than by involving the deity itself in a type of natural process. The characteristic feature of the positive philosophy, however, consists precisely in that it rejects all processes in *this sense*, namely in which God would not only be the logical but also the actual result of a process. To this extent, the positive philosophy is more properly speaking in direct opposition with each and every theosophical aspiration. —Hegel looks down at Böhme and in the preface to the second edition of his *Encyclopedia of the Philosophical Science* he speaks out against the renowned Franz Baader, who had imputed or accused the Hegelian philosophy of allowing matter to emerge immediately from God, so that this eternal issuing forth of God becomes the condition of matter's eternal retrieval, or return to itself, as spirit. Against this accusation, Hegel speaks out quite nobly: the emergence of things from God is not one of his categories—*he* makes no use of it since it is not a category at all but only a figurative expression. On the other hand, however, Hegel has the astounding [122] category of the release [*Entlassens*]. Yet is this release not a figurative expression? What this release itself is about is not explained. From the side of God, however, this release must nonetheless necessarily correspond to an issuing forth of that which is discharged (of that which God discharges from himself); thus, it must also correspond to an issuing forth of nature and to an issuing forth of matter out of God, just as, according to Hegel in his *Logic*, when God is still *enclosed* in his eternity, exactly the same matter must have issued forth out of his eternity into actual, extralogical nature.

In his *Philosophy of Religion*, Hegel speaks about the Trinity and specifically about the son as follows: "He is indeed the son, hence different from the father, but he may not remain the son; since as the son the distinction obtains, but as eternal it is again sublated; it is more or less only a game of love with itself [to be sure uncommonly edifying], it does not in this way come to be a serious matter of a different being [*Andersseyns*]."[xiii] So that it does become a serious matter it is necessary that the son contain the determination of a different being as a different being, that he must appear as an actual being *external* to God (but

---

xiii. *Hegel's Works*, vol. 12, 2nd ed. (Berlin, 1840), 248.

of course something that has proceeded out of God) and *lacking* God, that is, as the world. According to all philosophical concepts, it is here that the son is explicitly made into the matter of the world; for through this, that he is not merely a different being, but that he is also posited as a different being, will he become the world. Consequently, as long as he is still the son, as in the stated distinction, the son comports himself as the possibility, as the matter of the world to come. All this is just as theosophical as anything in J. Böhme could be, but with one difference: such fantastic ideas in Böhme are something original and are actually born of a magnificent intuition, whereas with Hegel it is tied into a philosophy whose indubitable character consists of being of the purest prose and a sobriety totally devoid of intuition. One forgives the individual who staggers when he is actually drunk with intuition, but not one who by nature is actually sober and only wishes to appear as if he too is staggering. [123]

One cannot help but say that J. Böhme is a miraculous appearance in the history of humankind, and particularly in the history of the German spirit. If one could ever forget what treasure lies in the natural depths of the heart and spirit of the German nation, then one would only need to remember this man, who in his own way is just as far above the explanations of popular psychology that one attempts of him, as it is impossible to explain mythology with popular psychology. Just as the mythologies and theogonies of the races preceded science, so too does J. Böhme with the birth of God as described by him precede all the scientific systems of recent philosophy. J. Böhme was born in 1575, Rene Descartes in 1596. In Spinoza, who passed away nearly one hundred years after J. Böhme's birth, that which in Böhme was intuition and like an immediate inspiration of nature appeared as a cultivated rationalism, but not without having driven completely out of the philosophy the great intuitions of nature that existed in J. Böhme's writings. For there was nothing in the physics of Spinoza that distinguished it from the utterly mechanical and soulless physics of Descartes. J. Böhme is truly of a theogonic nature, but precisely this prevented him from elevating himself to a *free* creation of the world, and thus to the freedom of a positive philosophy. As is well known, J. Böhme spoke often of a wheel of nature or of birth, one of his most profound apperceptions through which he expressed the dualism of forces in nature that, struggling with itself, wants to give birth but cannot. Yet he himself, however, is precisely this wheel, he himself is this nature that wants to give birth to this *science* but cannot. The rotation of his spirit arises from his futile attempt to escape from that substantial force in whose power he is, and to escape to a free science. If that substantial principle, which has gone through the whole of nature and experienced its entire process, again raises itself under the conditions of current human existence to know *directly*—that is, to replicate within itself that process from which it was once cut off (precisely this was the case for Böhme)— [124] if again it raises itself to know directly, without the help of a higher activity, namely, of the analytic understanding—to be, so to speak, directly begotten by that process—if this happens, then that principle can appear, as it were, only as a staggering and unconscious nature that is powerless over itself. The rotation of his spirit becomes outwardly apparent as well through the fact that in every one of his writings J. Böhme always starts at the beginning, repeatedly explicating the amply explained beginnings without ever going on any farther or ever even leaving that position. In these beginnings he is always astounding, a true drama of one whose nature is to wrestle with oneself, yearning for freedom and serenity, but who is incapable of ever changing over into real motion, instead circling around the very same point. As soon as J. Böhme goes beyond the beginning and into concrete reality one can no longer follow him; here every trace disappears, and even if one successively employs the concepts of Kant, Fichte, natural philosophy, or even Hegel, it will always remain a futile effort to transcribe the muddled concepts of his intuitions into any type of clarity.

We have advanced theosophy primarily as the antithesis of rational philosophy, and, thus, of rationalism in philosophy. Yet at bottom, theosophy *strives* to move beyond rationalism without, however, being capable of actually wresting away rationalism's substantial knowledge. The knowledge in which rationalism has its essence is to be called *substantial* [*substantiell*] to the extent that it excludes all *actus*. Rationalism can generate nothing through an action, that is, through a free creation; it is familiar only with pure *essential* relations. Everything merely follows from it *modo aeterno*, eternally, which means in a merely logical manner, through immanent movement. For it is only a falsified rationalism that explains the genesis of the world through a free divestment [*Entäusserung*] of the absolute spirit that as such wants to maintain a violent creation. For precisely this reason the false rationalism approximates theosophy, and is thus no less captive than theosophy to a merely substantial knowledge; theosophy [125] wants of course to overcome such a knowledge, but it does not succeed, as is seen most clearly with Böhme. No doubt, there has never been another spirit that has withstood the heat of this sheer substantial knowledge as well as J. Böhme; obviously for him God is the *immediate* substance of the world and he *wants* a free creation and a God that relates freely to the world, but cannot produce them. Although he calls it theosophy, thus making the claim to be the science of the divine, the content to which theosophy attains remains only a substantial movement, and he presents God only in a substantial movement. In its essence, theosophy is no less unhistorical than rationalism. The God of a truly historical and positive philosophy however does not *move*, he *acts*. The substantial movement in which rationalism is confused starts out from a negative *prius*, for example, starts out from something nonexistent [*einem nichtseyenden*] that must first move itself into being [*Seyn*]; but the historical philosophy starts out from something positive, that is, from an existing *prius* that does not first have to move itself into being. This *prius* thus posits only with *complete* freedom without being somehow required by its nature to posit a being. He does not directly posit his own being, but instead posits a being that is distinct from *his*, in which his being is more accurately negated or suspended rather than posited, hence his being is only indirectly posited in this being that is distinct from his. It is fitting for God to be indifferent toward his own being, but it is not fitting for God to trouble himself with his own being, to provide himself with a being, to beget himself within a being that—as J. Böhme expresses it—as the content of the highest science, for example, of theosophy, pronounces the birth of the divine essence, the divine birth, and, hence, a *real* theogony. Consequently, it would be justified if we explained the phenomenon of theosophy (for in any case it is a phenomenon, particularly with J. Böhme) as a regression into the process that preceded science, as the attempt to revert to a prescientific, theogonic process. That the positive philosophy cannot be theosophy is due to the fact that it is determined as a philosophy and as a science; [126] in that theosophy does not call itself *philosophy* and renounces science, it wants to speak from immediate intuition.

The question now, however, is in which way the science we have proposed—the positive philosophy—is a philosophy and in which way it will become a science.

If among the categories that stand at our behest for the designation of philosophical doctrines, empiricism can be opposed to nothing other than rationalism, then positive philosophy, as the antithesis of rationalism, will nevertheless be incapable of denying that it is also in some way and in some sense empiricism as well. The question thus returns to what type of relation the positive philosophy will have to experience: the same as that of a mystical doctrine, or an entirely different relation? What is common to all of these mystical doctrines is that they *start out* from experience—from something that occurs in *experience*. *What* this experience is is entirely irrelevant, for example, whether it starts out from the appearance or the miracles of Christ (as in an earlier time, when there was such a mindless historical theology, which avoided every contact with philosophy to the extent that it believed it could eliminate all philosophical arguments for the existence of God and could best prove the existence of God through the miracles of Christ), whether it proceeds from the presence of an exuberant feeling in us that is only to be satisfied through an existing God, or whether it proceeds from an immediate intuition of the divine—each of these always starts out from something given in immediate or mediated experience. I would now like only to briefly state—for it extends as far as a preliminary distinction, and we are concerned only with a preliminary distinction—that the positive philosophy starts out just as little from something that occurs merely in thought (for then it would fall back into the negative philosophy) as it starts out from some being that is present in *experience*. If it does not start out from something that occurs in thought [*im Denken Seyende*], and, thus, in no way from pure thought, then it will start out from that which is before and external to all thought, consequently from being [*Seyn*], but not from an [127] empirical being. For we have already excluded this, in that empirical being is external to thought only in the very relative sense, to the extent that *every* being that occurs in experience inherently carries with it the logical determinations of the understanding, without which it could never even be represented. If positive philosophy starts out from that which is external to all thought, it cannot begin with a being that is external to thought in a merely relative sense, but only with a being that is *absolutely* external to thought. The being that is external to all thought, however, is just as much beyond all experience as it is before all thought: positive philosophy begins with the *completely transcendent being* [*Seyn*] and it can no longer be just a relative *prius* like the potency that serves as the basis of the science of reason. For precisely as potency—as *nonbeing*—it has the necessity to pass over into being, and, thus, I call it the merely relative *prius*. If that being from which positive philosophy proceeds were also merely relative, then the *necessity* of passing over into being would inhere within its principle. Thus, through this principle, that being would be subordinated to the thought of a necessary movement and, consequently, the positive philosophy would fall back into the negative. If, therefore, the relative *prius* cannot be the beginning of the positive philosophy, then it must be the absolute *prius*, which has no necessity to move itself into being. If it passes over into being, then this can only be the consequence of a free act, of an act that can only be something purely empirical, that can be fully apprehended only a posteriori, just as every act is incapable of being comprehended a priori and is only capable of being known a posteriori.

The positive philosophy is not empiricism, at least insofar as it does not start out from experience—neither in the sense that it presumes to posses its object in an immediate experience (as in mysticism), nor in the sense that it attempts to attain to its object through inferences drawn from something given in experience, such as an empirical fact (for I must still exclude even this to distinguish positive philosophy from [128] rational dogmatism that, in its proof for the existence of God, makes partial use of empirical facts, such as the purposive arrangement of nature). But if positive philosophy does not *start out* from experience, then nothing prevents it from going toward experience, and thereby proving a posteriori what it has to prove, that its *prius* is God, that is, that which is above being [*das überseyende*]. For what it begins with is a priori—but a priori it is not God, only a posteriori is it God. That it is God is not a *res naturae*, something that is self-evident, but is a *res facti*, and can therefore only be proved factually. It is God. This proposition does not mean the concept of this *prius* is equal to the concept of God. It means that this *prius is* God, not according to its concept, but according to its reality. Of course, if positive philosophy does not start out from experience, then it must be an a priori science. To this extent it is thus again no different from the negative philosophy, for what we have ascribed to the positive philosophy also holds for the negative, namely, that it does not start out from experience but goes *toward* experience. They do indeed relate in this way, but the difference is this: positive and negative philosophy each has a position toward experience, but each is different. For the latter experience confirms but does not *prove* [*erweisend*]. Rational philosophy has its truth in the immanent necessity of its progress; as we said earlier, it is so independent of existence that it would be true even if nothing existed. If that which actually occurs in experience agrees with its constructions then this is something gratifying, something to which the construction indeed refers, but with which it does not really *prove* anything.[xiv] The position of positive philosophy is entirely different. It enters into experience itself and grows, as it were, together with it. It too is an a priori science, but the *prius* from which it proceeds is not simply *before* all experience, so that it must *necessarily* move [129] forward into experience, but rather it is *above* all experience, and thus there is no *necessary* transition into experience for this *prius*. From this *prius*, positive philosophy derives in a free thought and in an evidentiary sequence that which is a posteriori or that which occurs in experience, not as what is possible, as in the negative philosophy, but as what is real. It derives it as what is real, for only as such does it have the meaning and the force of proof. So that I make myself completely clear: not the absolute *prius itself* will be proved (this is above all proof, since it is the absolute and through itself indubitable beginning), thus, not it itself (the absolute *prius*) will be proved, but rather what the consequences are that follow from this, these must be *factually* proved, and only thereby do we prove the divinity of that *prius*—that it is God, and that *God* therefore exists. Consequently, we will say that the *prius*, whose *concept* is such and such (that of what is above being), will *be capable* of having *such* a consequence (we will not say that it will necessarily *have* such a consequence, for then we would fall back again into necessity, that is, *fall back into a movement* determined solely by concepts. We should rather only say it can have such a consequence *if it wishes*, since the consequence is contingent on its will). This consequence, however, really exists (*this* proposition is one founded now in experience: the existence of such a consequence is a datum, a fact of experience). This datum, thus, shows us—the *existence* of such a consequence shows us—that the *prius* itself also *exists in the way* we have *conceived* it, that is, that God exists. You see that in this manner of argumentation the *prius* is always the point of departure, that is, it always remains the *prius*. The *prius* will be known from its consequences, but not in a way such that the consequences had *preceded* it. The preposition 'a' in 'a posteriori' does not in this instance signify the *terminus a quo*; in this context 'a posteriori' means '*per posterius*': through its consequence the *prius* is known. To be known a priori means just this: to be known from and out of the *prius*; what is known a priori is, thus, that which a *prius* possesses and from which it is known. The absolute *prius*, however, is what has no *prius* from which it can be known. To be the absolute *prius* means, therefore, not to be known a priori. [130] Here, in the positive philosophy, lies the real empiricism insofar as that which occurs in experience itself becomes an element of and an assistant to philosophy.

---

xiv. Compare this to Schelling's remarks on page 60*ff*. above, and remarks made in the *Introduction to the Philosophy of Mythology*, I/5, 376.—ED.

To express this distinction in the sharpest and most concise manner: the negative philosophy is *a priori empiricism*, it is the *Apriori* [*Apriorismus*] of what is empirical, but, for this very reason, it is not itself empirical. Conversely, the positive philosophy is an empirical *Apriori*, or it is the empiricism of what is a priori insofar as it proves that the *prius per posterius* exists as God.

From the perspective of the world, positive philosophy is an a priori science, which is nonetheless derived from the absolute *prius*; from the perspective of *God*, it is a posteriori science and knowledge.[xv]

The experience towards which positive philosophy proceeds[xvi] is not just of a *particular kind*, but is the entirety of all experience from beginning to end. What contributes to the proof is not a part of experience, but all [131] of experience. For precisely this reason, though, this proof *itself* is not just the beginning or a part of a science (least of all some type of syllogistic proof posited at the apex of philosophy), it is the entire science, that is, the entire positive philosophy—and this is nothing other than the progressive, strengthening with every step, and continually growing proof of the actually existing God. Because the realm of reality in which this proof moves is not finished and complete—for even if nature is now at its end and stands still, there is, nonetheless, still the unrelenting advance and movement of history—because insofar as the realm of reality is not complete, but is a realm perpetually nearing its consummation, the proof is therefore also *never* finished, and for this very reason this science is only a *Philo-sophie*. For the science of reason is *philosophy* to the extent it seeks and possesses only at its terminus that which is the object of the most supreme knowing (that is, the σοφία) and possesses this only at the end of its path in a *concept*. The *other* side, which has the task of reaching this not merely as an object found or remaining to be known or cognized, but as an object actually known and cognized, the positive side is *philosophy* since it achieves its goal only when the proof is provided not in its individual components, but rather only in its continual development. Here, by the way, lies the

---

xv. One usually understands by a posteriori knowledge that type in which one, for example, infers backwards from the effect to the cause. The order of the proof here is the reverse of the actual matter, for the effect is as such only the conclusion, only the result; the cause, however, precedes it, it is the antecedent. In such an inference, what is the consequence according to its nature becomes something artificial in order to benefit the proof, and is, thus, accepted as what is logically antecedent (and for precisely this reason the proof means an a posteriori proof, that is, a proof in which what is actually the *posterior* is made into the logical *prius*, into the point of departure). Conversely, that which is the antecedent according to its nature—the cause—here in the proof becomes a logical conclusion, a consequence. In the positive philosophy, however, this is not an a posteriori proof in the usual sense of the word, for we progress not from the effect to the cause, but, conversely, from the cause to the effect; the cause, which according to its *nature* is that which precedes, is in this way here also the *prius* of the proof. It follows from this (natural) arrangement of cause and effect that here, while the *causa* (God) a posteriori or *per posterius* is proved or demonstrated, the conclusion (the world) is deduced or comprehended a priori.

xvi. In earlier lectures of the author, the positive philosophy was also designated as a progressive Empiricism, since it was not regressive, that is, it did not proceed backwards from experience toward that which is above experience.—ED.

central difference between philosophy and mathematics, in particular, geometry, which is a pure science of reason as well. For even the negative philosophy distinguishes itself from geometry, in that with every proposition it reaches or posits, the postulate of a consequence is simultaneously provided, and, thus, the reality of everything that has previously been posited can only be tentatively pronounced, since it is based on a consequence: the first potency holds only insofar as the second potency follows it; this, only insofar as the third follows it—whereas the first book, even the first, second, and third propositions of Euclid could stand on their own and would remain true even if the human understanding had never come across them. In particular, however, the object of the positive philosophy is the object of a proof that is, while of course sufficient at earlier levels, [132] nonetheless still incomplete; there could always arise in a resulting stage a contradiction of an earlier postulate. In this context, even the present is no limit, but is here a view that still opens onto a future that will also be nothing other than the progressive proof of the existence of the power that rules over being, of that which is no longer just the being with which negative philosophy busies itself, but is rather that which is above being. This entire philosophy is, therefore, an always advancing knowledge, always nothing other than a *philo-sophia*, never rigid or stagnant, and, thus, in this sense, a dogmatic science. For this reason, however, even this proof is only a proof for those who want to think and move forward, and, thus, only for the *wise*. It is not like a proof of geometry, with which one can coerce those of even the most limited abilities, and even the dumb, whereas I can coerce no one to become wise through experience if he does not want to, and this is why the psalm says: "the foolish speak in their hearts: there is no God."[41]

The positive philosophy is the truly free philosophy; whoever does not want it should just as well leave it alone. I propose it to everyone freely. I only maintain that if one wants the actual chain of events, if he wants a freely created world, and so on, he can have all of this only via the path of such a philosophy. If the rational philosophy satisfies him, and he longs for nothing beyond it, then he should just as well stay with it, only he must give up the desire to possess within the rational philosophy that which it by no means can possess, namely, the real God, the actual chain of events, and a free relationship of God to the world. The confusion that now reigns over this matter must cease. No one can appreciate the rational philosophy more than I; indeed, I would consider university students lucky if there was again a purely rational philosophy taught in the schools. For I do not concede that those who now boast of being rationalists are indeed rationalists; they are instead nothing less than this: those who produce a repulsive mixture of rational and suprarational philosophy, whereby neither of the two is done justice.[133]

There emerges at this point yet another difference between the negative and positive philosophy. The former is an entirely self-enclosed science that has arrived at an unchanging conclusion, and is, thus, in *this* sense a *system*; in contrast, the positive philosophy cannot in the same sense be called a system precisely because it is never absolutely closed. If, on the other hand, one understands by 'system' a philosophy that determines and distinguishes itself through positive assertions (in this sense, so many individuals long for a system and consider themselves lucky to be the proclaimers of such a thing, for everyone, even the most incompetent, loves to *proclaim* something, ignoring Lessing's words that in order to assert something there should be above all a something to be asserted, a fact because of which the negative philosophy—which, strictly speaking, is one that affirms nothing—must inevitably be driven beyond its limitations)—in this second sense, under which one understands a totality of knowledge that serves as the basis for a magnificent declaration, in this sense the negative philosophy is not a system. Positive philosophy, in contrast, as pre-eminently affirming, is in this sense, in an eminent way, a *system*. To note these different meanings of system is certainly worth the trouble.

Let us now assume that even something like revelation is found among the realities of experience to which positive philosophy advances. If this were so, positive philosophy could approach revelation no differently than it approaches real nature, real humanity, and real consciousness: namely, from and out of its *prius*. Revelation is thus neither its source nor its point of departure, as it is in the so-called Christian philosophy from which it is in this respect *toto coele* different. Revelation will be present within positive philosophy in no other sense than nature or the entire history of the human race is also present within it; revelation will exert on it no different authority than what every other object exerts on the science that deals with it. For example, the *empirically* observed movements of the planets are to such an extent an authority for the theories of astronomy that these theories for quite some time could not be considered to be perfectly exact and correct, since [134] the actually observed movements did not agree with those that had been predicted. Thus, every object of the natural sciences certainly exerts an undeniable authority on the science that is concerned with it.

Furthermore, and although so much is already apparent, namely, that this philosophy has the content of religion as its *own*, it will nonetheless refuse to call itself, or allow itself to be called, a *religious* philosophy. For it would then have to be called the negative, for example, the irreligious philosophy, and with this an injustice would be done to the negative, even though it can encompass religion only as the religion of absolute subjectivity, not as objective or, indeed, as revealed. If there is a truly irreligious doctrine, it should not be termed an irreligious *philosophy*, for to do so would be to accord it too much. An irreligious doctrine is just as little a philosophy as a fundamentally unethical doctrine can be a philosophy, since, on the contrary, and as often pointed out, only that philosophy has earned the right to call itself a philosophy that has fulfilled the truly scientific demand that all of its essential concepts have just as much a profound ethical significance as they do a speculative significance. This is also why the positive philosophy must refuse the title of a religious philosophy, since through it the *true* concept and content of religion will first be discovered. These concepts, therefore, cannot already be presupposed, and as soon as one does not presuppose them, this title becomes completely ambiguous. For while there are no different ethical systems, there are, no doubt, different religions: even the heathen has religion, and the modern Christian, who edifies himself according to the hours of his worship or other classical and insipid works, nonetheless believes that he too has religion. One could then go still further and site Christian philosophy, but there are so many very different viewpoints that call themselves Christian that one must, to speak quite decisively, go yet a step further and site Catholic philosophy (as has already occurred in a party in France and in some parts of Germany). One could then place this philosophy in opposition to Protestant science and Protestant philosophy, and somehow find it advantageous to use the first predicate mostly in a Catholic land and the other in [135] a Protestant land. But a philosophy that must call on Catholicism or Protestantism for help has either never been anything or, more to the point, has nothing more to be. One would thus have to leave the general title of a religious philosophy to those who somehow see an advantage in it so that they can, right from the start, cast suspicion on every other philosophy with which it finds itself in collision or is afraid of coming into collision with, and, in this way, to create for itself a privileged position.

One could, if we rejected revelation as a formal principle, as a *principium cognoscendi*, for *every* philosophy, and thus also for the positive (since one who wants to and can believe does not engage in philosophy, and one who does philosophize announces therewith that mere faith does not satisfy him)—one could, I contend, in order to show that a positive philosophy is nonetheless *necessarily* a Christian philosophy, point to the material dependency of all new philosophies on Christianity. For as one would say, philosophy of its own accord *would have never* come across these subjects and, still less, across this perspective toward these subjects without the preceding light of revelation. Yet to say even this would again prove too much. For in quite the same way one could thrust the title of *empiricism* on *every* philosophy, for neither would there have been a philosophy at all, nor a philosophy with this content, as in the ancients and moderns, if there were not such a world as is found in experience. If, however, a particular philosophy is meant that seeks to comprehend within itself that which lies beyond nature and the entire unending treasures of the human world, and thus especially encompasses the great historical phenomena of Christianity in both its development and as a part of that history—it goes without saying that such a philosophy, as *soon* as it lays its foundation, must have also thought about Christianity. Yet even this observation contains nothing that is particularly and especially characteristic about Christianity. For whoever proposes a comprehensive philosophy and can hope to really lead it to its conclusion must think far further, must have already surveyed everything beforehand and have [136] taken everything into his calculations. Nevertheless, if one considers this line of thinking that seeks to remind philosophy of its historical and material dependency on Christianity, if one thinks of a philosophy that has left Christianity completely outside itself, then the sense of this line of thinking is this: even this later philosophy could not have come this far if it had not had Christianity as its historical foundation. This is indeed something true, yet also something so general that it again loses all reference to the particular; for not only philosophy, but also the state or human affairs overall—where would *they* find themselves if Christianity had not existed? Can one, if the discussion is about the most insignificant phenomenon of the present, remove a piece of the immense past without promptly making the present impossible? Would it be possible to extract from a person, as through a chemical process, that which confers upon him a past and present? What would remain other than the merely vacuous title of 'self' or 'ego,' with which he could achieve little, or, to put it more accurately, absolutely nothing?

That person for whom *true* philosophy and *Christian* philosophy are synonymous expressions must above all form a higher idea of Christianity itself than the habitual notion that Christianity is a merely historical phenomenon that first appeared in the world approximately eighteen hundred years ago. He must grasp Christianity as that which is truly universal, that which, therefore, even serves as the very foundation of the world, and as a result of this say: It is as old as the world (in a different sense of course than the English deist Tindal who, as is well known, wrote a book with this title in which Christianity is made into a mere natural religion, about which it is then easy to say that it is as old as creation and human reason[42]). If Christianity is understood merely as a historical phenomenon, our philosophy would then be dependent on it, even if we see in Christ only a Socrates of a higher type; for without a Socrates, and without a Plato and Aristotle, our philosophy would be an entirely different one. Who [137] could it occur to in this sense to deny the external historical dependency of our entire culture and, to this extent, of philosophy, on Christianity? Through this dependency, even the *content* of our thought, and thus even the content of philosophy, is determined; it would not, however, be the content of philosophy if it remained perpetually in this dependency, that is, if it were only to be accepted on authority. If Christianity is really the content of philosophy, then with this it becomes the content *of our own thought*, it becomes for us our own insight, independent of all authority. I would like to explain myself further on this subject through a simile. As is well known, the four moons of Jupiter are only visible for normal eyes through a telescope; yet there are nonetheless people with such farsighted vision that they can see the moons without a telescope. This fact first came to my attention through Zimmermann's book on experience. Thereafter I often had the opportunity to observe this myself and have known a woman, among others, who is still alive who actually saw the four satellites with her naked eye. Put to the test in the presence of an astronomer and a physicist, she sketched a drawing of the momentary positions of the satellites vis-à-vis each other and Jupiter; a sketch that was then found to be in the most precise agreement with the positions as they appeared in the telescope. Now it is further the case that a small fixed star, which we could not perceive with the naked eye, can be immediately seen even with the naked eye when one has caught sight of it beforehand through a telescope. I do not doubt that there are more people than one thinks who in this way could see the four moons of Jupiter with the naked eye. Such people, however, are no longer dependent on the telescope. They really see the four stars with only their eyes. In precisely the same way, philosophy would not have known some things without revelation, or at least it would not have discerned them as it has. Yet philosophy can now see these objects with its own eyes, since in regard to all truths, even the revealed, it is only *philosophy* to the extent that it transforms them into independent truths known for oneself [*selbsterkannte*]. [138] Of course, if a philosophy proposes not to exclude the great phenomenon of Christianity, but, rather, to comprehend it if possible just like other things and in connection with everything else, then philosophy must necessarily expand its concepts beyond their previous limits in order to be a match for this phenomenon, just as, in exactly the same manner, other objects impose upon the science that relates to them the necessity to correct their concepts, and to augment them according to circumstances, until they find themselves at the same expanse as that of their objects. As one would now declare any philosophy incomplete that had excluded nature from itself, so too would a philosophy in no way be complete that could not comprehend Christianity. For Christianity is one of the greatest and most significant phenomena of the world. It is in its way just as good a reality as nature and has the right, just as every other phenomenon, to be left in its singularity and not to be misrepresented only in order to be capable of the next best thing, that is, of applying to it an explanation accessible to everyone. In recent times, Christianity has *actually* been included among the objects of philosophical consideration. Yet the sincere inquirer soon discovers that it is not to be gotten hold of with the merely logical systems, no matter how unnaturally they extend themselves beyond their borders. For it is then a matter of robbing not only its external character, but its internal and historical character as well—a direction at which all previous attempts to rationalize Christianity have ultimately aimed. Still it is by no means just revelation that requires philosophy to advance beyond the merely logical systems; as we have seen, it is a necessity that lies in philosophy itself that propels it beyond the merely logical.[xvii] With this, the concept of the philosophy of revelation as such is already justified. [139]

---

xvii. I have also, albeit only in preliminary expositions, posited positive and negative philosophy in opposition to each other as the *historical* and the *ahistorical* [*ungeschichtliche*], and then explained what these expressions mean; only the expressions circulate, whereas the explanations most often do not proceed beyond the immediate circle [of students]. Accordingly, historical philosophy was understood as if, within it, knowledge was drawn directly out of historical matter as through an alchemical process and all a priori procedures abandoned. Others thought that historical philosophy was to be understood as what one would otherwise call the philosophy of history, and brought

One has sought to make the expression 'philosophy of revelation' acceptable, and spoken of a '*revealed philosophy*' [*Offenbarungsphilosophie*]. This offered an immediate advantage, namely, to create the belief that it is a question of a philosophy drawn from revelation, subject to the authority of revelation that it consequently ceases to be real philosophy, a freely created science. Whoever followed the development of this philosophy immediately discovered that this is not so, since 'philosophy of revelation' is meant in exactly the same sense as in similar constructions—philosophy of nature, philosophy of history, philosophy of art and so on—that is, that in this construction, revelation is proposed as an object and not as a source or authority. Thus, according to what has just been said, it is at best an authority in the same sense as every [140] object of nature and history is an authority that, when intellectually considered, exercises an authority over thought. The mistaken opinion, therefore—intentionally or unintentionally aroused by the expression 'revealed philosophy'—disappeared for those who informed themselves further; for most of those who did not have the opportunity or the will to inform themselves, this prejudice remains in place. One knows how much is superficially won against a subject—whose refutation one gladly avoids since one has not yet comprehended it—through the arousal of such a prejudice. One now says without hesitation 'natural philosophy' instead of 'philosophy of nature,' and this long-lived habit has made the misunderstanding impossible, as if 'natural philosophy' were somehow the antithesis of 'art philosophy' [*Kunstphilosophie*], and as if one could speak in the same manner of 'natural philosophers' and 'art philosophers,' just as one has had the opportunity in recent times to hear of 'nature poets' and 'art poets.' But to say, instead of the 'philosophy of government,' the 'government's philosophy,' one will guard against this, if only because under the latter one may well understand a philosophy protected and supported by the government or one arranged according to the momentary principles of the government's administration—a philosophy of which one has certainly also had examples.

(*continued*) in connection with this *The Ages of the World*, which they arbitrarily—without providing any reason for doing so—called 'the four ages of the world.' A different misunderstanding was that in the future, instead of philosophy, there will be instituted and taught just a genetic development of philosophy that would have as its basis the history of philosophy. I must allow my contemporaries to once again experience justice, so that at least in this matter you will have not, through too great expectations, put me in an embarrassing position. When the geometrician proves from the nature of the triangle that the sum of its angles equals two right angles, this follows from the nature of the triangle devoid of any other movement save that of my thinking: between the object itself and its attributes there is nothing in the middle save my thought. The triangle itself does not somehow precede these attributes, nor does something precede it through which it would assume these attributes. The triangle exists only according to its concept, that is, it is more truly logical than its attributes. If Spinoza used this geometrical truth as an example to illustrate how, in his opinion, the individual finite things follow from God's nature, namely, in just as timeless and eternal way, then his explanation of the world was indeed ahistorical, and, in contrast to it, the Christian doctrine that the world is the result of a free decision, of an *action*, is to be called a historical explanation. The expression 'historical,' when used by philosophy, refers, thus, not to the manner of knowing *in it*, but exclusively to *the content* of the knowing.

Accordingly, one could have just as well let the matter stand with the title philosophy of revelation. But some have gone still further and have used revealed philosophy as the title of an entire philosophical system, of which the philosophy of revelation was only a *component* or an application, as one, in precisely the same way, once termed 'natural philosophy' not merely a component of the system that dealt primarily with nature, but an entire system, with the intent, in part, to make the entire system suspect, as if it were a doctrine like that of the French encyclopedists, for which material nature, and thus matter as such, would be the only reality. Regarding revelation, one can distinguish two different kinds of philosophy: one for which the content of revelation is something absolutely incomprehensible, and so not appropriate for thought, and the other that has the means [141] to comprehend its content. Yet *on this account*, one will not specifically call the latter a revealed philosophy, for it will extend to and comprehend still *more and different objects* than simple revelation will, and it will comprehend these only because it has already grasped something different, namely, the actual God. For a God who is merely an idea of reason does not allow an actual religion or, much less, an actual revelation to be conceived. Let us call the philosophy that comprehends the actual God—and, thus, in general, not simply the possibility, but the actuality of things—the positive philosophy, and so the philosophy of revelation will be a consequence of, or even a component of it, but the philosophy of revelation will not be the positive philosophy itself, which, in the former sense, one had gladly advanced as a revealed philosophy, that is, a philosophy drawn solely from revelation.

Next, I would like to correct yet another *possible* misunderstanding. Whoever hears the word 'revelation' can imagine simply the act through which the divine becomes the cause or author of representations in any one individual human consciousness. Those theologians who do not find the content of Christian revelation to be *inherently* true, but only because those individuals through whom the content was proclaimed had been inspired from God himself, must lay particular importance on this act. Now I do not want to deny that in the philosophy of revelation a point may well arise in which the possibility or impossibility of revelation in this sense is also investigated. Yet in the philosophy of revelation, this question will always only be a subordinate one, and if it receives an answer at all then it will be answered as a consequence of the investigation that extends beyond this particular question. The philosophy of revelation refers not to the merely formal element of a divine act, which in any case would only be a particular one. It refers to what is *general* in revelation, and, above all, to its content and to the great, general context in which this content alone is comprehensible. The [142] content of revelation is first of all a historical content, but not in the vulgar or temporal sense. It is a content that indeed is *revealed* at a determinate time, that is, intervenes in worldly phenomena. Yet according to its subject matter it is nonetheless veiled and hidden, as it was present and prepared "before laying the foundation of the world," before the foundation of the world had been laid, whose origin and proper understanding thereof leads back to that which is beyond this world.[43] It is this type of content that should become the content of philosophy within the philosophy of revelation. If this is seriously meant, that is, should this content in its entire truth and authenticity become the actual content of philosophy, then you see that a philosophy capable of incorporating this content in this way must be constituted totally differently from those that have previously ruled in most circles. This is, however, seriously intended with the philosophy of revelation. As its first principle, it must be proposed (and was proposed) that this combination of philosophy and revelation does not occur at the cost either of philosophy or of revelation, that neither component will relinquish anything nor suffer any violence. Let us consider revelation only in a certain improper sense, in which every unexpected expansion of human consciousness or unforeseen enlightenment could become a part of a science so that it could be called the revelation of the spirit of this science—to comprehend a revelation in this sense would indeed be an easy task, but not one that is appropriate for philosophy. Just as if one acknowledged as the content of revelation (and it is above all a question of this *content*, for with the content the chain of events will be comprehended as a matter of course) only general or so-called rational knowledge, so that to be capable of resolving the highly particular truths of revelation into such general truths one had to take refuge in the distinction of content from *form* or *garment*—once again it would not be worth the trouble to deal with revelation. If revelation contained nothing more than what is in reason, then it [143] would have absolutely no interest; its sole interest can only consist in the fact that it contains something that exceeds reason, something that is more than what reason contains. How something that exceeds reason can be conceived and how it can even be actually thought in many instances will be shown later. Is not everything that one learns only through experience something that exceeds reason? And what occurs in the general history of humankind, often in the acts and deeds of exceptional individuals, is this not something that cannot be comprehended through reason alone? A reasonable man is, thus, still no hero of world history.

In practice, it would not be worth the trouble to concern oneself with revelation if it were not something special, if it contained nothing more than what one already had without it. I should probably not, right at the beginning, state my rejection of this means of instruction by which others are used to being helped. Some could feel from the outset already rebuffed, or at least disinclined toward the investigation. I do not at all expect to be judged according to prejudices and provisional remarks alone. Whoever seeks to listen to me listens to the end. It could very well be that in this case he would find something completely different from what, commensurate with his existing and somewhat narrow opinions, he expected to find, something against which the customary (and these days well-known) objections to everything that exceeds reason would find no use. I would like, however, to point out the following. If revelation is a reality and is actually something factual—and we must presuppose this, for if what is factual in it were merely its general wording, then normal knowledge would be sufficient to comprehend it—to realize that it is *actually* something factual no doubt requires still other historical mediations and corroborations than what until now have been a part of revelation. If it is to be substantiated at all, it will only be substantiated in a higher historical context, in a higher context that extends beyond itself and Christianity as a special phenomenon, thus, in a context different [144] from the one we usually have in mind. In this regard, I refer for the moment to the lectures on theology in my talk *On University Studies*, the fundamental thought of which is that the concept of Christianity as a revelation is possible only in the context not merely of earlier (Old Testament) revelations, but only within the context of religious development overall, and especially of Heathendom. For my part, I blame no one who, without thinking of this mediation, without being familiar with it, is prepared and, indeed, even determined to abandon revelation as *fact*, and with this solve the problem in the quickest manner, through the removal of its object. However, in what follows even this—the historical mediation of the fact—will be addressed and taken care of. The great and central question will always be how, given the presuppositions, exactly as they are stated regarding the reality of revelation, a philosophy could be consistent with this, and yet not be second-rate, but rather one worthy of this name. Although it would seem natural to first secure the facts correctly, before one undertakes an investigation into the means of comprehending revelation philosophically, in this context the matter comports itself differently. For I have already conceded, and others will concede it still more willingly, that such an undertaking cannot be executed with a philosophy as it now exists. To be sure, no philosophy has yet been able to neglect seeking a relationship revelation, and even Kant allowed this to be his final principle that established the relationship of his philosophy to Christianity (for presumably Kant's *Religion within the Limits of Pure Reason*—the primary foundation of vulgar rationalism—has not yet been fully forgotten). Yet the relationship that real philosophy and revelation found with each other was still, for both elements, such a forced and awkward one that it dissolved itself again of its own accord. It could never last, and on the contrary, every sincere thinker must prefer the manifestly antagonistic relationship that philosophy has (earlier and otherwise often enough) assumed toward Christianity to such a false [145] and untrue relationship. From this follows what has already been stated: that a philosophy of revelation is not conceivable without an expansion of philosophy beyond its current limits. Yet an expansion of philosophy intended *just* for the sake of revelation would, no doubt, have quite an ambiguous reputation. We have nonetheless already substantiated such an expansion in our previous lectures, an expansion that appears to us as the consequence of a necessity *present within philosophy itself*. But precisely the last point of this discussion has again placed us before that seemingly insuperable duality, according to which philosophy cannot help but be both negative and positive. We were led to this last development through the intent to show that both of these clearly distinguishable lines of thought, in ancient philosophy just as (and even more definitely) in recent times, have always existed *beside each other*. And attempts at a positive philosophy, as well as attempts at a purely rational philosophy, have until now not succeeded in the one overcoming or assimilating the other—a situation that nonetheless would be required for the unity of philosophy. The entire history of philosophy (that I entered into in the previous discussions only for this reason) presents a struggle between the negative and positive philosophies. Even Kant in his *Critique of Pure Reason* advanced a very important lesson that he titled 'the antithesis of pure reason' in which he specified the antinomies, that is, the self-contradictions, that reason allegedly falls into regarding the cosmological ideas. Yet what are these antinomies other than precisely the many manifestations of the opposition of the negative and positive philosophies? The thesis of the Kantian antinomies positions itself consistently on the positive side, the antithesis on the negative side. Nothing is required to allow the world to continue into infinitude or indeterminacy—for in doing this, strictly speaking, nothing is posited, since to posit the absence of all limits [*Grenze*] ultimately means not to posit something, and, thus, properly speaking, to posit *nothing*. In contrast, to posit a limit is to do something; it is an *assertion* [*Behauptung*]. Yet the antinomy as contradiction arises only through the fact that what [146] is really not an assertion (the antithesis) is put forth as an assertion, whereas the other one, which is actually an assertion (the thesis), is put forth as an assertion of reason. Reason, which according to its nature cannot assert, can also not posit a limit, and, conversely, the philosophy that asserts a limit must proceed beyond reason and know more than what by virtue of reason alone is *to be known*. The so-called antinomy is, therefore, not an opposition, a collision of reason with itself, as Kant assumed, but is rather a contradiction between reason and that which is more than reason, the true positive science.

I believe thus far to have supported my proposition that both lines of philosophy have until now always coexisted, even through the eminent example of Kant, who indeed recognized the existence of this opposition, but who of course did not think of the possibility of a positive philosophy. And this although his philosophy ended with the *demand* (with the postulate, as he said) for an actually existing God, and, thus, basically with the demand for a positive philosophy, for an extension that ends beyond the mere science of reason. Only the prejudice that theoretical philosophy must be a science, in which reason starts out purely from *itself*, that it can only be a pure science of reason, prevented him from seeing this. As a result, for him this demand only had significance for action [*die Praxis*], for the ethical life, but none for science. [147]

THE GROUNDING OF POSITIVE PHILOSOPHY

Will we, however, allow this antithesis of two philosophies to stand? You remember that we have only for the moment assumed but not conceded the conclusion in this form. Here is now the place to decide. But in order to decide we must return to a standpoint that lies beyond this antithesis and is, thus, still completely free of it; this standpoint can be no other than precisely that of philosophy as such: the standpoint of one who just now comes to philosophy, without yet having to decide anything definite about it. But even from this standpoint, and even if all other preliminary determinations and explanations are still held at a distance, one must realize that among all the sciences, philosophy is the only one that can receive its object from none of the others, which must provide its object for itself, must determine it for itself, and must therefore also create itself. Philosophy is indeed the only science that leaves in its wake nothing undiscussed and always proceeds to the ultimate causes; thus, it must first secure and ground its object, for philosophy cannot accept a merely contingent object, nor one provided by experience or from another higher science. From this standpoint, it can be said that the discovery and grounding of its object must be the first order of business for philosophy. Mathematics, on account of its object, can refer to a universal need or to philosophy. No one demands that it must justify itself on account of its object. [148] Philosophy, however, must first search for its object. But since it searches for *its* object, that is, the object that is singularly appropriate for it, from the outset it cannot already be engaged exclusively with its object, for from the beginning it can exclude *nothing* at all and must instead traverse all possible objects in order to, through the exclusion and removal of all others, arrive at that *one object* that *philosophy itself* seizes as the object of *its* own cognition. It should, however, not even accept these possible objects randomly as they occur in experience, nor should it even allow them to be provided from somewhere else, rather, it must *secure* them as well; to secure not merely their *content*, but simultaneously to secure their complete enumeration and consistent arrangement.

It can do this, however, only if it proceeds from the *universal* possibility, hence from being as the immediate content of reason, and finds how everything comes into being from this, finds what is first in being, what is second, and so on, whereby that which has come before must serve as the step to what follows.

But with this, right at the start, where it still has to seek and create its object, philosophy is placed at the standpoint of possibility, or of the universal *prius*, and thus assumes an a priori position towards all being. And this position is precisely that of the rational or negative philosophy, from which it is clear that philosophy, if it wants to describe its entire sphere, can really only begin as rational philosophy. In this progression, it will finally arrive at an ultimate [*ein Letztes*] beyond which it can no longer continue and because of which it cannot also refer to experience in the same way as with everything which has preceded it. For in experience there is only that which goes beyond pure thought, whereas this ultimate is that which no longer has the capacity to be (empirically) *outside* of thought and in which philosophy will first recognize *its object* as that which is singularly appropriate to it. This ultimate is that which stands above being, which no longer passes over into being, which we have called being itself [*das Seyende selbst*]. It is no longer just being, but is rather being itself, [149] being in its truth, and, therefore, that which was really wanted from the very beginning—not just *cognoscible* (for everything else is this as well), but rather the *maxime cognoscendum*, that which is most worthy of knowing: τὸ μάλιστα ἐπιστητόν (to use in this context an expression of Aristotle's, which he of course applied to something else). It is not just that which is most worthy of knowing, but it is also that which is to be known in the purest knowing, since, according to its nature, it is *entirely* being, not potency, but rather entirely *actus*, pure actuality, whereas everything else (that which passes over *a potentia ad actum*), precisely because it is only a mixture of nonbeing and being (of potency and *actus*), can therefore only be the object of a knowing that mixes knowing and unknowing, and thus of an impure, imperfect knowing, the type which we therefore call empirical. How everything empirically cognized is just as much known as not known allows itself to be shown quite easily, since according to its *nature* everything empirical is to be known only partially, whereas that knowing in which the pure *actus* is thought is not a mixture of *potentia* and *actus*, but is rather the pure ἐνεργεί ὄν of Aristotle, that which is entirely being, in which there is absolutely nothing of nonbeing, that is, of that which cannot be known. This is, thus, necessarily also that which can be *entirely* known, according to the Platonic expression, as παντελῶς ὄν, but also as the παντελῶς γνωστόν, as that which *entirely* is, which can thus be *entirely* known. Just as it is that which is most worthy of knowing, it is also that which is the most, indeed, that which is alone worthy of *existence*. For everything else that negative philosophy leaves to the other sciences for real knowledge is only, so to speak, admitted to being in view of this ultimate, posited as a stage of the same, and, thus, has as a preparatory moment no meaning in itself and, therefore, no truth in itself but, rather, only truth in reference to this ultimate.

After philosophy has arrived at this ultimate, composed to be known only in a pure knowing since it alone *entirely* is, it can leave the actual knowledge of this being to a *different* science as little as it can leave this being itself unknown. Philosophy will instead reserve *this being* for itself *as* its own [150] object, in light of which it has regarded everything that preceded it as nothing, as not being. Regarded as such, philosophy will take on [*anziehen*] this object in order to bring it together with this being to an actual knowledge that, as now can be clearly seen, can no longer happen in the same line of science, but rather only in a new science that starts from the very beginning. As is *now* clear, with this ends the function of philosophy in which it was the science of all sciences, which by means of its reciprocal superposition, in accordance with a certain and—when properly employed—even infallible method, was capable of providing a representation of reality—just as, for instance, geology is capable of representing the reciprocal ordering of the lower and upper plates out of which the earth's crust is composed. As the science of all sciences, philosophy has the peculiar characteristic of positing *actual* knowing not in itself, but in the very sciences of which it is the science. To this extent, philosophy is also a not knowing and, in this sense, also a negative science. From this point on, however, philosophy no longer posits knowing outside itself, but rather within itself. It is no longer unknowing, but is rather itself knowing and, thus, a positive science. Yet as the *former* and as the *latter* it is philosophy: there (as negative science), since it *seeks* what is beyond everything and is thus the greatest thing to be known, here, because it has to bring that which has been uncovered, the object of the highest knowing, of σοφία, to an actual knowledge. And its astonishing challenge [*Aufgabe*] in this is to prove that what the ultimate principle of the negative science was, and what in reference to everything else that exists, is that which is beyond existence, is not merely the highest idea, but is that which *actually exists*.

According to these determinations, and before we move completely beyond the aforementioned antithesis, the following can be established about the difference between both philosophies. In the negative science, everything that lies between the beginning and the end is only relatively true, and so is not what is genuinely and properly true, *truth itself*; every moment is no doubt true as a point on the way to what is true, but it is not what is true, being itself [*Seyende selbst*]. As the science that has truth only at its *terminus*, the negative itself is not yet in the truth, and so is also not yet the true science. Yet it is not a mistaken philosophy because of this (for it is [151] after all on the perpetual path to truth). As opposed to the true science, namely, that science which does not have what is true at its end, but is rather itself within the truth, the negative science, taken in isolation or in its own right, is not capable of making a claim to the name philosophy: it only becomes worthy of this name in its final moment, through its relationship to the positive science. This is a very important point that finally leads us to completely sublate this duality within philosophy. For the negative philosophy is, in its own right, not yet philosophy, but rather only in its relation to the positive. Vis-à-vis the positive science, it will always be satisfied with the name of the first science (πρώτη ἐπιστήμη). However, if for itself it is satisfied with the name of the *first* science (that it is the science of all sciences), it will confer upon the positive the name of the *highest* science. Just as that from which the negative philosophy proceeds—from that which is before being—is alone the *primum cogitabile*, so will that which is *beyond* being (and in *this* sense also before being), and that which is the task of the positive philosophy, be the *summum cogitabile*. Between these two, the *first* and the *highest* sciences, lie all the other sciences in the middle: as negative, philosophy precedes all sciences, just as when positive, it resolves all sciences, so that in this way the entire sphere of the sciences is set between these philosophies.[xviii] In this last insight into the necessary advance to *positive* philosophy lies its difference from Kant as well as from the philosophy of identity, to the extent [152] that it had developed earlier. If, at the end of his critique, Kant dismisses from reason everything that is positive (dogmatic), the very same thing occurs from the viewpoint of the correctly understood negative philosophy; it differs from Kant only in that it *positively* excludes what is positive, that is, it *posits* it in a different knowledge, which Kant had not done. But although we realize in an indubitable manner that philosophy only completes itself in two sciences, the semblance, nonetheless, of two different philosophies existing side by side, which certainly would have to be called a scandal of philosophy, now disappears through this last exposition. For it has become apparent that the negative philosophy must posit the positive, but *by* positing this it only makes itself into the consciousness of the positive, and is *to this extent* no longer *outside the positive*, but rather belongs to it itself, so that there is in fact but one philosophy. Where it is only a matter of the presentation of the positive philosophy, the negative will be found only in this respect, and then, admittedly, as an introduction and, therefore, in an abbreviated and condensed form; this does not, however, nullify its demand to be presented as an independent science. Beyond question, it will be the rational philosophy that must take over the position of the former *Schulphilosophie* and which must supply the universal dedication to scientific studies in general and to every particular science. As a pure science of reason, as something extracted from its own resources, a creation of the human spirit woven out of its own material, it will always endure and maintain its independent worth.

It is a proud name with which it is entitled to adorn itself when it calls itself the science of reason. But what is its content as such a science? Properly speaking, only the constant *overthrow* [*Umsturz*] of reason. And its result? Simply that reason, inasmuch as it merely takes itself as its source and principle, is capable of no *actual* knowledge. For that which always simultaneously becomes what is and what is knowable for it is something that goes beyond reason, namely experience, which it must leave [153] to another science. In

---

xviii. Negative philosophy is only a *philosophia ascendens* (ascending from below), from which one immediately realizes that it can only have a logical significance, whereas positive philosophy is a *philosophia descendens* (descending from above). Both together first complete the entire sphere of philosophy, as one could, if one still required further explanation or elucidation, easily trace this duality back to the customary division in the schools of theoretical philosophy between logic and metaphysics, in that the first is fundamentally only logic (logic of becoming), while everything truly metaphysical fell entirely into the other division (the positive philosophy).

The Grounding of Positive Philosophy 197

this advance, then, reason possesses nothing *on its own account*, it only watches as its content *dissipates* [*entwerden*], and even with the one that remains, *it can*—on its own account—begin nothing or bring this one thing together with its content to knowledge. To the extent that the positive philosophy brings to knowledge precisely that which remained in the negative as something incapable of being known, to this extent it is precisely the positive philosophy that straightens out reason *contorted* [*gebeugte*] by the negative, in that it helps bring it to the actual knowledge [*Erkenntniß*] of that which it had become acquainted with as its singular, *enduring*, and inviolable content. If the negative philosophy would have remained alone and by itself, if it would have had no positive result for reason *itself*, then this knowing reason would have remained unsatisfied regarding its own content and would have departed empty-handed. In the positive philosophy, the negative triumphs as the science in which thought, after it has liberated itself from its immediate, that is, accidental content, first really attains its goal whereby its necessary content becomes dominant, and upon which thought now looks on in freedom (for previously, thought did not see this necessary content in freedom, since the accidental content, so to speak, stood between reason and its necessary content). Therefore, in its truth, that is, to the extent it is *philosophy*, the negative is itself positive since it posits the latter outside itself, and, thus, there is *no longer* a duality. From the very beginning our earliest aspirations have sought a positive philosophy. History shows how late the origins of all purely rational inquiries are and how early the human spirit concerned itself with representations [*Vorstellungen*] that, considered from the rational standpoint alone, are transcendent. The positive philosophy is the one philosophy that has always and originally been wanted, but because it was unsuccessful or was sought for in the wrong manner it prompted the *critique* from which, in exactly the same manner as I have shown, the negative philosophy then emerged as a philosophy that has its worth and meaning only *as* negative, that is, insofar as it does not want to be positive itself, but rather posits the positive outside itself. This positive philosophy could begin of its own accord since it starts out from the absolute *prius*, from that which, through itself, is the certain beginning. It is, to this extent, simply its own [154] will when it presupposes the negative. And this one, the negative, could exist of its own accord and know nothing of the positive if it were in the position to renounce all actual knowledge, but how could it do this if it defines itself *as philosophy*? For then it would have to cease calling itself philosophy, just as Kant did not call his *critique* philosophy, but rather a critique. If it calls itself philosophy, how will it be able to resist the demands commonly connected with this? One will demand from it the *actual* God, not the mere idea of God. How will it furnish this, which within its philosophy is left standing as something unknowable? To begin with, it will perhaps say: "The God that is in reason is a mere *idea*, and must become real for us through *feeling*." But then what? If one for whom this bankruptcy of reason is acceptable—because it is acceptable for him to limit his thoughts to the sensible world—if this person uses the appeal to feeling to show that the real God is but a creation of our emotions and of the heart, of our power of imagination, and that he is altogether nothing objective—then will not only Christianity but also *every* religious idea have at the very most a psychological significance? (It is justifiably amazing when one now struggles against this result, after Jacobi and others, who had known of no *other philosophy* than the rational and only negative, had been earlier praised and even recognized as Christian philosophers because of the appeal to the faculty of emotion, for which the God whom reason only knows how to deny could alone exist.)

Will one find this other approach, that only an exclusively negative philosophy can still obtain to a real God, any better? I mean *the* opinion that precisely through the development of the *human* spirit, through *its* progress to ever greater freedom, that is, basically to ever greater negativity, that through this progress alone God will be realized, that is, so that outside human consciousness God does not exist at all—that man is really God, and God is only man, which one subsequently even designated as the incarnation of God (to which corresponds a becoming God of man). One sees [155] to what sort of entirely untenable confusion this struggle has progressed, seeking to obtain Christian ideas with an allegedly purely rational philosophy. Instead of saying that positive philosophy presupposes the negative as its foundation, one would like, on the contrary, to declare the inverse: the negative is only grounded through the positive because through the positive it first becomes certain of its status and is put in the position to remain with and equal to itself, thereby remaining within the limits accorded by its nature.

I have already said that negative philosophy will predominately remain the philosophy of the *academy*, whereas the positive will be the philosophy for *life*. The complete dedication that one demands from philosophy will only be provided through the two in combination. As is well known, the Eleusinian dedication distinguished between the major and minor mysteries, whereby the minor were regarded as a preliminary stage to the major mysteries. The Neoplatonists even called the Aristotelian philosophy the minor, and the Platonic the major mysteries of philosophy, an ordering that is not fitting insofar as the Platonic philosophy cannot follow from the Aristotelian, as the major must follow from the minor mysteries. However, the positive philosophy is the necessary result of the correctly understood negative philosophy, and, thus, one can indeed say that in the negative philosophy the minor mysteries of philosophy are celebrated; in the positive, the major mysteries.

It now only remains to show in more detail the transition from the negative to the *principle*, to the *beginning* of the positive philosophy.

The rational philosophy does not concern itself with what really exists, with that which has the capacity to exist. The ultimate [*das Lezte*] that can exist, however, is *the* potency that is no longer potency but, rather, since it is being itself, is pure *actus*; for this reason we could call it the *existing* potency [*die seyende Potenz*]. Yet this ultimate is, for the present, only a concept in the

The Grounding of Positive Philosophy 199

negative philosophy. But certainly it can be asked, and it can always be considered a priori, *in what way* this ultimate can exist. Here it becomes immediately clear that the potency, which is not a potency, but is rather itself the *actus*, [156] does not exist via the transition *a potentia ad actum*. *If* it exists, then it can only *be* a priori, having being as its *prius*. We could, therefore, also call it the inverted capacity to be, namely, that capacity to be in which the potency is the *posterius* and the *actus* is the *prius*.

Up to this thought—that at the highest point the *actus* is first and the potency follows—up to this thought *in general*, the former metaphysics had also advanced, but, of course, it had applied this thought of a being that precedes all potency incorrectly, even inverting it as in the ontological argument (it is called ontological because this being should be derived from the *essence* of God a priori, without incorporating anything from experience). One has attempted to give the ontological argument different expressions, precisely because it was seen as the most metaphysical and, so to speak, as the *citidal* [*arx*] of the so-called rational theology. Even Gottfried Wilhelm von Leibniz had attempted to reduce it to the form of what in his opinion was an irrefutable syllogism. But in this attempt as well, the argument's entire strength depended on the definition of God: *Deus est Ens, ex cujus essentia sequitur existentia* [God is one, from whose essence existence follows]. But in eternity there follows from the essence, from the nature, from the concept of *God* (these are all synonymous expressions) nothing more than this: that God, *if* he exists, must be that which a priori, in no other way can he exist; but *that* he exists does not follow from this concept. If, however, one understands under *ex cujus essentia sequitur existentia* [from whose essence existence follows] nothing other than that which *necessarily* exists, then *to the extent that it is nothing other than this*, in which one thinks of nothing save that fact that it is precisely that which exists, its existence, of course, requires no proof, since it would be nonsense to want to prove that what is only thought of as existing in a verbal sense actually exists. That which is nothing, however, which has no *concept* other than to be that which exists (and with this, with that which precedes its concept, positive philosophy begins), this is still in no way God. This can be easily seen in Spinoza, whose most supreme [157] concept is precisely that which *just* exists [*jenes bloß Existirende*], which he himself describes as follows: *quod non cogitari potest, nisi existens* [of which nothing can be thought except that it exists], in which nothing at all is thought other than existence. Spinoza indeed calls this concept God, but it is certainly not God in the sense that Leibniz and the metaphysics he defended understood the term. While one must concede that Spinoza was correct *in that* the only thing positive from which one may begin is precisely that which just exists, his error lies in the fact that he posits this being immediately equal to = God without having shown, as true philosophy must, how one can get from that which just exists as *prius* to God as *posterius*, that is, he had not shown how that being which simply exists (which to this extent is not *God*, indeed, is not *natura sua*, since this is impossible), is as *actu*, as effective, according to its actuality, a posteriori God. Spinoza had to this extent come to the most profound fundament of all positive philosophy, but his mistake is that he did not know how to proceed beyond it.

The oldest (Anselmian) formulation of the ontological proof was this: the most supreme being beyond which nothing is, *quo majus non datur* [nothing larger is allowed], is God, but the most supreme being would not be the most supreme if it did not exist, since we could then imagine a being that had existence before it, and, thus, the former would no longer be the most supreme being. What else can this mean but that in the most supreme being we have already thought of existence? In this way, of course, the most supreme being exists, but take notice: if there is a most supreme being in the sense that it includes existence, then the proposition *that it exists* is certainly nothing other than tautological. In the Cartesian formulation, one can demonstrate even more formally the paralogism (for it is but an error in form) committed in the ontological argument as follows: the premise states that the essence of God refuses to exist contingently; in this the discussion is simply about necessary existence, that is, about one *manner* of existence. In the conclusion, consequently, the discussion cannot be about existence in general, but, likewise, only about necessary existence, only about one *manner* of existing. [158] This is quite clear. The conclusion can only read, "Therefore, God exists in a necessary manner, that is, *if* he exists, which then still leaves undecided whether he does or does not exist. Yet as little as the ontological argument—which I have introduced only on account of its connection with the fundamental idea of positive philosophy—could prove the existence of God, it must have, if it had been correctly understood, nonetheless led to the beginning of the positive philosophy. That God cannot exist contingently means he cannot exist *per transitum a potentia ad actum* [in transition from potency to *actus*], for otherwise he would not be the *existing* potency, the upright capacity to be, as we could also say. Thus, *if* he exists, he can only be *in* and, as it were, *before* himself,[xix] that is, *he can only* be that which is [*das Seyende seyn*] *before* his divinity [*Gottheit*]; but if before he is divine he is that which is, then for this very reason he is that which precedes his concept, and, thus, all concepts. In the positive philosophy, therefore, I do not proceed from the concept of God, as the ontological argument and the former metaphysics had attempted to do. Rather, I must do away with precisely this concept, the concept of *God*, in order to proceed from that which just exists [*dem bloß Existirende*], in which nothing at all is thought other than just that which just exists, to see whether the divine is to be reached from it. Thus, I cannot really prove the existence of God (whereby I somehow proceed

---

xix. To say "in and for itself" (so that the 'in itself' and the 'for itself' designate different concepts) is not correct (this was mentioned earlier: cf. *Philosophy of Mythology*, I/6, 28.—ED.). This is, in fact, counter to the genius of the German language, which, in such manners of speaking, loves to combine only synonyms, not disparate expressions.

from the concept of *God*), and the only concept given to me is of that which precedes all potency and, therefore, indubitably exists. I call it that which indubitably exists [*das unzweifelhaft Existirende*]. Doubt is wherever there are two cases, two possibilities. That which is intrinsically doubtful is, for precisely this reason, the potency: what can and cannot be. Doubtful and precarious is also the being of all things that have emerged out of the potency, and that indeed now *are*, as we say, but only contingently; thus, they do not cease to be capable of also not being and hang in the constant danger of [159] ceasing to be. But from *this* being, from which every *potency*, which is the sole cause of all doubt, is excluded, for precisely this reason all doubt is likewise excluded: it is that which indubitably exists and can, as it is free from all potency, be nothing but an individual being [*Einzelwesen*], an individual being like no other.

The concept of God as it occurs at the end of the negative philosophy also provides me with the *prius* of divinity [*Gottheit*]. This *prius*, however, is *in itself* that which is irrefutably, indubitably certain, from which on its own account I can likewise proceed if I discard the concept of *God*. I cannot, therefore, proceed from the concept of *God* to prove the existence of God, but I can proceed from the concept of that which indubitably exists and conversely prove the divinity of that which indubitably exists. Now, if the divinity is the *what*, the essence, the potency, then I proceed not from potency to being, but rather, conversely, from being to essence: being is here *prius*, essence *posterius*. But this transition is not possible without a reversal, without changing the entire direction of the science that proceeded from that which has the capacity to be, and to break off from it, and to start from the very beginning a new science, which is precisely the positive philosophy.

One is usually content to call God the necessarily existing being [*Wesen*], but this is not precise. The true relationship is this: the most supreme being (the most supreme being that can be, which is to this extent, of course, the most supreme potency), in a word God, *if* he exists, *can* only be that which necessarily exists. This expression shows that God is not merely the necessary being, but is rather *necessarily* the necessary being; this, however, is a critical distinction. Just as that which has the capacity only to be round is that which is necessarily round, so too that which has the capacity only to necessarily be, as God does, is that which is necessarily necessary being. This simple necessary being, about which Spinoza alone knows, is not God, but is, no doubt, the *prius* of divinity. If God—I ask that you comprehend this precisely—is that which has the capacity *only* to exist necessarily, [160] then only that which necessarily exists is what God *can* be. But with this it is only that which God *can* be, *insofar* as the *prius* of God is understood not as the *prius* of his being, but rather as the *prius* of his divine being [*Gottseyns*], of his divinity [*Gottheit*]. To this determination, according to which the discussion is about a *prius* of the divinity, one cannot oppose something like the old dictum: *In Deo nil potentiale*. This dictum, on the contrary, supports us, since it says that in God there is no potency, as there is in contingent being, which is more possible than actual (in God it is the reverse). The proposition *In Deo nil potentiale* states that God a priori is not like every other *potency*, that he is a priori *actus*. We rather agree with this principle, for in the positive philosophy, what we call the *prius* of the deity is not potency, but rather *actus*; we exclude everything potential, in the sense just specified, *as that which precedes the actus*. If God has his *prius* in *actus*, then he will have his divinity in the potency, in that he is the *potentia universalis*, and as this is that which is above being, the *Lord* of being [*Herr des Seyns*]. But for precisely this reason—in order to actually reach God, that is, to prove as far as it is possible the actual existence of the divine, we must proceed from that which I have called that which *just* exists: from the immediate, simple necessary being, that necessarily is because it precedes all potency and all possibility.

I ask you to be sure to notice the point of departure is only the necessary being. I do not say the necessarily subsisting essence, since this would have already said too much. In this necessary being there *should* be nothing thought of other than that which exists [*das Existiren*].

The negative philosophy can also reach this concept of that which necessarily exists, preceding all concepts, or, rather, it has led us in its final inference, which is the only justifiable one of the ontological argument, to this concept of that which purely and simply exists. From this, it could seem as if the beginning of the positive philosophy is nonetheless provided by the negative, [161] the positive nonetheless grounded by the negative. But this is not so; for with that which, devoid of any preceding potency, *purely* and *simply* exists, with being in this sense, philosophy has come across that which requires no foundation at all, indeed, whose very nature excludes every foundation. For it would not be that which exists, which is itself the absolute *prius*, if one could reach it from anything else, for then of course this something else would be the *prius*. The nature of that which just is [*das bloß Seyende*] is precisely to exist independent of every idea, thus, even from the final idea of negative philosophy. Thus, that which just exists detaches itself from the presupposition it had in but an accidental manner in the preceding philosophy, just as in the same way the positive philosophy detaches itself from the negative philosophy in that, as I said, it lets go of the concept and retains only that which purely is, devoid of all whatness. With *this* principle of that which just exists, the positive philosophy *could* also begin entirely on its own, and begin even if no rational philosophy preceded it. For I, at the very least, did not know that one had disputed Spinoza's right to simply begin with that which infinitely exists, for we can also call that which infinitely exists that being which is not limited by any anterior potency. That which just—that which only—exists is precisely that which crushes everything that may derive from thought, before which thought becomes silent, and before which reason itself bows down; for thought is only concerned with possibility and potency; thus, where these are excluded, thought has no authority. That which infinitely exists is precisely for this reason—because it is this—also positioned securely against thought and all doubt.[xx] A principle however, cannot be something that promises upheaval

[*Umsturtz*]. A principle can only be that which guards against every subsequent possibility, thus, indubitably *exists*—[162] that which can never perish, abiding and necessary, which above all endures, come what may and regardless of what subsequently happens.

What has once begun in thought can only continue in thought and can never advance any further than to the *idea*. What shall reach reality must then also proceed directly from reality and, indeed, from *pure* actuality, thus, from the actuality that precedes all possibility. One could object: an actuality that precedes all possibility cannot be *thought*. One can concede this in a certain sense and say that for precisely this reason it is the *beginning* of all real thought—for the *beginning* of thought is not yet itself thought. An actuality that precedes possibility is surely also an actuality that precedes thought; but for precisely this reason it is the first proper *object* of thought [*quod se objicit*]. All the more important, however, is the question of what type of relation it could then have to reason if reason bows down before it. It surely has *on its own* a relation to reason, but as is clear from the expression just used, a negative relation.

That which infinitely exists can certainly put one in an embarrassing situation if one must explain whether it is also to be called an idea, a concept of reason. For the moment, it seems undeniable that one must call it an idea, since for the moment there seems to be no proposition and no assertion connected with it. That which just exists is in its way also that which exists of itself, αὐτὸ τὸ ὄν, that is if we accept this Greek ὄν in its verbal sense. To this extent, one cannot attach being to it as an *attribute*; what is *elsewhere* the predicate is here the subject: it is itself in the position of the subject. Existence, which appears as accidental in everything else, is here the essence. The *quod* is here in the position of the *quid*. It is, thus, a pure idea, and nonetheless it is not an idea in the sense this word is understood in the negative philosophy. That which just is [*das bloß Seyende*] is being [*das Seyn*] from which, properly speaking, every idea, that is, every potency, is excluded. We will, thus, only be able to call it the inverted idea [*Umgekehrte Idee*], the idea in which reason is set *outside* itself. Reason can posit being [163] in which there is still nothing of a concept, of a whatness, only as something that is absolutely *outside itself* (of course only in order to acquire it thereafter, a posteriori, as its content, and in this way to return to itself at the same time). In this positing, reason is therefore set outside itself, absolutely ecstatic. And who has not, for example,

---

xx. It would, indeed, be a contradiction to put before what comes first in thought another first thought, but it is not a contradiction to subordinate what is first in being, insofar as it is that which outstrips and, so to speak, surpasses all thought—to subordinate what comes first in thought to this, or to think of it as *posterius*. For it is not because there is thinking that there is being, but rather because there is being that there is thinking.

experienced the ecstatic dimension of Spinoza's philosophy and of all the other teachings that begin with that which necessarily exists![xxi]

Kant calls the unconditional necessity that, as he says, we so indispensably require as the *supporter of all things*, (no doubt Kant has the well-known argument in mind: if anything exists, if, at the very least, *I myself* exist, then there must also be something else that necessarily, and thus groundlessly, exists)—Kant calls the unconditional necessity of being, which precedes all thought, the true abyss for human reason. "Eternity itself," he continues,

> in all its terrible sublimity, as depicted by Haller,[44] is far from making the same overwhelming impression on the mind; for it only *measures* the duration of things, it does not *support* them. We cannot put aside, and yet also cannot endure the thought, that a being, which we represent to ourselves as supreme amongst all possible beings, should, as it were, say to itself: I am from eternity to eternity, and outside me there is nothing *save* what is through my will, *but whence then am I?* All support here fails us; and the greatest perfection, no less than the least perfection, is unsubstantial and baseless for the merely speculative reason, which makes not the least effort to retain either the one or the other, and feels indeed no loss in allowing them to vanish entirely.[xxii]

I quote these words because they express Kant's profound feeling for the sublime nature of the being that precedes all thought, in whose place in our own time being has indeed also been posited as the beginning of philosophy, but as just a moment of thought, whereas in this unavoidable and most deeply implanted thought of human nature, it is a matter of *the* being that exists *before* all thought. [164]

We can produce everything that occurs in our experience a priori in mere thought, but as such it exists, of course, *only* in thought. If we wanted to transform this into an objective proposition—say, that everything in itself likewise exists only in thought, then we would have to return to the standpoint of a Fichtean idealism. If we want anything that exists outside of thought, then we *must* proceed from a being that is absolutely independent of all thought, which precedes all thought. Of this being the Hegelian philosophy knows nothing—it has no place for this concept. Kant has in mind that which necessarily exists, to the extent that it is at the same time *God*. At the beginning of the positive philosophy we must still disregard this, and, seizing it as that which just exists, we discard the concept of *God* precisely because it is a contradiction to posit on the one hand that which just exists and, yet, also to posit

---

xxi. The mystic also wants to know *ecstatically* the *Whatness*.
xxii. *Critique of Pure Reason*, 470–71. [A 613/B 641.]

it as *something* with a *concept*. For either the concept must come first and being must be the result of the concept, so that it would then no longer be the unconditional being, or the concept is the result of being and we must then start from being, devoid of the concept, which is precisely what we want to do in the positive philosophy. But in God it is precisely *that* by virtue of which he is what groundlessly exists, which Kant calls the abyss of human reason, and what is this other than that before which reason stands motionless, by which reason is devoured in the face of which it is momentarily nothing and capable of nothing?

Kant still distinguishes the groundless necessity of existence in God from eternity, but the absolute eternity, eternity insofar as it is not yet *opposed* to time, but is rather before and above all time—absolute eternity is itself nothing other than precisely this existence, of which we know no *prius* and no beginning. For eternal is that which is preceded by no concept, against which thought has no *freedom*, as it does against finite being, which is of course anticipated in thought, and which philosophy can comprehend a priori.

One would completely misunderstand Kant if one wanted to see in this questionable position a *rejection* of that idea (of groundless necessary [165] existence). On the contrary, what he wants to express is merely its incomprehensibility, since he himself is overcome by the unavoidable necessity of reason to assume some kind of groundless being [*ein grundlos Seyendes*]. Incomprehensible—this existence is indeed that, if by incomprehensible one understands what is not comprehensible a priori. With the latter, with what is capable of being comprehended a priori, the negative philosophy busies itself while the positive deals with what is not capable of being comprehended a priori. But the positive philosophy concerns itself with this only in order to transform precisely that which is incomprehensible a priori into what is a posteriori comprehensible: what is incomprehensible a priori becomes comprehensible in God.

As long as reason makes itself into an object (and this direction was provided and profoundly impressed upon it by Kant), it can discover as its immediate content only the infinite potency of being—through which it sees itself posited in an a priori position toward all being, but only toward finite being. It cannot, however, come to terms with this on its own—it cannot bring itself to completion without demanding that which is above being [*das Ueberseyende*], but *this* has an entirely different *prius*: not the potency, but, rather, being, and indeed *that* being in which no thought can discover a ground or beginning. If reason is itself its object, if thought directs itself towards the content of reason as in the negative philosophy, then this is something accidental, and, thus, reason is not in its pure substantiality and essential nature. But if reason abides in *this* (that is, does not draw back into itself, thereby seeking the object within itself), then it can, as the infinite potency of cognition, only correspond to the infinite *actus*. According to its pure *nature* it posits only infinite being. Thus, conversely, if in positing this it becomes motionless, paralyzed, *quasi attonita*, it is paralyzed by that being which overpowers everything, but only *in order* that through this subordination reason may reach its true and eternal content, which it cannot find in the phenomenal world as something actually known, and which, for this reason, it even now *eternally* possesses.

That which infinitely exists is, thus, the *unmediated* concept of reason, to which reason free of itself, that is, no longer its own object, does not have to arrive at by first [166] proceeding through the very natural and unavoidable inferences of which Kant, in his naive manner, says: "There is something very strange in the fact, that once we assume something to exist we cannot avoid inferring that something exists necessarily."[xxiii] Kant calls this a natural and, for this reason, not a *certain* inference, and he is quite right to apply his critique to the cosmological proof that wants to ascend regressively from condition to condition to the unconditioned; but the simple and *immediately* posited concept of that which necessarily exists is precisely that which excludes all critique. The critique of a concept brings the possibility of its object into question. But it would be nonsense, as already pointed out, to ask whether that which necessarily exists *could* exist, although this is what has been asked. For if it only *could* exist it would, of course, not be that which necessarily exists. For this very reason, it is that which necessarily exists, since it excludes every *anterior* possibility and precedes every potency. One may well wish to submit the concept of that which necessarily exists, when it is the result of an argument (and particularly of the cosmological argument), to a critique, but no one has been able to submit to a critique the concept directly put forth by Spinoza, just as no one can escape from it, but, rather, all must submit to it. Only in this concept, not in the system itself, lies the alleged irrefutability of Spinoza's philosophy.[45]

No less absurd than the question of whether that which necessarily exists *could* exist would also be the question: "*What type of being [Wesen]* can that which necessarily exists be? How would this being have to be constituted so that it can be that which necessarily exists?" Such questions arose in the cosmological argument, where one first proves the unavoidable supposition of a necessarily existing being, and afterwards seeks to show that this necessarily existing being can only be the most perfect being, that is, God. It is, therefore, absurd to ask: "What type of being *could* exist necessarily?" For in doing this, I assume that that which necessarily exists is preceded by an essence, a what, a [167] possibility, whereas, on the contrary, I must posit this as that which just exists and in which still nothing of an essence, of a what, is to be comprehended.

In the way that the old metaphysics dealt with this concept, this illusion always arises, due to the fact that in the pure concept of that which necessarily exists, in which still nothing of an essence should be thought, one distinguishes

---

xxiii. Ibid., 515. [A 616/B 643.]

an essence (namely the deity) and does not, as we earlier instructed, abandon this *concept* entirely in order to arrive at that which just is. Kant states in his critique of the cosmological argument that the entire challenge—namely of the transcendental ideal—is a matter of either finding the absolute necessity of a concept, or of finding in the concept of any kind of thing the absolute necessity of that thing. "If either task be possible," he proceeds, "so must the other; for reason recognizes only that as absolutely necessary which follows of necessity from its *concept.*"[xxiv] Regarding this last point, I deny that any kind of being [*Wesen*] will be realized as necessary on account of its concept. For if this being should be God, then it is to be realized from its *concept* not that he necessarily exists, but, rather, that he *can only be* that which necessarily exists, and, thus, that he is necessarily that which necessarily exists—that is, *if* he exists—but it does not follow that he exists. Is it, however, a question of that which simply and necessarily exists, then one cannot again say that existence *follows* from its concept, for its concept is precisely to be that which just exists: existence here is not the consequence of the concept or of the essence, but, rather, that which exists [*das Existirende*] is here itself the concept and itself the essence.

But regarding the second part of the Kantian either-or (the first was that necessary existence is sought in the concept of some type of being, which happens in the ontological argument, the second conversely sought the concept of absolute necessity), this would be the proper business of a positive philosophy that seeks to get from that which necessarily exists (as a still nonconceptual *prius*) to the *concept*, [168] to the essence (*God*) as *posterius*. As one sees, this strategy is exactly opposite to that of the ontological argument; however, to be capable of executing it, one must first make up one's mind about the concept of that which just simply is, and have completely nullified the false dependency in which this concept was held to the idea of God in the former metaphysics. For that which necessarily exists is not that which necessarily exists because it is God; for then it would not be that which necessarily and thus groundlessly exists, since in the concept of God there would have then been found a *ground* for its necessary existence. That which necessarily exists is precisely that which exists not in consequence of an antecedent concept, but rather exists *of itself*—as one used to express it, *a se*, that is, *sponte, ultra*, and which exists without an antecedent ground. Here lies the confusion of the former metaphysics, which is only to be resolved if both concepts are held apart. Kant was so close to achieving this resolution, since, on the one hand, he acknowledged the impossibility of denying of that which necessarily exists as an immediate concept of reason, and he, on the other hand, recognized the concept of the most supreme being [*Wesens*] as the final, lasting content of reason. In this way, Kant failed to connect the absolutely *immanent* concept, that of the most supreme being (for *everything else is only* relatively

---

xxiv. Ibid., 513. [A 612/B 640.]

immanent to the extent that it can pass over into being), and the absolutely *transcendent* concept (of that which necessarily exists), leaving one *beside* the other, *both* as concepts of reason, but without being able to explain their *being* beside one another. Here there really is a hole in Kant's critique. Yet both concepts must limit one another, because the first (that of the most supreme being) is the end of the negative philosophy, and the other (of that which necessarily exists) is the starting point of the positive philosophy. Both concepts are consequently also connected in the former, as well as in the later, but in the former in a different way. In the negative, one says: "The most supreme being, *if it exists*, can only a priori be that which is [*das Seyende seyn*], thus, it must be that which necessarily exists, it must be that which *is* before its concept, and, thus, before every concept." This is the one and only truth that remains to be [169] found in the ontological argument. In the positive philosophy they are connected in such a way that one says: "That which necessarily exists (that is, that which simply and necessarily exists) *is*—not necessarily, but rather *factually* [*faktisch*] the necessarily necessary existing being [*Wesen*], or God." This is proved a posteriori in the manner already indicated, namely, in that one says: "If that which necessarily exists is *God*, then this and that consequence—we want to say, then *a*, *b*, *c*, and so on—become *possible*; but if according to our experience *a*, *b*, *c*, and so on, really exist, then the necessary conclusion is that that which necessarily exists is *really* God."

I have, therefore, called that which is devoid of anterior potency the absolutely transcendent concept. Since Kant, there has been so much favorable discussion of immanent knowledge, immanent knowing and thinking, and only unfavorable discussion about the transcendent that one cannot mention the latter without a kind of apprehension or fear. However, this fear is only fitting for the standpoint of the former metaphysics, which we have superseded [*aufgehoben*]. Consider the following. Everything transcendent is actually something relative, since it is this only in reference to something that is transcended. If I infer from the *idea* of the most supreme being its *existence*, then this is a transcending: I first posited the idea and now wish to pass from it over into existence—here is then a transcendence. If, however, I *proceed* from that which is anterior to all concepts, then I have surpassed nothing, and, on the contrary, if one calls this being transcendent and I advance within it to its concept, then I have surpassed the transcendent and *in this way* again become immanent. The transcendence of the old metaphysics was merely relative, that is, timid and half-hearted, whereby one wanted to remain with one foot stuck in the concept. The transcendence of the positive philosophy is an absolute transcendence, and for precisely this reason is *not* transcendent in the sense in which Kant had forbidden it. Once I have made myself immanent, that is, enclosed myself in pure thought, then a transcendence is hardly possible; however, if I start from the transcendent (like the positive philosophy), then there is nothing that I have to exceed. [170] Kant forbade metaphysics transcendence, but he forbade it only for dogmatizing reason, that is, for reason that of

The Grounding of Positive Philosophy 209

itself seeks, by means of inferences, to reach existence; he did not forbid reason to proceed conversely from that which *simply* and, thus, infinitely *exists* to the concept of the most supreme *being* as *posterius* (he had not thought of it, for this possibility had not even presented itself to him). However, as we said earlier, reason can posit that *simple* being (ἁπλῶς ὄν) absolutely *outside* itself, precisely because only in this simple being is there no trace of a concept, since it is that which is opposed to all concepts. But reason posits this simple being only with the intent to make what is external to and above reason once again into the content of reason: it will do precisely this because a posteriori it is God (is known as God). It posits nonconceptual being [*begrifflose Seyn*] in order to reach from it to the concept; it posits the transcendent in order to transform it into the immanent and to have that which is *absolutely* immanent simultaneously as something that exists and that is only possible in this way, since reason indeed already has that which is absolutely immanent in the negative philosophy, but not as something that exists.

The pure or infinite potency (the beginning of the negative philosophy) is the content *identical* with thought, which, because it does not go *toward* thought (since it is identical to it), only proceeds out from thought. In contrast, that which *simply* is is the content that is not identical with thought; indeed, it is excluded from the very start and, for this very reason, it can and must be first conveyed to thought *since* it is originally external to thought. God is not, as many imagine, the transcendent, he is the immanent (that is, what is to become the content of reason) made transcendent. In that this has been overlooked lies the great misunderstanding of our time. As I have already said, what is a priori incomprehensible, because it is conveyed through no anterior concept, will become a comprehensible being in God, or it arrives at its concept in God. That which infinitely exists, that which reason cannot hide within itself becomes immanent for reason in God.

Until now we have called the negative philosophy primarily a [171] science of reason. This can make the positive philosophy appear as if it were a science opposed to reason. But the true relationship is this: in the former, reason proceeds from its immediate but contingent content, progressively liberating itself from that which is contingent, so that in a necessary progression it arrives at its enduring content. But it arrives at this without having to reach it as something actual: the content remains stuck in the mere idea.[xxv] The *positive* philosophy proceeds from that which is entirely outside of reason, but reason submits to this only in order to immediately enter again into its rightful domain. It has already been said earlier: the science of reason cannot demonstrate its final idea—which is precisely that content of reason which always remains *in* reason—as it can with everything else that has occurred to it in experience. And yet it is precisely *this* concept that has the distinction of being

---

xxv. Although it is *its* idea; c.f. the *Introduction to the Philosophy of Mythology*, I/5, 562.—ED.

the one that does not allow indifference about the actual existence of what it demands, as was the case for the philosophizing subject in regard to whether everything else that preceded it exists. Here this means *Tua res agitur* [your matter is done]. Because of this, reason, which cannot demonstrate its final idea in experience, *must* now turn to the being [*Seyn*] that is itself outside and above experience, to the being that relates to reason as the *pure* faculty of knowing in the same exact way as the being occurring within experience relates to the sensible faculty of representation.

Of itself, reason cannot realize or prove any actual, real being even in the sensible world; it cannot realize or prove any *present* existence, for example, the existence of *this* plant or this stone. If reason wants a real being, if it wants as something real any type of object discovered within itself in a concept and, thus, as something merely possible, then it must submit to the authority of the senses. For the testimony of the senses is nothing other than an authority, since through it we know the present existence, the plant that exists *here*, which cannot be realized from the mere *nature* of things, and thus from reason. If one now wishes to [172] call *this* submission to authority belief, then this is the correct term: through belief (namely, through the sheer authority of our senses, not through reason) we know that things outside us *exist*. This word, to the best of my knowledge, comes to us from F.G.Hamann, but it only has meaning, as was said, insofar as *every* submission to an authority can be termed belief. A different word of Thomas Aquinas's also distinguishes quite clearly what allows itself to be known from the mere *nature* of things and what does not. To the latter, of course, he ascribes only *ea quae divina autoritate traduntur* [the things bequeathed by divine authority]. These, however, are also *supra naturam*, that is, they are more than what can be realized in the mere nature of things as a result of only conceptual necessity. However, more generally, it can be said that everything that refers to existence is more than what can be realized from the mere nature of things and, thus, also with pure reason. With pure reason I cannot, as was said, even realize the existence of some plant that if it is an actual plant, exists necessarily in a definite location in space and at a definite point in time. Under given conditions, reason, *of itself*, can know quite well the *nature* of this plant, but never its actual, present existence.

One can also trace this antithesis back to the distinction made quite some time ago between *thought* and *representation*. This distinction originally comes to us from Reinhold and, after many others, Hegel also made use of it in order to say, among other things, that religion, and revelation in particular, contains what is true only in the manner of representation [*Vorstellung*], that is, not even in the *form* of truth, since it is only *like this* in thought. In this way, even the concept of God belongs merely to representation, since in pure thought God is the conclusion, the result. *God*, however, what one really calls God (and I believe that even the philosopher must direct his employ of language according to general usage), can only be he who is the creator, who can begin something, who thus exists before everything, and who is not just an

The Grounding of Positive Philosophy 211

idea of reason. A God who does not *exist* could also not be called God, but since existence can never be realized in mere thought, even the [173] God who really is it, according to Hegel, belongs to mere representation. But even Hegel himself in his own philosophy could remain no less than true to this restriction to pure thought and exclusion of everything that belongs to representation: he himself remains in pure thought as long as he is immersed in the logic whose contents, however, are mere abstractions and, thus, nothing real. Yet when he passes over into reality, into real nature (and the philosophy of nature also qualifies for him as a part of philosophy, and indeed as an essential element), he is compelled to reach for explanations that, according to his own views, can only belong to the modality of representation, so that one truly does not realize with what right he specifically determines religion as the *form* that contains truth only in the modality of representation. Pure thought, in which everything develops of necessity, knows nothing of a decision, of an act, or even of a deed. Even this antithesis between representation and thought, like so many others, does not achieve clarity in Hegel.

Originally, representation [*Vorstellung*] was spoken of only in reference to objects of *sense* perception. As the result of a received impression, we put before us an object in space. The next content of this representation is only the *existence* of something in general [*etwas überhaupt*]. *What* it is that we represent, the *quid*, first comes with the second representation; the *quod* is thus in the representation, which, because of this, may have received the name *before* the *quid*. Representation and thought relate to one another, therefore, as existence and essence; the content of pure representation is being [*Seyn*] and the content of pure thought is essence, but, with this, it becomes immediately clear that both cannot subsist in this abstract and reciprocal exclusion and the one must immediately proceed into the other. The being that precedes all thought is to this extent precisely that which is absolutely represented [*absolut Vorgestellte*]. But opposed to this, against this pure *thatness*, thought immediately rises up and inquires about the *whatness*, or about the *concept*. This is also the path of the positive philosophy, whose genesis we have finally once again addressed.

This concept, the concept of that which is represented absolutely, is to be that [174] of the universal essence, the *potentia universalis*. The same one that is before every potency, in which there can be nothing universal, and which, therefore, can only be the absolute individual—precisely *this* is the embodiment [*Inbegriff*] of all principles and comprehends all being. He is, this means, this one who is not (μὴ ὄν), who is the sheer totality of all possibility, and who is the cause of being (αἰτία τοῦ εἶναι), for the very reason that he is this. In this the being of being [*das Seyende-seyn*] (as we earlier called being [*das Seyende*] the embodiment of all principles) resides his eternal divinity,[xxvi]

---

xxvi. ἡ ἀίδιος αὐτοῦ θειότηςγκ [His eternal Godhead—an allusion to Romans 1:20].

and it is through this that he makes himself knowable. For, of itself, the One is unknown, it has no concept through which it could be designated, but rather only a *name*—therefore, the importance placed on the name—in name *He* is *himself*, the singular being who has no equal. The One is known as the universal essence, the πᾶν, being according to its *content* (not effective being). It is thereby known and distinguished from other individual beings as *the* individual being who is *everything*.

To bring this concept into view is the task of a positive philosophy that is certain of its beginning. It is this concept, the concept of that which is capable of all things, of the absolute spirit—for what is an embodiment of the principles of being can only be spirit, and what is the embodiment of all principles can only be *absolute* spirit.

It was remarked earlier that the philosophy of revelation, to which we now pass over, is nothing other than an application of the positive philosophy itself. According to its universal and philosophical content, the former coincides with the later.

The first part of the philosophy of revelation proceeds to the point where, as the intelligibility of the *content* of revelation is provided, the possibility of a philosophy of revelation is also given. The second part concerns itself with making this content comprehensible.

NOTES

TRANSLATOR'S INTRODUCTION

All Schelling citations are my own, except for passages taken from Peter Heath's translation of Schelling's *System of Transcendental Idealism* (1800). I have used the following form when citing Schelling's collected works: (II/3, 163) refers to part, volume, and page of *Schellings Sämtliche Werke*, ed. K.F.A. Schelling (Stuttgart-Augsberg: J.G. Cotta, 1856–64). Abbreviations for other Schelling texts are found in the notes below.

1. Schelling, *Grundlegung der Positiven Philosophie: Münchener Vorlesung WS 1832/33 und SS 1833*, ed. Horst Fuhrmans (Turin: Bottega D'Erasmo, 1972), 99 (hereafter cited as GPP).
2. Ibid., 100.
3. Ibid., 93.
4. Claude Lévi-Strauss, *The Naked Man: An Introduction to a Science of Mythology*, vol. 4, trans. John and Doreen Weightman (New York: Harper and Row, 1981), 625.
5. Schelling, *Philosophie der Offenbarung 1841/42*, ed. Manfred Frank (Frankfurt am Main: Suhrkamp, 1977), 170 (hereafter cited as PO). I depend mightily in much of what follows on Frank's insightful and comprehensive introduction to the *Paulus Nachschrift*. The supplementary historical documents he has collected in this volume are required reading for anyone who wants to understand the complexities of the situation surrounding Schelling's first lectures in Berlin.
6. Terry Pinkard takes such a position in his recent treatment of Schelling, when he writes that "any presentation of 'Schelling's Philosophy' can only be either a presentation of some time-slice of it or else display the developmental history of a train of thought that was cut short only by Schelling's death." Terry Pinkard, *German Philosophy 1760–1860: The Legacy of Idealism* (Cambridge: Cambridge University Press, 2002), 172.
7. Christian Daniel Rauch to Sulpiz Boisserée, Berlin, 1 November 1836, cited in *Schelling im Spiegel seiner Zeitgenossen*, ed. Xavier Tilliette (Turin: 1974), 627–8.

8. Friedrich Wilhelm, as quoted by Max Lenz, *Geschichte der königlichen Friedrich-Wilhelm Universität zu Berlin*, Bd. II, 2 (Halle a.d.S.: Berlin, 1918), 9–10; cited in PO, 72, n. 6.

9. In his sixty-sixth year, Schelling made it clear that he would make the move from Munich to Berlin only on his terms. Money was an issue, and by the end of negotiations Schelling was scheduled to receive 5,000 Taler instead of the average professor's salary of 1,980 (PO, 73).

10. Adolf Harnack, *Geschichte der Kgl-Preußischen Akademie der Wissenschaften zu Berlin*, Bd. I/2, (Halle a.d.S.: Berlin, 1900), 919; cited in PO, 11.

11. Christian Carl Josias Freiherr von Bunsen, *Aus seiner Briefen und nach eigener Erinnerung geschildert von seiner Witwe*. Deutsche Ausgabe von Friedrich Nippold, Bd. 2 (Leipzig: 1868), 133; cited in PO, 408. The cited words are not those of the king himself but of his ambassador, C. J. Bunsen.

12. Frederick Beiser, *The Fate of Reason: German Philosophy from Kant to Fichte* (Cambridge, MA: Harvard University Press, 1987), 81, n. 108.

13. Karl Jaspers, *Schelling: Größe und Verhängnis* (Munich: 1955); cited in PO, 1, n. 1.

14. Schelling, *System der Welalter: Münchener Vorlesung 1827/28 in einer Nachschrift von Ernst von Lasaulux*, ed. Siegbert Peetz (Frankfurt am Main: Vittorio Klostermann, 1990), 85 (hereafter cited as WMV).

15. *Über Schelling und Hegel. Ein Sendschreiben an Pierre Leroux* (Königsberg: 1843), 7; cited in PO, 14.

16. *Le Semeur. Journal religieux, politique, philosophique, et litéraire*, Paris, Tome X, Nr. 9. (3 March 1841), 66; cited in PO, 412.

17. Friedrich Engels, *Telegraph für Deutschland*, Nr. 207/8, December 1841; cited in PO 459.

18. Anonymous publication of a Hegelian supporter, cited in the *Augsburger Allgemeinen Zeitung*, Nr. 236, July 24, 1841; cited in PO, 13.

19. Friedrich Engels, *Telegraph für Deutschland*; cited in PO 460.

20. Karl Marx, *Zur Kritik der Hegelschen Rechtsphilosophie*, MEW Bd. I, 378; cited in PO, 11. Frank makes this case in his introduction to the *Paulus Nachschrift*, and I follow his argument here quite closely. Any distortions and dubious leaps in reasoning are of my creation.

21. G. Bacherer, cited by Helmut Pölcher, *Schellings Auftreten in Berlin (1841) nach Hörerberichten*, in: ZRG VI (1954) Heft 3, 197; cited in PO, 11.

22. Arnold Ruge to Robert Prutz, Dresden, 21 October 1841; cited in PO, 421. The characterization of Schelling as an apologist "for the contemporary state-sanctioned Christianity and for the authority of the monarchy" (Pinkard, 330), does not stand up to critical scrutiny in light of both the historical record and Schelling's political philosophy. The fact that Schelling openly defied the government of Bayern's edict banning philosophy instructors from addressing theological issues complements his insistence that he have complete academic freedom in Berlin. Philosophically, Schelling called for the shrinking of the state, a position he contrasts sharply with Hegel's "deification of the state," which he characterizes in the following manner: "The spirit that is thoroughly conscious of itself however, can no longer 'lower itself' to art… After this there can no longer be poetry and art. Instead of history and art containing all of this magnificence there is, however, still one surrogate: this philosophy ends with the deification of the state… But even in this deification of the state, this philosophy shows

itself as being fully trapped in the immense error of [our] time. The state, [no matter] how much it includes that which is positive within itself, still belongs to the side of the most negative forces that are against all that is positive, and against all manifestations of the higher spiritual and ethical life. The state is but the carrier of a higher life. The state is the organism that is determined to support a higher, spiritual, ethical, and religious life. And just as the body is more healthy when it is less aware of its organism, so are those peoples, who have to fight for their external organism [the state], denigrated to a lower level of life. The true, but greatly misunderstood task of our time is to shrink the state itself…in every form. Thus whoever makes the state into the absolute highest, has a system which is essentially conservative, in that he subordinates everything that is higher [in life] to the state" (GPP, 234–35). Schelling's independence from, and philosophical critique of state power, stands in marked contrast to Hegel's open—in the words of Fries, "sycophantic"—dedication to the Prussian state, demonstrated perhaps most clearly in the words he personally wrote in a copy of his *Philosophy of Right* given to Chancellor von Hardenberg in 1820. According to the note his main goal in this work is "to demonstrate the harmony of philosophy with those principles which are generally required by the nature of the state, but most immediately with the principle which the Prussian state—belonging to which is a source of the greatest satisfaction to me—has had the good fortune of having upheld and continuing to uphold under the enlightened government of His Majesty the King and the sagacious leadership of Your Highness." Cited in Horst Althause, *Hegel: an Intellectual Biography*, trans. Michael Tarsh (Malden, MA: Polity Press, 2000), 151.

23. The difficulty of translating the word *Geist* itself points to this tension between integration and alienation. Sometimes we translate this term into English as mind, in the rational and intellectual sense, and other times we must use that most awkward of terms for philosophers, spirit, as in the religious sense of spirituality. Either way, the translation cheats the complex richness of meaning of the German term *Geist*, which has the capacity to unify both the intellectual and the spiritual.

24. G. W. F. Hegel, *Lectures on the Philosophy of Religion*, trans. and ed. P. Hodgson et al. (Berkeley: University of California Press, 1987), 92, n. 42.

25. G. W. F. Hegel, *Logic: Part One of the Encyclopedia of the Philosophical Sciences (1830)*, (Oxford: Oxford University Press, 1975), sec. 70, 104, n. 1.

26. Ibid., sec. 70, 104.

27. G. W. F. Hegel, *Lectures on the Philosophy of Religion*, 100. Hegel's unrelenting insistence on there being just one true method led Pierre Leroux to charge that Hegel was "the inventor of the specialized technical discipline of philosophy." Following the example of the successful retailer, Hegel realized that focusing one's business on one narrow specialty is the secret to success. "Hegel has behaved exactly like those retailers who write in large letters on their storefront 'Specialties.'—'I restrict myself to one single selection,' the retailer says, 'I follow the principle of the division of labor, and my products are therefore better and more exclusive.' According to Leroux, Hegel argues in the same fashion: 'We are moving philosophy forward (more cultivated), and leave it to our neighbors to deal with religion; we do not maintain that the wares of our neighbors are bad,…they have their specialties and we have ours; the consumers are different: the masses go to them—the higher classes to us.'" Pierre Leroux, *La Revue Indépendante*, trans. Jochen and Renate Hörsche, June 1842, 582; cited in PO, 482.

28. Pierre Leroux, *La Revue Indépendante*, May 1842, 330; cited in PO, 480.

29. Goethe to Seebeck, 28 November 1812. *Vom tätigen—Goethes Briefe aus der zweiten Hälfte seines Lebens*, hrsg. Ernst Hartung (Ebenhausen: Wilhelm Langewiesche-Brandt, 1919), 128.

30. Pierre Leroux, *La Revue Indépendante*, 29; cited in PO, 477–8.

31. "When philosophy paints its grey on grey, then has a shape of life grown old. By philosophy's grey on grey it cannot be rejuvenated but only understood. The owl of Minerva spreads its wings only with the falling of the dusk." G. W. F. Hegel, *Elements of the Philosophy of Right*, ed. Allen Wood, trans. H. B. Nisbet (Cambridge: Cambridge University Press, 1991), 13.

32. M. A. Bakunin, *Sobranie socinenij I pisem 1828–1876*, trans. Barbara Conrad, Red. Is prim. Ju. M. Steklova (Moskva: 1934), Bd. 2, 66; cited in PO, 461.

33. Sören Kierkegaard, *Die Tagebücher*, Bd. 1 (Düsseldorf: 1962), 273; cited in PO, 452.

34. Pierre Leroux, *La Revue Indépendante*, April 1842, 7; cited in PO, 477.

35. Pierre Leroux, *La Revue Indépendante*, May 1842, 344; cited in PO, 481.

36. Schelling is referring to his *Philosophical Letters on Dogmatism and Criticism*, begun while he was still a student at the Tübingen Stift in 1795 (I/1, 281).

37. Beiser, *The Fate of Reason*, 47.

38. Immanuel Kant, *Critique of Pure Reason*, trans. N. K. Smith (London: Macmillan and Co., 1964), A 800/B 828 (hereafter cited as *CPR*).

39. That his *Naturphilosophie* was more important than his work on transcendental philosophy is clearly demonstrated by the fact that he generated twice as many pages on the subject: roughly 1600 pages on his *Naturphilosophie*, to 800 on transcendental philosophy.

40. Hamann held that all men had the possibility of enjoying a direct experience of God's presence anywhere and at any time if they allowed themselves to be open to such immanent transcendence. The world of nature itself thus becomes the most important medium through which the divine presence is mediated; God's presence manifests itself in, and speaks through, the world of nature, at least "to those who have eyes to see and ears to hear" (Hamann, cited in Isaiah Berlin, "Hume and German Anti-Rationalism," in *Against the Current*, [New York: 1980], 167). Although a close friend of Kant, Hamann repeatedly charged his fellow Pietist with creating a theoretical "castle in the air," which mistakes "words for concepts, and concepts for realities" (Hamann to Jacobi, 14 November 1784, ibid., 168). While such conceptual analysis may play an essential role in logic, economic, and technical activities, it fails to provide an adequate access to the real world. Instead of diving into Goethe's "stream of the world," the conceptual analyst remains trapped within a "virtual" world of possible experience.

41. Following Lessing and Herder, Schelling built his *Magister* (his master's thesis) around the then prevalent reading of the Fall in the Garden of Eden as a symbol of the simultaneous birth of freedom and knowledge (II/1, 40–41).

42. In the following citations from Schelling's *System of Transcendental Idealism*, I am using Peter Heath's translation of Schelling's *System of Transcendental Idealism (1800)* (Charlottesville: University Press of Virginia, 1993), 95.

43. It was most likely Bardilli, and not Hölderlin, who was responsible for this etymological wordplay.

44. Schelling's point is the inverse of Fichte's position that the knowing subject must have a different cognitive status than what it knows: the ground of consciousness must have a different cognitive status than consciousness itself.

45. "λόγου ἀρχὴ οὐ λόγοσ, ἀλλά τι κρεῖττον," Greek as found in Aristotle, *Eudemian Ethics* (Loeb Classical Library: 1934), 1248a28. Schelling makes this reference in 1797. In 1854, some fifty-seven years later, he again calls on Aristotle's passage to emphasize that "what truly exists is first, what is external to the idea, that is not the idea, but is rather more than the idea, κρεῖττον τοῦ λόγου" (II/1, 566).

46. Again: philosophy cannot account for our consciousness, reason, or thought without calling on a ground that transcends the phenomenon under consideration. Under threat of circularity, the ground of thinking cannot itself be thinking, and as stated above, all such attempts at an immanent grounding will ultimately prove to be a form of self-involved fiction.

47. Contrary to Derrida and other Post-Structuralists, Saussure called upon the subject as the central agent responsible for providing an actual ground for self-consciousness and meaning. According to the *official version* of the Saussure's *Cours*, it is the individual person who speaks words: "The vocal sound is not a word except to the exact, constant extent that a meaning is attached to it [...]. Thought is what delimits units; sound itself does not delimit them in advance: there is always a relation to thought" (*Cahiers Ferdinand de Saussure* 15 [1957], 8, 68). Derrida based his readings on the vulgate version of Saussure's *Cours*, a collection of lecture notes edited and published in 1915 by two former students, Bally and Sechehaye. In this inaccurate version of Saussure's lectures, the role and importance of the thinking and speaking subject hardly even appears. In the quote above, taken from the *critical edition* of Saussure's works, the significance of a meaning conferring consciousness clearly emerges. In light of the fact that the critical edition had been available since 1957, that is, since before Derrida began to deconstruct the Structuralists, Derrida was repeatedly challenged to correct his readings of Saussure. Unfortunately, he never even addressed the issue. For more on this, see Ludwig Jäger, "F. De Saussures historisch-hermeneutische Idee der Sprache: Ein Plädoyer für die Rekonstruction des Saussureschen Denkens in seiner authentischen Gestalt," *Linguistik und Didaktik* 27 (1976): 210–44.

48. Schelling paraphrases two passages from Plato's *Cratylus*. The first reads: "Those on the other hand, who say οὐσια would agree, well enough with Heraclitus that all things move and nothing remains still" (401d). The second is: "Heraclitus says, you know, that all things move and nothing remains still, and he likens the universe to the current of a river, saying that you cannot step twice into the same stream" (402a).

49. This unceasing movement of discursivity compares nicely with Derrida's belief in the infinite deferral of meaning within the diacritical system of linguistic signs, which, for him at least, exhaustively account for language, and thus meaning. This comparison supports Schelling's contention that negative philosophy is a continuous presence with philosophy in general.

50. Schelling refers to Aristotle's substantive treatment of Parmenides in *Physics* 1.3, the conclusions of which are referred to in *Metaphysics I*, v. 12–14.

51. Schelling cites *The Republic* 6.22.511f. See 511b for Plato's presentation of what Schelling here calls a "*Denkwissenschaft*."

52. Consequently, negative philosophy will always be "the philosophy of the academy, whereas the positive will be the philosophy for life" (II/3, 155).

53. *CPR* (B xxxv).

54. Immanuel Kant, *Logic*, trans. R. S. Hartman and W. Schwarz (New York: Dover, 1988), 79 (hereafter cited as L). When viewed from the context of this distinction between a positive and a merely formal knowing, Schelling believes he can make sense of Socrates' claim of ignorance: "Thus the knowledge which according to Socrates' assertion has something in common with the other forms of knowing, but which he regarded as ignorance, may very well be the pure science of reason; a science he knew as well or even better than the Eleatic philosophers, and from which he distinguished himself precisely through the fact that whereas they wanted to make their logical knowledge into a knowing knowledge, in Socrates' opinion it could only be maintained as an ignorant knowing" (II/3, 99).

55. *CPR* (B xxv).

56. *Grundlegung der Positiven Philosophie: Münchener Vorlesung WS 1832–33 und SS 1833*.

57. GPP, 223. Schelling makes the obvious point that if philosophy were really the science that presupposes nothing, "then it would have to deduce language itself. The philosophy that absolutely presupposed nothing would have no other option than to refrain from all speech" whatsoever (*ibid*).

58. Following his method of construction, the production of this initial concept is a creative act whose legitimacy can only be determined by others if they themselves have also produced such a concept.

59. Kant to J. H. Lambert, 2 September 1770, AK 10:98; B xxv.

60. The question here is obvious: how can a regulative ideal serve as the ground of reason's edifice and its alleged necessary certainty? That is, how can a regulative ideal serve as the basis of reason? Kant holds that the apodeictic use of reason is dependent upon the transcendental ideal's power to supply systematic unity to reason. But "the unity of reason is purely hypothetical" because this unity is dependent upon an ideal, which reason nonetheless must always "presuppose" in order to function (A 650/B 678). Kant is compelled by the design of his construction "to presuppose a transcendental principle whereby such a systematic unity is *a priori* assumed to be necessarily inherent in the objects" of reason's consideration (A 651/B 679). And finally: "the law of reason which requires us to seek for this unity, is a necessary law, since without it we should have no reason at all, and without reason no coherent employment of the understanding, and in the absence of this no sufficient criterion of empirical truth. In order, therefore, to secure an empirical criterion, we have no option save to presuppose the systematic unity of nature as objectively valid and necessary" (A 651/B 679). With this, we again encounter the circular dynamic generated by Kant's regressive method.

61. *Inbegriff* is a most difficult word to translate. In Latin, one might say it is a *comprehension*, whereby we mean it is a collection or aggregation of things. It is, in this sense, that Kant here speaks of the transcendental ideal as encompassing the unconditioned totality of all possible determinations of things. Here at least, *Inbegriff* does denote a sum, and therewith, the result of a process.

62. Immanuel Kant, *Schriften zur ästhetik und Philosophie*, hsg. Manford Frank und Véronique Zanetti (Frankfurt am Main: Deutscher Klassiker Verlag, 1996), 582 (hereafter cited as the third *Critique*).

63. The third *Critique*, 582.

64. The third *Critique*, 592.

65. Schelling to Hegel, in Gustav Plitt, ed., vol I, 71.

66. As Schelling's son notes, "In earlier lectures of the author the positive philosophy was also designated as a progressive empiricism, since it was not regressive" (II/3, 130, n. 2).

67. As the logical form of the category of reciprocity, the disjunctive relation binds its members simultaneously together and apart. This relation is "not, however, of logical sequence, but of logical opposition, in so far as the sphere of the one excludes the sphere of the other, and yet at the same time [it is a relation] of community, in so far as the propositions taken together occupy the whole sphere of the knowledge in question" (A 73/B 99). There is, however, no additive sequence in the first moment of this disjunctive logic of opposition. The first moment is the relation of community, which supports the opposition between different members; a common whole that, while it unites and coordinates the oppositional relations of its constituent parts, cannot be treated epistemologically as its constituent parts are: the whole is transcendent, and thus heterogeneous, to its constituent *membra disjuncta*. And it is for this very reason that the logic of disjunction is problematic: it works through a nonlinear logic of reciprocity whose simultaneous interaction of ground and consequent explodes the linear sequence of ground and consequent required by exponible concepts (B 441/A 414; cf. L, sec. 117, 149). To parse its simultaneity Kant would have to qualify the form of inner sense and its time sequence (something that he will only later allow in his treatment of the sublime and its subsequent *Aufhebung* of the time conditions (third *Critique*, 593)). As Kant repeatedly emphasizes, since the synthesis of the disjunctive form of judgment generates unities that "contain nothing on which to base a series [*keinen Exponenten einer Reihe haben*]," reason can find "no ground for proceeding regressively to conditions" (A 414/B 441).

68. "This unity of reason has always presupposed an idea, namely, that of the form of a whole of knowledge—a whole which is prior to the determinate knowledge of the parts and which contains the conditions that determine a priori for every part its position and relation to the other parts" (A 645/B 673).

69. L, sec. 30, 114–15.

70. As he does in articulating the logic of freedom, organism, and reflective judgment, Kant here employs the disjunctive syllogism in his effort to finally account for how all the individualized parts of our reality cohere as one unified system. He maintains that this logical form somehow employs both the principle of the excluded middle and a principle of complementarity. Coordinating and not subordinating relations of sequence and reciprocity, he explains that the sphere of a disjunctive syllogism is divided into parts "thought as co-ordinated with, not subordinated to, each other, and so determining each other, not in one direction only, as in a series, but reciprocally" (B 112). The law of contradiction follows from the categorical form of syllogism that requires a linear relation among members of a series, thereby excluding the reciprocal connection among *membra disjuncta*. The disjunctive form allows Kant to entertain the possibility of thinking an oppositional dynamic between the members of a whole that, "taken together," constitute "the sphere of the whole as parts of the sphere of a cognition, each [part] being the complement of the other (*complementum ad totem*)." We can see with this definition why this is the form that the dynamic unconditioned must take. He continues: "The division in disjunctive judgments thus indicates the coordination not of the parts of the whole concept, but all the parts of its sphere. There I think many things through one concept; here one thing through many concepts, e.g., the definitum through all characteristics of coordination" (L, sec. 39, 114–15).

Schelling follows Kant very closely in his Würzburg lectures of 1804, when he posits the disjunctive form of logical relation as the highest principle of his logic: "The disjunctive *Schluß* presents the highest totality divided, so to speak, in that it contains all the conditions to the determination of its object" (II/6, 526).

71. The full passage reads: "The subject of the categories cannot by thinking the categories acquire a concept of itself as an object of the categories. For in order to think them, its pure self-consciousness, which is what was to be explained, must itself be presupposed" (B 422).

72. Albrecht von Haller (1708–1777), a Swiss botanist who also wrote poetry.

73. The third *Critique*, 582. Yet while Kant perhaps does appreciate these sublime experiences, he nonetheless finds them, just like other inexponible concepts, to be "unsubstantial and baseless" for a "speculative reason" that "feels indeed no loss in allowing them to vanish entirely" (A 613/B 641). And it is here that Schelling perhaps most strongly objects to Kant's refusal to integrate the positive facticty he demands yet refuses to provide, in that the ultimate ground of all his determinations, the *ens originarium*, is ultimately no more than a necessary idea whose actual existence we can never know.

74. *Eudemian Ethics*, 1248a28; cited at I/2, 217.

75. II/3, 232; cf. I/10, 181; II/2, 50,52.

76. "The mystic also wants to know ecstatically the Whatness" (II/3, 163, n. 1).

77. This is a reflective form of judgment that Kant, however, still understands in a reflexive sense.

78. In his first published philosophical essay, *On the Possibility of a Form of Philosophy in General*, Schelling writes that this "is a circle—of course, but one which would only be avoidable if there were nothing absolute in human knowledge" (I/1, 92, n. 1). His point in 1794 is precisely his point in 1842: at the edge of predication, reason is brought to a standstill, and knocked outside its domain of possible experience, into the arena of actual experience and the hands of a historical individual, who must then realize the truth of this idea in his or her moral life.

79. Schelling, *Initia Philosophiae Universae: Erlanger Vorlesung WS 1820/21*, ed. Horst Fuhrmans (Bonn: H. Bouvier u. Co., 1969), 47. In this ecstatic moment, in which we know nothing yet experience everything, there is an inverse relationship between the Absolute Subject and my knowledge: "there is precisely just as much reality in the Absolute Subject as there is no reality in my knowing, ... [a relationship of] reciprocal interaction," which is "only possible through the fact that both were originally one, in that the eternal freedom was originally within our consciousness, or ... that that eternal freedom has no other place where it can come to itself, other than in our consciousness" (ibid.).

80. Plato, *Symposium*, 203–4.

81. G. W. F. Hegel, *Briefe von und an Hegel*, ed. K. Hegel (Leipzig: Dunker & Humboldt, 1887), Bd. I, 138.

82. As Schelling pointed out years earlier regarding Kant's own experience with his purely negative science: "All of those theories are contrary to experience that abstract from experience and explain with causes that they do not know *an sich* or independent of the very experience that is to be explained. For when this is the case, nothing occurs other than one just puts everything into the principles that is sufficient to explain the (already familiar) experience—one thus creates the causes and arranges them in precisely the manner that one will employ them afterward. Indeed, disregarding the

circular explanation formed in this [procedure], in that one first derives the causes from the effects, and then derives the effects again from the (self-created) causes, it will nonetheless turn out that because experience of course increases daily, that those assumed causes will momentarily become insufficient, so that one must then again always posit new conditions" (II/4, 529).

83. G. W. F. Hegel, *Wissenschaft der Logik I und II*, Werke 5 und 6 (Frankfurt am Main: Suhrkamp, 1969), I, 68.

84. Calling to mind Kant's distinction between the absolute and potential unconditioned, it is clear that Hegel is operating with only the potential unconditioned in mind, since only this unconditioned, understood as the additive result of a series, can be reduced to its constituent negative members from that series. As a result, since Hegel does not begin with an actual unconditioned, but rather only with a potential unconditioned, there can be no actual opposition. In light of the ease with which this potential being converts to potential nothingness, Schelling fails to locate any "real dissonance" between the two, and instead sees Hegel's beginning "acting like a mere minus, an absence," in which, however, "there is as little to overcome as there is in filling an empty vessel" (I/10, 137). It all just happens too "peacefully" in an alleged dialectical process where there is, however, no opposition and thus "no struggle at all" (ibid.).

85. Dieter Henrich, "Hegel's Grundoperation: Eine Einleitung in die 'Wissenschaft der Logik,'" *Der Idealismus und seine Gegenwart*, ed. von Ute Guzzoni et al. (Hamburg: 1976), 215.

86. G. W. F. Hegel, *Logic*, II:27. See also Heinrich, "Grundoperation," 215.

87. G. W. F. Hegel, *Phenomenology of Spirit*, trans. A. V. Miller (Oxford University Press: 1977), 23–24.

88. Plato, *Sophist*, 255d; 248e–249.

89. Schelling points to this prereflective layer of our thinking as early as 1795 when he writes: "In accepting this reality we are not aware of any freedom; we are constrained to admit that it exists with as much certainty as we assume our own existence to be true. We cannot be deprived of this reality without being deprived of ourselves." And again, his earlier pleas for transcending "discursive thinking" must be understood in this light: "For all the failed attempts to answer this question share the mistake of attempting to explain conceptually what effectively precedes all concepts; they all betray the same incapacity of the spirit to tear itself away from discursive thinking and to ascend to the immediacy that exists within spirit itself" (I/1, 376).

90. The feeling engendered by this experience at the outermost limit of predication corresponds to our "religious feeling," which, for Schelling, "is the primal feeling of humanity, the thought that pounds every heart" (WMV, 121).

91. Following Schelling, I am referring to the Ancient Greek terms *exstasis* and *existêmi*.

92. If communicating the inner meaning of the world's existence is the primary work of philosophy, then far from philosophy being the science that presupposes nothing, it is instead the one science that must presuppose everything. Conversely, Schelling argues that "[i]n short, a philosophy that totally presupposed nothing could talk about only nothing, and in desperation about this, one could say that philosophy is the science that must instead presuppose everything" (GPP, 223).

93. The influence Schelling had on Peirce was "enormous," or so he says in a letter he writes to William James on January 28, 1894: "Dear William,...You ask whether I know of anybody but Delboeuf and myself 'who has treated the inorganic as a sort of

product of the living'? This is good. An instance, no doubt, of that wonderful originality for which I am so justly admired. Your papa, for one, believed in creation, and so did the authors of all the religions. But my views were probably influenced by Schelling,—by all stages of Schelling, but especially by the *Philosophy of Nature*. I consider Schelling as enormous; and one thing I admire about him is his freedom from the trammels of system, and his holding himself uncommitted to any previous utterance. In that, he is like a scientific man. If you were to call my philosophy Schellingism transformed in the light of modern physics, I should not take it hard." R. B. Perry, *The Thought and Character of William James* (Boston: Little Brown, 1935), II:416.

94. Charles Sanders Peirce, *Logic, Regarded As Semeiotic*, MS L75, memoir 19, draft E, *On Arguments* (The Carnegie application of 1902), ed. Joseph Ransdell, http://www.cudenver.edu/~mryder/mem19.html.

95. Ibid.

96. Ibid., memoir 24, draft E, http://www.cudenver.edu/~mryder/mem24.html.

97. Ibid.

98. Immanuel Kant, *Opus postumum*, ed. Eckhart Förster, trans. Eckhart Förster and Michael Rosen (Cambridge: Cambridge University Press, 1993), 246, 21:79.

99. Werner Beierwaltes makes this point succinctly when he notes that "for Schelling the essential relation of philosophy and theology has, since his beginning in the *Systemprogramme*, never been questionable: true philosophy is simultaneously theology or philosophical religion." Werner Beierwaltes, *Platonismus in Idealismus* (Frankfurt am Main: 1967), 68. See also Joseph Lawrence's insightful discussion of Schelling's idea of a philosophical religion in his essay "Philosophical Religion and the Quest for Authenticity," in *Schelling Now: Contemporary Readings*, ed. Jason M. Wirth (Bloomington: Indiana University Press, 2004), 13–30.

TRANSLATOR'S NOTES

1. Schelling, *Grundlegung der Positiven Philosophie: Münchener Vorlesung WS 1832/33 und SS 1833*, ed. Horst Fuhrmans (Turin: Bottega D'Erasmo, 1972), 44, n. 2 (hereafter cited as GPP).

THE GROUNDING OF POSITIVE PHILOSOPHY

1. Horace, *Odes*, book 4, canto 9, line 25. As is his practice, Schelling provides a loose paraphrase. The actual text reads: "Vixere fortes ante Agamemnona...[Brave men lived before Agamemnon]."

2. Friedrich Schiller, *Wallensteins Tod*, act 3, scene 18, lines 2051–52 (translation mine).

3. Johann Wolfgang von Goethe, "Studienzimmer," in *Faust I*, lines 1776–84 (translation mine). These lines are spoken by Mephistopheles, thus the "us" refers to negative spirits, whereas the "you" refers to humans.

4. Goethe, *Faust I*, "Nacht," lines 550–51 (translation mine).
5. Cf. Matthew 11:30.
6. Feder, *Logik und Metaphysik; nebst der philosophischen Geschichte im Grundrisse* (Göttingen: J.C. Dietrich, 1769). Feder lived from 1741 to 1821. The student to whom Schelling refers to is of course himself, at the age of thirteen.
7. Gottfried Wilhelm von Leibniz, *La Monadologie. Vulgo: Principia Philosophia seu theses in gratiam principis eugenii conscriptae* (1714).
8. In 1843, Heinrich Eberhard Gottlob Paulus (1761–1851) issued an unauthorized reproduction of notes he had taken of Schelling's lectures entitled *Die endlich offenbar gewordene positive Philosophie der Offenbarung oder Entstehungsgeschichte, wörtlicher Text, Beurtheilung und Berichtigung der v. Schellingschen Entdeckungen über Philosophie überhaupt, Mythologie und Offenbarung des dogmatischen Christentums im Berliner Wintercursus von 1841–42* (Darmstadt: Carl Wilhelm Leske, 1843). Schelling sought to repress this unauthorized reproduction of his lectures and brought a suit against the publisher—a suit he eventually lost. These notes formed the basis for the text found in *Philosophie der Offenbarung 1841/42*, edited and introduced by Manfred Frank (Frankfurt am Main: Suhrkamp, 1977).
9. Antisthenes (445–365 BCE) was a pupil of Socrates and the cofounder of the Cynic school of philosophy in Athens.
10. Goethe, *Faust I* "Studienzimmer," lines 1868–2048 (translation mine).
11. Read as one word, καινοῦ is the genitive form of an adjective meaning 'fresh' or 'new.' But since Ancient Greek was written in one continuous stream of letters with no spacing or punctuation to indicate separate words, clauses, and sentences, καινοῦ could also be read as the two words και and νοῦ, meaning 'and understanding.'
12. Raimondo conte di Montecucculi (1609–1680) was an Austrian general and prince of the Holy Roman Empire.
13. Christian Gottfried Ehrenberg (1795–1876) was a German scientist whose work with microscopic organisms—mostly a unicellular group of protists called diatoms—laid the foundations for modern micropaleontology.
14. William Shakespeare, *King Henry IV*, Globe edition part one, act 5, scene 1, lines 130–42.
15. Friedrich Schiller, *Don Carlos, Infant von Spanien*, act IV, scene 21, lines 4289–96 (translation mine).
16. Johann Friedrich Herbart (1776–1841) was a prominent German philosopher heavily influenced by Johann Gottlieb Fichte and Schiller (particularly his *Letters on the Aesthetic Education of Man*), whose work in the field of pedagogy established teacher education as an academic discipline in Germany and elsewhere.
17. Johann Schultz (1739–1805), *Erläuterungen über des herrn professor Kants Critik der reinen Vernunft* (Königsberg: C.G. Dengel, 1784).
18. Published under the title *Nouveaux essais sur l'entendement humain* (1765).
19. Schelling is alluding to the discovery of Neptune in 1846.
20. Schelling incorrectly refers to the work as "David Hume oder ein Gespräch über Idealismus und Realismus." It was actually published under the title *David Hume über den Glauben, oder Realismus und Idealismus: Ein Gesprach, in Fredrich Heinrich Jacobi's Werke*, vol. 2 (Leipzig: 1815), 1–310.
21. Schelling cites the work as "Grundlage der Wissenschaftslehre." It was published as *Wissenschaftslehre, 1804*, trans. Peter Heath and John Lachs (Cambridge: Cambridge University Press, 1982).

22. Schelling gives the title as "Anweisung zum seligen Leben." It was published as *Die Anweisung zum seligen Leben, oder auch die Religionslehre* (*The Way Towards the Blessed Life; or, the Doctrine of Religion*, trans. William Smith (London: John Chapman, 1849).

23. Schelling refers to the work as "Sonnenklarer Bericht oder Versuch das Publikum zum Verständniß der Wissenschaftslehre zu zwingen." It was actually published under the title *Sonnenklarer Bericht an das grossere Publikum über das eigentliche Wesen der heutigen Philosophie; ein Versuch, die Leser zum Verständniß zu zwingen* (Berlin: 1801).

24. This is Virgil's description of the difficulty of returning to Avernus after the descent: "This is really work, this is really labor" (Virgil *Aeneid* 6.129).

25. Cf. *Metaphisics* 1037a25ff: "There is no formula involving the matter, for this is indeterminate; but there is a formula in accordance with the primary substance."

26. Schelling, *Philosophical Letters on Dogmatism and Criticism* (I/1, 281).

27. Schelling is referring to what became known as his "System of Identity," a title that makes use of a term—*Identitätsystem*—that Schelling used just once, in a hastily composed and very brief essay from 1800 (cf., I/3, 105).

28. *Denkmal der Schrift an der göttlichen Dingen usw. Des Herrn Friedrich Heinrich Jacobi 1812* (1/4, 19).

29. Cf. note 55 in the Translator's Introduction.

30. Schelling refers to Aristotle's substantive treatment of Parmenides in *Physics I* (iii), the conclusions of which are referred to in *Metaphysics I* (v.12–14).

31. τῦφον occurs in Plutarch's *Alcibiades* (4.3), to describe the "vain and foolish pride" of the philosopher who claims to possess wisdom.

32. Blaise Pascal's *Pensées* (1660), § 327: "The other extreme is that reached by great intellects, who, having run through all that men can know, find they know nothing, and come back again to that same ignorance from which they set out; but this is a learned ignorance which is conscious of itself."

33. Schelling cites *The Republic* VI xxi (511f). See 511B for Plato's presentation of what Schelling here calls a "*Denkwissenschaft*."

34. In *Metaphysics* (992a25), Aristotle critiques Plato's idea of participation as being "χενῶς"—translated as 'worthless.' Εν τοις λογοις is taken from B995a: "We must ask whether the first principles are limited in number or in kind—both those in the definitions and those in the substrate."

35. Aristotle uses this term twice to describe Plato's doctrine of participation in the *Metaphysics* at A991a20 and M1079b25.

36. The term εφεξῆς ('in order, in a row, one after another') appears seventeen times in the *Metaphysics*, though never associated with the other terms in the phrase as presented by Schelling. Fluent in Ancient Greek since the age of ten, Schelling is most likely providing his own interpretation of Aristotle on this point.

37. Cf. *Metaphysics* (Q1048a10). In describing how potencies are acquired and actualized, Aristotle reaches for "desire or conscious choice" to serve as the deciding factor that "pulls" potentiality into actuality.

38. Cf. *Metaphysics* L1072b7: "Now if a thing is moved, it can be otherwise than it is. Therefore, if the actuality of 'the heaven' is primary locomotion, then in so far as 'the heaven' is moved, in this respect at least it is possible for it to be otherwise; i.e. in respect of place, even if not of substantiality. But since there is something—X—that moves while being itself unmoved (αὐτὸ ἀκίνητον) existing actually, X cannot be otherwise in any

respect. For the primary kind of change is locomotion, and of locomotion circular; and this is the motion which X induces. Thus X is necessarily existent; and qua necessary it is good, and is in this sense a first principle."

39. "For the final cause is not only 'the good for something,' but also 'the good which is the end of some action.' In the latter sense it applies to immovable things, although in the former it does not; and it causes motion as being an object of love, whereas all other things cause motion because they are themselves in motion."

40. Schelling is synthesizing Aristotle's fragmented doctrine of divine nature, which is that since only what is pure form can be unmoving, divine nature must be noetic instead of dianoetic. Mind thinking itself no longer accepts the discursive separation of subject and object but instead unites both as one (cf. *De Anima* 429b5f and 430a3f.). Schelling uses this contrast to show how his distinction between logical thinking and real thinking —between a negative and positive philosophy—is as old as philosophy itself.

41. Psalms 14:1.

42. The Christian deist Matthew Tindal (1650–1733) published a very influential book in 1730, entitled *Christianity as Old as the Creation*.

43. John 17:24.

44. Albrecht von Haller (1708–1777) was a Swiss botanist who also wrote poetry.

45. Spinoza, *Ethics I*, prop. XI.

Index

abduction, 68
   proof of God, 74
absolute
   idealism, 2-4, 16
   prius, 26, 34, 43, 127, 179–181, 197, 202
   spirit, 153, 164, 177, 212
Absolute, 26, 39, 40, 51, 63-64, 80
   Idea, 55-58, 65-66
   Subject, 48, 51–53, 58, 220
Aristotle, 3, 18, 22-25, 27, 49, 106, 113, 120, 131, 156-164, 185, 194, 217, 224, 225

Bacon, F., 116, 166
Böhme, J., 51, 163, 174-177

copula, 30, 35, 79

Descartes, R., 23, 31-34, 77, 97, 100, 116, 176

ecstasy, 5, 50-56, 67, 173-175, 203
   experience of, 41, 50, 62, 64, 204, 220
   and the future, 68, 80, 182
   and overthrow of reason, 49, 59, 67-68, 196, 203
   philosophical experience, 52
   and Spinoza, B., 204
   as transcendence, 53, 82, 203, 209
empiricism, 75, 117, 161, 165-169, 171-196
   a priori, 167, 179-181
   metaphysical, 7, 197-203
   philosophical empiricism, 167-169, 171
   progressive, 219

supersensible, 75, 173-175
evil, 17-18
existence, 2-8, 13-30, 37, 41-44, 49-64, 67-71, 81-85, 124-125, 129-131, 145-149, 155, 162, 165, 168, 194-195, 199-202, 205-211, 221
   divinity of, 82
   and dynamic categories, 43, 83
   ecstatic nature of, 80, 220
   as essence, 85
   extra-logical nature of, 16, 27-28, 71
   facticity of, 28, 53
   of God, 177, 180-182, 194
   groundlessness of, 49
   inverted idea, 50
   meaning of, 52, 70, 76, 79-82
   necessary, 69-71, 200, 207
   ontological proof, 200
   philosophy of, 29, 67, 86
   purpose of, 7, 113
   in relation to essence, 211
   before representation, 18
   simple, 72, 76, 82
   of supersensible, 171-173
   system of, 124
   transcendence of, 82
   as unconditioned, 43

Fichte, J. G., 6, 20-23, 48, 63-65, 98, 124-131, 143, 146, 151, 177, 204, 214, 217, 223
final cause, 65, 162-164, 225
freedom, 2-4, 14-17, 23, 26, 30-31, 41-44, 51-55, 66-67, 76, 81, 93, 102, 105, 113, 153, 155, 176-177, 197-198, 205, 216, 219-221, 222
   of being, 51

freedom (*continued*)
    from censors, 6, 10
    coming age of, 31
    emergence of, 5
    Essay on Human Freedom (1808), 30
    philosophy is a work of, 4
    positive, 48
    risk of, 54
    third antinomy, 26

German Idealism, 1, 2, 12, 23, 26, 29, 32, 85
God, 29-31, 45, 48, 63-64, 70, 74, 80, 113-121, 131, 138, 145-148, 162-165, 169-182, 197-211
    abductive proof of, 74-75
    Aristotle's idea of, 162-164, 225
    Böhme's idea of, 176-177
    as creator, 164
    cosmological proof of, 206
    Godhead, 211
    Hegel's idea of, 210-211
    as individual, 201
    Jacobi's proof of, 172-173
    as necessary idea, 146
    ontological proof of, 29, 81, 199-209
    in positive philosophy, 201-211
    revelation of, 183, 190, 210-212
    Spinoza's idea of, 199
    three ages of, 30
    transcendental theology, 38
Goethe, J. W. von,, 12, 97-99, 101, 151, 216, 222, 223

Hamann, J.G., 17, 210, 216
Hegel, G. W. F., 1-17, 27, 32-33, 40, 48, 54-66, 72, 85, 129-133, 145-146, 149-154, 168, 175-177, 204, 211
    Encyclopedia of the Philosophical Sciences, 129
    Logic, 12, 61, 65, 150, 175, 215, 221
    Phenomenology of Spirit, 11, 57, 221
    Philosophy of Nature, 199
    Young Hegelians, 9-10
Henrich, Dieter, 61, 221
history, 2, 41, 66, 80, 93, 181, 197
    of God, 80
    modern philosophy, 59, 77
    of philosophy, 159
    pragmatic history, 80
    post-Kantian philosophy, 26
    of self-consciousness, 18-21
Hume, 55, 117, 119, 122, 124, 216, 223

idealism, 2, 17, 23, 66, 123, 126, 204

Jacobi, F. H., 7, 15, 51, 124, 148, 163, 171-173, 198, 216, 223, 224
judgement, 15, 19, 22, 44
    aesthetic, 39
    disjunctive, 44, 219
    emphatic, 79
    reflective, 79, 219
    synthetic, 54
    teleological, 55
    Urtheil, 19-20

Kant, I., 3, 16-55, 70-83, 100, 110-113, 117-139, 147-152, 163, 177, 190-197, 204-208
    abyss of reason, 47, 68, 204
    cosmological proof of God, 206-207
    Logic, 29, 44, 218
    Opus Postumum, 78, 222
    unconditional necessity, 47, 204
Leibniz, G. W., 4, 57, 67, 77, 85, 97, 102, 117, 119, 163, 199
Locke, J., 117, 119, 122

mythology, 13, 31, 156, 159, 164, 174, 176
    demythologixing, 59
    of Hegel's *Idea*, 55
    historical age of, 31
    and ideology, 54
    mythic consciousness, 4
    and negative philosophy, 31
    philosophy of, 31, 116, 144, 159, 164, 180, 200, 209
    and positive philosophy, 162
    truth of, 83

nature, 5, 9, 12, 16, 22, 30-31, 59, 65, 71, 80, 92, 125, 148, 175, 183, 222
    as the other of the Idea, 56

Index

negative philosophy, 16, 28-43, 50-53, 60, 65-71, 81, 145-149, 160-162, 178-183, 194-199, 202, 207-209
Neoplatonism, 164, 198

Peirce, C. S., 74-75
   abduction, 74-75, 221, 222
philosophical experience, 167, 169, 171
Plato, 27, 51, 53, 63, 68, 85, 94, 102, 108, 131, 148, 156-160, 163-64, 185, 194, 198, 217, 220, 221, 224
   absolute nothingness, 63
   and positive philosophy, 28, 159
   relative nothingness, 63
   Timaeus, 159
   wonder and genesis of philosophy, 51, 68
positive philosophy, 1, 4, 6, 8, 10-16, 24-26, 28-36, 44-46, 52-56, 58, 65-67, 68-74, 80, 92-100, 141-147, 155-161, 180-187, 209
progressive method, 40-44, 70-75

rational theology, 120, 199
reality (*Wirklichkeit*), 16, 49, 59, 121, 131

reflection, 21-24, 42-44, 49-50, 60-62, 65, 67-70, 97, 117, 126
regressive method, 40-46, 70-73, 218
revelation, 31, 80, 121, 174, 183-190, 210-212
   philosophy of, 10, 31, 76, 87, 186-190, 212

Schelling, F. W. J. von, works of
   Letters on Dogmatism and Criticism (1795), 7, 15, 40, 146, 216, 224
   Philosophy of Mythology, The, 31, 116, 144, 159, 164, 180, 209
   Philosophy of Nature (1799), 9
   Philosophy of Revelation, The, 31, 87
   System of Transcendental Idealism (1800), 9, 68, 80, 213, 216
scholasticism, 97, 113, 133
Spinoza, 22, 24, 46, 50, 55, 66, 126, 148, 176, 187, 199-206, 225

theosophy, 173-178

Wolff, C., 58, 77, 98, 120, 133
wonder, 51-54, 67-68, 73, 76, 80, 91, 222